W9-CCJ-371

WITHDRAWN

Urban Life and Urban Landscape Series

Main Street Blues

The Decline of Small-Town America

RICHARD O. DAVIES

7/00

Ohio State University Press

Columbus

Cover illustration: The abandoned train depot, 1967. It was torn down in 1972 to make way for a small restaurant. Photograph by Bruce Goldflies.

"My Hometown" by Bruce Springsteen. Copyright (c) 1984 by Bruce Springsteen. Reprinted by permission.

Library of Congress Cataloging-in-Publication Data

Davies, Richard O., 1937–
Main Street blues : the decline of small-town America /
Richard O. Davies.
p.   cm.—(Urban life and urban landscape series)
Includes bibliographical references and index.
ISBN 0-8142-0781-2 (cl : alk. paper).—
ISBN 0-8142-0782-0 (pa : alk. paper)
1. Camden (Ohio)—History.   2. Camden (Ohio)—Social conditions.
3. Camden (Ohio)—Social life and customs.   4. City and town life—
United States—Case studies.   I. Title.   II. Series.
F499.C177D38 1998   97–51225
977.1'71—dc21   CIP

Text and jacket design by Paula Newcomb.
Type set in Stone Serif by G & S Typesetters, Inc.
Printed by Thomson-Shore, Inc.

9 8 7 6 5 4 3 2 1

There are values in a small town you cannot get in a big one. There are neighbors and their problems, their affection, their kindliness. There are crops and cattle in the nearby country which are the stuff of life.
—Sherwood Anderson

Contents

Preface

This project began innocently enough at a family get-together one evening in 1992 when my daughter suggested that the many humorous
stories I told about growing up in the small southwestern Ohio town of
Camden should become the basis for a book. The particular Camden
that I described was emerging from the dislocations of World War II
and grappling with unsettling economic and political changes. It was a
secure and pleasant community, its streets guarded by mature maple
and elm trees, its modest brick and wood frame houses providing shelter for a population of slightly more than one thousand that was 100
percent white, overwhelmingly Protestant, and middle class. An additional one thousand persons lived on farms located within the twenty
square miles that made up Somers Township. Its five churches and small
school system provided coherence and continuity for the ebb and flow
of daily life.

At mid-century Camden was a typical midwestern farm town with
no compelling features to distinguish it from other communities of
similar size and function. It supported one weekly newspaper, four service stations, an independent bank, a drugstore with a soda fountain
complete with black marble counter, small Ford and Chevrolet dealerships, four modest mom-and-pop grocery stores, one butcher shop, three
taverns, two barbershops and three home-based "beauty shoppes," and
at any given time several marginal enterprises struggling to survive. A
part-time and untrained "police chief" occasionally patrolled the streets
to deter hot-rodders, and a volunteer fire department stood at the ready
whenever the siren perched atop the Town Hall alerted the community.

The nearest hospital was twenty miles distant. Two beloved general practitioners often performed minor surgeries in their home-based offices and routinely made home visits to the sick and maimed. The life and rhythm of the town revolved around weddings and funerals, planting and harvest seasons, church and school affairs, Saturday night shopping and Friday night high school basketball. Norman Rockwell never visited Camden, but his popular paintings that graced the covers of the *Saturday Evening Post,* which I used to read at Bert Umbaugh's barber shop waiting my turn in the chair, captured the community and its people with unerring accuracy.

I knew most everyone who lived there, especially during the several years that I covered the entire town each day by bicycle while running my newspaper route. Although I did not comprehend it at the time, I was privileged to be permitted to grow up in a community that embodied the values, virtues, and foibles of an older America that was rapidly disappearing. Camden was certainly a stereotype of the towns that Sinclair Lewis lampooned and Sherwood Anderson lamented. Serious crime was virtually unknown, although occasional rumors about spousal abuse made the rounds. Neighbors routinely assisted each other in times of need and distress, families were eagerly assimilating television into their living rooms and their lives, and the local gossip mill not only vigorously enforced a rigid moral code but also transmitted important news with incredible speed, if not always with equal accuracy.

The offhand suggestion by Jennifer Hoy that Camden was worthy of my attention as a historian started the process of conceptualization that eventually led me to attempt an examination of this small town within the broader context of regional and national history. Although I hold many special memories of this place I still call my hometown, I have not lived there for more than forty years and visited only rarely until I undertook this project. In the narrative that follows, I have attempted to transcend sentimentality to ask the questions of the research historian. I hope that I have asked the right questions and have been able to move beyond my own assumptions and memories to produce accurate answers.

As I pondered the significance of this nondescript town, I came to realize that while my upper division and graduate courses in American urban history and modern American history have routinely examined the growth of metropolitan America, they have never considered the obverse—the pervasive impact that the forces of modernization and urbanization have had on small towns. The historian William Cronon's

monumental study of Chicago's far-reaching impact on distant hinter-
lands greatly influenced my conceptualization of this project. I am also
indebted to historians John Mack Faragher, Catherine Stock, and Joseph
Amato, who have in recent years demonstrated the possibilities in
herent in community studies. My years spent on the editorial board
of *Locus,* an academic journal devoted to local history, further exposed me to emerging research methodologies. The pioneering work of
three urban historians—Charles Glaab, Richard Wade, and A. Theodore
Brown—contributed substantially to the analytical framework and research methodology employed in this study. I also salute Lewis E.
Atherton, the distinguished professor at the University of Missouri,
whose pioneering *Main Street on the Middle Border* (1954) has become a
classic against which all subsequent studies of American towns must be
measured. His course "Teaching History in College" greatly influenced
my development as a professional historian.

The controlling assumption upon which this study rests is that the
fate of the American small town has been the by-product of regional and
national forces. The Camden that emerges in these pages is not the same
community Ruth Neff described in her brief history of the town written
as a master's thesis in 1955. Her Camden was a strong, proud, successful,
vibrant, and ruggedly independent community that controlled its own
destiny. It was apparently also devoid of social classes, racism, intolerance, discrimination, and poverty. Her glowing narrative is similar to
the many local "booster" histories I have consulted in my research.
These volumes are guided by a faith in the American Dream and the
inevitability of Progress. Their publication often coincides with a centennial or other significant community celebration, and they are filled
with legends of brave white settlers confronting angry Indians, sanitized
summaries of prominent families, the achievements of a select few
daughters and sons, glowing profiles of prominent (i.e., surviving) businesses, and recapitulations of the most horrible floods, fires, tornadoes,
and other disasters, natural or otherwise, that visited themselves upon
the sturdy town. Invariably written by local residents with selective
memories, these brief books, while interesting and useful, tend to look
inward and seldom mention external events, except when local heroes
march off to help win a distant war. They avoid, if at all possible, conflict
and divisions and emphasize positive rather than negative events.

The Camden that my research has revealed is a much different community, one that has always been vulnerable and subject to rapid and
substantive change produced by distant forces over which it had no

control. The narrative that follows is an attempt to look at the role of this unexceptional town within the broader context of American history. Why and how did Camden develop as it did? To what extent was it unique, or to what extent is Camden representative of other small towns? I make no professions that Camden is "typical." I do believe, however, that the core themes identified in this study are consistent with those that would be uncovered in studies of similar-sized towns anywhere in the continental United States, and as such provide the historian with concepts that have applicability beyond southwestern Ohio.

~

Although I began my university teaching career in 1960, it was not until 1995 that I had the opportunity to take a sabbatical leave. I am extremely grateful to the Board of Regents of the University and Community College System of Nevada for granting me a leave, during which time a substantial amount of research for this book was completed. I am indebted to several members of the faculty and administration of the University of Nevada, Reno, who supported my proposal. My colleague and department chair, Professor Jerome E. Edwards, virtually demanded that I submit a sabbatical application, an opportunity that I had not even contemplated before. I gratefully acknowledge his support and encouragement. It has been my experience that those of us in the professoriat frequently overlook the role administrators play in providing an academic environment in which a professor can grow and mature as a teacher and researcher. The University of Nevada, Reno, has been blessed with many such administrators, and I especially acknowledge the support of Deans Ann Ronald and Robert Mead of the College of Arts and Science, former Vice Presidents for Academic Affairs Robert Hoover and David Westfall, and President Joe Crowley. I also express appreciation to my friends in the Department of History, a group of fifteen stimulating and dedicated professional historians who exemplify the ideal of what the word *colleague* means.

The sabbatical leave made possible visits to research libraries in Ohio, around which I sandwiched an extended trip to explore several American small towns selected at random to serve as an informal control group. My wife, Sharon, accompanied me on that delightful but arduous journey. In the spirit of William Least Heat-Moon and Charles Kuralt, we zigged and zagged our way over many more than fifteen thousand miles of less-traveled roads, staying as far from the interstate highway system as possible. Our trip eventually took us to forty-one states and into hundreds of small communities of less than 2,500 residents. Visits to these towns were not intended to produce data for a massive statistical examination of the condition of small-town America. My objective was not to write another anthropological treatise on class structures, economic conditions, race relations, and gender issues within a community. Rather, my trip was intended to provide me with a perspective for my study of the town where I spent my childhood and graduated in a senior class of thirty in 1955.

We poked around stores, chatted with waitresses and bartenders, examined local history collections and newspaper files in town libraries, culled information from town officials and newspaper editors, walked quiet streets, explored a wide variety of neighborhoods, pondered the deteriorating condition of business districts, and contemplated the dearth of modern medical facilities and the frequent lack of either dentist or physician. We assessed the condition of housing, schools, churches, and businesses in small communities from Nevada to the Florida coast, from Maine to Oregon. Not only has Sharon happily supported this project by making invaluable suggestions and providing insights into local conditions, but after I reached the writing stage, she read draft chapters with an informed and critical eye. Throughout thirty-five years of marriage she has cheerfully supported my many adventures in the curious world of academia. I appreciate these things and much more.

I am deeply indebted to the 165 present and former residents of Camden who completed and returned a detailed questionnaire about their past and present perceptions of their town. Many of these persons who took the time to complete this lengthy document also appended comments and reminiscences. The Camden Archives, located in what is now a branch of the Preble County Library System, is special. It contains a rich storehouse of newspaper files, photographs, local government and school district documents, and other materials. This small but impressive collection was started by the late Nell Jones when she retired to her hometown after a long professional career in the Library of Congress. Her work has been continued by a dedicated group of volunteers. In particular, I extend my appreciation to librarians Yolonda Murphy and Norma Wilson and to archives volunteer Joy Donohoe Rhoden for their assistance. The contributions of many other persons are also acknowledged: Michael Simpson, Drake Bush, Paul Starrs, Ted Cook, Robert and Judy Kany, William and Maxine Eikenberry, Jack White, Julia Deem, Herschel Brown, Dewaine Gahan, Garris Edwards, Mabel Temby, Randy Murphey, Dan Satran, and John Brewer. While these individuals have helped make this book a reality, any possible errors of fact or interpretation are my responsibility.

Camden

In Camden where my heart is
And where I spent my youth
Where I met with many parties
Who loved honor bright and truth.
Tho' I wander by the lakeside,
And love its breezes well,
In Camden, where my heart is,
My mind delights to dwell.

In Camden where my heart is,
I shared life's early joys;
Where culture, music, art is,
And charming girls and boys.
There, true friends of my childhood,
Now, fair women and brave men:
In Camden where my heart is,
Is friendship's deathless den.

O noble men of Camden
And fair daughters of the plains
The mem'ry of life's morning
Like a pleasant dream remains.
Like I rake in the dollars,
And grow rich by-and-by,
In Camden where my heart is,
I hope to live and die.

—John McCord, *Camden Gazette,* 1901

Plainville, U.S.A.: The Towns We Left Behind

They still dot the map of America, some 11,897 of them according to the Census of 1990. Often quaint reminders of an earlier and more ebullient time, with populations ranging from several hundred to a few thousand, they are the incorporated small towns of America. Now shunted to the margins of national life, located in rural areas that lie beyond the borders of metropolitan America, they live a present that is less and less appealing while confronting futures that are bleak at best. A century or more ago, they occupied a central place in the overall scheme of things, but modern America, with its dominant urban culture, has now passed them by, relegating them to the cruel obscurity that comes from being abandoned by a railroad or left off the federal interstate highway map. Their economic base has been eroded, and their slowly shrinking populations have become increasingly older and poorer as the best of their younger generations have departed. These communities now contain less than 10 percent of the American people.

This is the history of one such town. Camden, Ohio, lies in a small valley some forty miles north of Cincinnati close by the Indiana border, surrounded by fertile farm land that each year yields bumper crops of wheat, oats, corn, and soybeans. Its dairy farms are large and prosperous, and its beef and pork bring premium prices on the Cincinnati commodities market. Its once thriving business district, however, has become a veritable slum, a microcosm of the devastated sections of our much publicized inner cities, and many of its homes, once classic examples of Victorian architecture, have fallen into various stages of neglect and dilapidation. It offers energetic young adults few economic

1

opportunities, driving them to nearby cities. Its population, although increasing, is also an aging one; upon retirement many of the more affluent move to Florida or other Sunbelt states. One gets the distinct impression that the town is caught up in a slow but sure downward spiral from which there is no escape. The town will not die, but neither will it flourish. A mood of quiet resignation seems to hover over the small valley in which it is located.

Camden's story is not especially exciting or special, but it is one that is replicated throughout the United States. Camden is merely one of thousands of small towns that modern America has left behind. Its history contains, perhaps, a few special quirks that give it a modest claim to uniqueness, but the overall pattern of settlement, growth, and eventual stagnation is familiar. This same book could just as easily have been written about many other towns, and the essential story would not have been all that different. Camden was selected as a prototype for this study for several reasons; one is that it was in this typical midwestern small town that I was born and raised. The three houses I lived in during my youth were all situated on Main Street. I left in 1955 after graduation from high school and seldom returned. Between 1960 and the time I decided to undertake this project, I had visited the town briefly only three times.

The pages that follow attempt to relate this particular town to the broader themes of American history. Like most such communities, Camden produced no presidents or senators, no famous artists or captains of industry, although it has long proudly proclaimed itself as the birthplace of the novelist Sherwood Anderson. His reputation as a writer, however, is based primarily on his critical dissection of another Ohio town, Clyde, located some 150 miles to the north. Anderson's parents moved from Camden when he was still an infant, and he did not return until his fifty-eighth year. Camden did provide a goodly number of successful farmers, artisans, businessmen, athletes, industrial workers, teachers, and soldiers. The more I delved into the history of the town, the more fascinated I became with just how strongly Camden's history was shaped by external forces. This study attempts to describe and interpret the historical role of the American small town by focusing upon one particular community.

This is not a success story; in fact, there is a tragic element suggestive of a "rise and fall" theme lurking throughout the narrative. Like many small American towns, Camden has been in a period of decline for nearly half a century; as such, it is merely one example of the period of stagnation and decay that descended upon America's Main Streets following the Second World War. There are, of course, thriving towns that stand as exceptions to this story of atrophy and decline, and my travels and research have uncovered some notable success stories. These special communities have been blessed by a combination of imaginative leadership and unique advantages provided by an anomaly of history or geography. Such examples are the exception to the rule, however, because both the quantitative and qualitative data lead to the inescapable conclusion that the American small town has fallen on hard times, with the prognosis for the future anything but encouraging.

≈

This pattern of steady erosion is neither new nor shocking, because throughout much of the twentieth century journalists and social scientists have first predicted and then described the demise of the American small town. With the assurance that comes from the cold reality of census data and government reports, they have traced the slow but steady loss of young persons, the stagnation and aging of populations, the diminution of political clout, a fading economic viability, and an increase in social pathologies. As early as 1906, the progressive reformer Frederick C. Howe perceived what would become a veritable truism during the latter three-quarters of the twentieth century, namely, that the rise of the metropolis would eclipse the small town and the agricultural society it served: "The city has become the central feature in modern civilization and to an ever increasing extent the dominant one." This development, Howe concluded, meant that the "rural civilization, whose making engaged mankind since the dawn of history, is passing away. The city has erased the landmarks of an earlier society. Man has entered an urban age."[1]

The Census of 1920 confirmed the trend that Howe had observed. For the first time, more than half of the American people lived in cities. Social and economic trends during the 1920s did nothing to change this. As the cities grew, so did their economic and political power. Then came the Great Depression. "There is no hope for the small towns of America. They are doomed." So wrote an anonymous elected official of a small Illinois town in 1934. For many years he had been warily observing the disturbing trends that increased the vulnerability of the small towns of Illinois. He believed that these converging trends, which predated the depression, spelled the end to the dominance of agrarian America: "The small towns and villages of America, together with the farms, represent the real strength, the support, and the reserve power of the United States." But now he detected a "dull apathy" that presaged the end to an era. This trend, he concluded, was sapping the strength of one of America's greatest resources, the "steady, moderately conservative, industrious, independent, and frugal" men and women who lived in the towns.[2]

This sad lament would be repeated many times in the years to come. For example, the journalist Alfred Sinks identified a pattern of "decline and decay" in an article in *Colliers* magazine in 1947. "The small centers in most parts of the country are dying," he wrote, noting the steady flow of workers, shoppers, and, especially, young people away from the towns of America to the rapidly growing postwar cities. Sinks warned that "the single, most wholesome, democratic way of living," America's "root and stock," was facing extinction.[3] Journalist Morrison Colladay reported the same story a few years later after visiting his (unidentified) hometown in upstate New York. "These little towns are slowly dying, though they are hard to kill. They lose many of their young people but the older folk have nowhere to go. How they manage to exist in a world that seems to have no place for anything between the corporate farm and the city suburb perplexes even their inhabitants."[4]

The research findings of several social scientists confirmed the decline of Main Street. The anthropologist Carl Withers was able to report on a relatively self-sufficient and viable rural society in "Plainville," Missouri, on the eve of the Second World War.[5] Fifteen years later, another anthropologist, Art Gallaher, spent a year in "Plainville" and reported a greatly changed community. The gathering forces of postwar urban society had already had a severe impact on this once thriving town in southwest Missouri. Gallaher concluded that "Plainville" (actually the farm town of Wheatland) was losing many of its more industrious residents to the nearby cities of Springfield, Joplin, and Kansas City. Worse, Plainville's business community had come under intense pressure from outside forces, the result of improved transportation and communication systems. At the same time, writing not far from Wheatland at the University of Missouri in Columbia, the historian Lewis E. Atherton lamented, "Americans everywhere think of country towns as museum pieces. They argue that Main Street has not only lost population, but also the hope, daring, and originality necessary to fight back." Himself a native of the town of Bosworth, Missouri, Atherton noted, "They point to vacant store buildings and sagging, unpainted houses, to numerous old people vegetating in village homes, and to boys and girls anxiously looking forward to the time when they can join the rush to the cities."[6]

Subsequent studies by social scientists conducted in other sections of the country during the 1960s confirmed Gallaher's conclusions about "Plainville." The sociologists Arthur Vidich and Joseph Bensman, in *Small Town in a Mass Society* (1968), described the many ways in which the independence and viability of the small upstate New York town of "Springdale" had been eroded by the relentless pressure emanating from the expanding urban centers of the state of New York.[7] A study by Don Martindale and Galen Hanson during the late 1960s in the community of Benson, located in the fertile western farmland of Minnesota, led to a similar conclusion. Powerful "translocal" forces, they reported, were undercutting the economic, political, and social independence of this once proud community.[8]

Writing about the same fertile agricultural region of western Minnesota in the early 1990s from the perspective of a social historian, Joseph Amato reported an irreversible pattern of decline that had taken hold during the 1960s and showed no signs of abatement more than a quarter century later. He wrote that this decline could be seen in such factors as "a disproportionate number of old people, with no source of income other than Social Security; dying towns, which steadily lost not only population but also their schools and businesses; an absence of good jobs; and a whole generation of youth who were emigrating because of low-paying jobs." Amato described an education system operated by discouraged teachers and weak administrators who encouraged outmigration by their best students. "The teachers accepted a passive role; their goals [are] . . . to make a living, to avoid controversy and politics, to be discreet, and to have the glory in preparing students to go on to college. In effect, they assured the exit of the brightest and most-needed youth."[9]

In 1994 a *New York Times* journalist visited western Nebraska and discovered that even if good jobs were available, many of the area's youth would nonetheless depart for distant cities upon graduation from high school or college. "The failure of these places to retain their young people has traditionally been explained by a shortage of jobs," reporter Dirk Johnson noted. "But the talk among teen-agers on the Great Plains now reveals something deeper, a lament that no job in a small town is worth staying for." His research indicated that the small town had been undercut by powerful images projected by the modern media, images that implicitly proclaimed the superiority of urban lifestyles. "It's a tragedy that people in small towns feel the only way they can be successful is to leave," a business executive told Johnson. "In the age of cable television, rural kids get all these messages and images that suggest that all these exciting things are happening far away from them, and it's hard to explain that it's not necessarily the truth." The head of a small chamber of commerce office in Arnold, Nebraska, concurred with this assessment: "Too often, you're considered a loser if you don't leave." [10]

In 1995 a *Washington Post* writer reached the same conclusion in his examination of the central Nebraska community of Anselmo, describing a town that had lost its bank, school, newspaper, most businesses, and half its population since 1960. "This is the slow lane," the mayor glumly concluded, as he noted that nearly all twenty-five of the town's 1995 high school graduates had already left for jobs elsewhere. [11]

~

During the 1920s it became fashionable in urban intellectual circles to satirize and ridicule the societies clustered along the nation's many Main Streets. Leading the attack was the son of the town doctor from Sauk Centre, Minnesota, the gangly, red-haired Sinclair Lewis. When his novel *Main Street* appeared in 1920, it quickly hit the best-seller lists. Although some readers found his stridently sarcastic dissection of the American small town offensive, most readers, and especially literary critics, proclaimed it to be a refreshing departure. Finally, someone had dared to challenge the long-standing myths about the supposed morally superior way of life that existed in America's farming communities. "Red" Lewis's characters were drawn from his memory of a less-than-happy childhood spent on the Minnesota prairie, but he assured readers that they could be found in any town in the United States. As he explained in a brief introduction: "This is America—a town of a few thousand, in a region of wheat and corn and dairies and little groves. The town is, in our tale, called 'Gopher Prairie, Minnesota.' But its Main Street is the continuation of Main Streets everywhere. The story would be the same in Ohio or Montana, in Kansas or Kentucky or Illinois, and not very differently would it be told Up York State or in the Carolina hills." [12]

Lewis's heroine, the urbane and cultured librarian from St. Paul turned doctor's wife, fights the good fight against the dullards in Gopher Prairie, but ultimately she is overwhelmed by the forces of mediocrity that permeate the community. Carol Kennicott's spirited, if modest, efforts to elevate the quality of life in Gopher Prairie fail miserably. The didactic Lewis offers no hope or relief as he describes a civilization that is beyond redemption. In the end Carol essentially surrenders, accepting her fate to live in this depressing community. The jeremiadic picture that Lewis presented was soon echoed by other writers and social commentators, but this cultural assault did not last for long, losing most of its steam by the end of the Second World War. Social critics now had new fish to fry, primarily the gathering "urban crisis." As America's intellectuals contemplated the "exploding metropolis" and the "death and life of great cities," along with the immense implications of the new suburban way of life that was sweeping all before it, the American small town virtually disappeared from the cultural radar screen.[13]

Thus the harsh critiques of the small town that became fashionable during the 1920s gave way after the Second World War to a gentle nostalgia. As depicted by television and motion pictures, the towns of America reverted to being more or less idealized places where everyone is friendly (if perhaps a little eccentric), life is lived at a relaxed, humane pace, and no one locks their doors at night. National Public Radio audiences smiled knowingly at Garrison Keillor's whimsical tales about the decent, if somewhat plodding folk of Lake Wobegon, Minnesota ("where the women are strong, the men are good-looking, and all the children are above average"), and television audiences warmed to the quaint characters sitting on the porch of a dilapidated general store in some out-of-the-way village, whittlin' and spittin' while chatting with roving CBS commentator Charles Kuralt. Americans lamented the showing of the "last picture show" in the dusty postwar town of Thalia, Texas, with novelist Larry McMurtry, and roamed America's uncrowded "blue highways" to such obscure communities as Nameless, Tennessee, and Dime Box, Texas, with William Least Heat-Moon. They accompanied John Steinbeck and his dog Charlie in an aging pickup truck camper to intriguing places. The American small town even became the stuff of recreational theme parks, perhaps a surefire indication of its ultimate demise. Each visitor to Disneyland must enter and depart the Magic Kingdom via "Main Street USA," a pristine replica drawn from Walt Disney's not-so-accurate memory of the town in which he spent his youth, Marceline, Missouri.[14]

~

When I was a high school student in Camden during the early 1950s, a motorist approaching the town on the two paved highways that intersected in the town's center would encounter a sign that proclaimed:

Welcome to Camden,
Birthplace of Sherwood Anderson,
Famous Author

I was somewhat bemused, but not surprised, to find no copies of Anderson's books in the high school library and to see that both of the school's English teachers neglected to assign or discuss his books in their classes. I located a dusty copy of *Winesburg, Ohio,* tucked away on a special shelf in the town library under a small black-and-white picture of the author. It had not been checked out in many years. Although Anderson's novel was based on his experiences growing up and working as a young journalist in another small Ohio town—Clyde, located fifty miles southeast of Toledo—the legacy of Sherwood Anderson hovered, however vaguely, over the town of his nativity.

In the final chapter of *Winesburg, Ohio,* the young newspaper reporter George Willard departs on the train for Chicago, intent on building a career and making the most of his life. Willard is caught up in the emotions of leaving the town in which he grew up, but he understands that if he does not leave he will be condemned to the same plight of so many of the people whose desperate lives he has come to know intimately. The conductor punches his ticket, smiling, for he "had seen a thousand George Willards go out of their towns to the city." George now takes one last fleeting glimpse back at the town in which he had grown to manhood, just at it disappears from view. At that moment, he realizes that "his life there had become but a background on which to paint the dreams of his manhood." [15]

Perhaps that was the fate to which the small towns of America were destined all along—to produce generation after generation of George Willards, talented men and women who would grow up there but then feel compelled to move on to the city to paint their dreams of the future. Now, it seems, these towns, once the proud backbone of a young and vibrant democracy, are near exhaustion, incapable of producing many more George Willards. It is sad but true: there is not a great deal of hope left in the small towns that remain.

1

Dover: The Building of a Community

In 1874 Emma and Irwin Anderson moved from the crossroads community of Morning Sun, Ohio, to the nearby town of Camden, where they set up housekeeping at 142 South Lafayette Street. It was in this modest southwestern town of 850 residents that their third child, a boy they named Sherwood, was born on September 13, 1876. The Andersons' single-story white frame cottage was located a few doors from the red brick Methodist Church where Irwin sometimes taught Sunday school, and just a five-minute walk from the ramshackle shop on North Main Street where he lethargically pursued his trade of harness maker. Residents would later recall that Irwin seldom showed the same enthusiasm for his business as he did for music. When customers stopped by his shop they were often greeted by the sounds of his cornet coming from the back room. A crackerjack musician, Irwin seemed to be most happy when practicing on his brass instrument or marching down Main Street with the Camden community band in holiday parades. He was often featured as a soloist during the band's regular Thursday evening summertime concerts held at the town's main intersection.[1]

Without any notice to the community, the year following his son's birth, Anderson moved his family to northern Ohio. Some Camden residents thought that Irwin had a line on a better job, but others said that he departed to avoid a stack of bills he could not pay. After brief stays in Mansfield and Caledonia, in 1880 the Andersons settled into the bustling northwestern agricultural town of Clyde, which had become a major center for the production of vegetables and fruit, shipping produce to

New York City, Cleveland, Toledo, and Chicago on the New York Central Railroad, which sliced through the northern edge of town. Clyde had already become well known for its high quality sauerkraut made from the bountiful cabbage crops produced each summer by area farmers.

By the time he entered the third grade, young Sherwood regularly took on odd jobs to help his perpetually financially strapped family, earning the nickname of "Jobby" from residents who took notice of his persistence in seeking employment. After graduation from high school he worked for a few years as a reporter for the *Clyde Enterprise* before departing for Cleveland and what would become a relatively successful, but emotionally exhausting, business career. In 1912 Anderson suffered what was termed a "nervous breakdown" and, after obtaining a divorce from his first wife, relocated to Chicago, determined to pursue a career as a writer.[2]

By 1915 Anderson had already settled into writing a series of biographical sketches based on his observations of the human condition as reflected in the lives of Clyde residents. These character sketches evolved into the novel that established his reputation as a serious writer of considerable talent. Although *Winesburg, Ohio* (1919) received high praise from literary critics, it never enjoyed much success at cash registers, selling only six thousand copies. Anderson never publicly expressed envy over the enormous sales and popularity that Sinclair Lewis received from *Main Street* (1920), but he privately fumed over the lack of recognition and financial rewards he felt his writings merited.

What irritated him most, however, was being lumped into the emerging vanguard of intellectuals, led by Lewis and journalist H. L. Mencken, who were making the small towns of America their special target for ridicule. The popular Mencken delighted readers with his sarcastic descriptions of the "sweating anthropoids" of communities like Dayton, Tennessee, as he flailed away against what he perceived to be the full flowering of the distorted culture of small-town America: prohibitionists, Kluxers, and fundamentalist preachers. And Lewis's early novels—*Main Street, Babbitt, Elmer Gantry*—amounted to an outright repudiation of the small town and everything it symbolized. A careful reading of Anderson's works, however, indicates that to identify him with such writers was unfortunate. Unlike Lewis, Anderson expressed deep regret over the way the rapidly expanding business system was warping the special way of life of the American town. Underlying his writing was an appeal for a return to the ideals and lifestyle of the mid-

Sherwood Anderson, Camden's most famous native. Anderson was born in 1876 in a small cottage on South Lafayette Street, and although he moved to northern Ohio at age one, he always cherished a pristine preindustrial image of his place of birth. Courtesy Camden Archives.

nineteenth-century farming community, coupled with a protest against the dehumanizing forces of modern American commerce.[3]

Anderson had originally entitled his novel "The Book of the Grotesque," and the lives of the individuals he depicted in *Winesburg, Ohio* were indeed grotesque: among them were a former schoolteacher who had fled from Pennsylvania after his career was shattered when young male students fabricated charges of homosexual advances; a middle-aged woman who waited expectantly, but in vain, for the return of her long-departed lover; a Presbyterian minister who used his church belfry to peer into the bedroom of a lady schoolteacher possessed of "a neat trim-looking figure"; and a telegraph operator whose "immense girth" and steadfast refusal to bathe made him "the ugliest thing in town." When Anderson's novel first appeared in 1919, older readers condemned it for its emphasis on the twisted and deformed lives of the inhabitants of what Anderson suggested was an ordinary midwestern community. Younger critics, however, delighted in its exploration of the haunted and desperate lives being lived in a place long assumed to be the repository of virtuous behavior and good old-fashioned neighborliness. Nearly all readers, much to Anderson's dismay, viewed the novel as a caustic criticism of life in small-town America.

These readers greatly oversimplified Anderson's complex message. Anderson viewed small towns with sympathy and compassion, not with the sardonic contempt that filled Lewis's novels. True, the characters about whom Anderson wrote were beset with loneliness, dark secrets, and emotional exhaustion, and at times their behavior approached the bizarre. But Anderson considered such individuals to be the norm for all of modern American society, not just the small town. He had simply discovered that he could write best about the people he had observed while growing up in Clyde. Much to the anger (or amusement) of locals, depending on one's point of view, his novel resembled reality all too closely: the names of prominent characters, locations, and businesses described in *Winesburg, Ohio,* either were identical to or closely resembled actual persons and places in Clyde.[4]

It is significant that, unlike Sinclair Lewis, who described Gopher Prairie in a contemporary setting, Anderson placed his novel four decades in the past. The 1880s were, he believed, a critical juncture in American history when the disruptions and corruptions of modern commerce began to shatter the tranquillity and erode the independence of once secure, relatively self-sufficient towns. The real "grotesque" that Anderson sought to expose was not the decadence and shallowness of the small town but the corroding influence of a dominant new American social and economic order that was bereft of a moral compass.[5]

Anderson continued this powerful theme in his next novel, *Poor White* (1920). In many respects this less well known work is more successful in achieving his objectives than the more widely acclaimed *Winesburg, Ohio.* The narrative describes the life of Hugh McVey, who was raised in the small Missouri river town of Mudcat Landing. As a young man he moved to Bidwell, Ohio, to build a career. Once again Anderson set his novel in the defining years of the 1880s, and once again he described the damage being inflicted on the town and its people by commercial and industrial development. In one poignant scene near the end of the novel, an embittered harness maker, whose time-honored craft was being destroyed by machine technology, kills a visiting salesman in a fit of frustration and rage. Academic explorations of Anderson's literature would later make much of the fact that Anderson's father had been, however fitfully, a harness maker.[6]

Although Anderson's writing did not attract a wide popular reader-ship, it had a profound impact upon a new generation of writers, including William Faulkner and Ernest Hemingway. Henry Miller perhaps best expressed the debt of many writers of his generation when he wrote, "I always think of [Anderson] as the one American writer of our time who has walked the streets of our cities as a genuine poet."[7]

∼

The fondness with which Sherwood Anderson embraced the small town is revealed in his fantasies about the place of his birth. He had, of course, no memories of the town from which his parents had moved when he was still an infant, and he did not return until 1934, by which time his writing career had already assumed a distinctly downward trajectory. Throughout his adult life, however, Camden held a deep fascination for Anderson. In the early pages of the semiautobiographical *Tar: A Midwest Childhood* (1926), he provided a detailed description of the town as he imagined it. It was an isolated farming village, pristine and secure, "a little white town in a valley," inhabited by hardworking and honest folk whose uneventful lives indicated that they were at peace with themselves and content with their place in the grand scheme of things.[8]

Throughout his life, as his biographer Kim Townsend explains, the often troubled Anderson found solace in fantasized retreats to the "Camden" that he created in his mind. He fled to this imaginary haven whenever the pressures of business, his writing, or his four marriages pressed in on him too heavily. In the initial pages of *Tar,* Anderson recalls that "he left [Camden] in his mother's arms," and "never as a conscious human being . . . saw the town, never walked its streets and later when he grew to manhood . . . was careful never to go back."

This imagined town of "Camden" thus became a special place for this introspective and sensitive man, a refuge from the travails of his turbulent life. "As a man Tar sometimes lay in his bed in a city and thought of Camden, the town in which he was born and which he never saw and never intended to see, the town filled with people he could understand and who always understood him." It was a sparkling little village, located among lovely wooded hills, "a place of mystery—the home of romance." Anderson's imagined "Camden" was, most important, untouched by the heavy hand of modernism, "The town of Tar's birth, this purely fanciful place, which has nothing to do with the real Camden, has no electric lights, there was no waterworks, no one there owned an automobile. By day men and women went into the fields to plant corn by hand, they harvest wheat with a cradle. At night, after ten o'clock, the little streets, with the poor houses scattered about, were unlighted."

Consistent with the major themes of *Winesburg, Ohio,* and *Poor White,* Anderson's vision was of a preindustrial farming village. "To tell the truth," he writes, "Tar was trying through the creation of a town of his own fancy, to get at something it was almost impossible to get at in the reality of life. In real life people never stood still. Nothing in America," he laments, "ever stands still for very long." But this romantic, preindustrial image of his birthplace did stand still in Sherwood Anderson's mind, and it provided the standard by which he judged his own life and the world in which he lived. "Tar kept the town of Camden as something special in his life. Even when he had become a grown man and was called successful he clung to his dreams of the place."

Despite his depiction of "Camden" as a pleasant farming village, Anderson feared that in reality it had been transformed into yet another commercialized sort of place, the unwitting victim of modern technology. Perhaps, he speculated, "It is on a railroad. Tourists go through there, stopping to have their gas tanks filled. There are stores that sell chewing gum, electric fixtures, automobile tires, canned fruits and vegetables." Only occasionally, during those times when he was overcome by doubt, did Anderson ask himself the toughest of questions: "Perhaps . . . Camden wasn't a very progressive a town as Tar saw it, in dreams."[9]

∾

As Sherwood Anderson reluctantly conceded in this moving and introspective autobiographical novel, the place of his birth was not the frozen-in-time community of his dreams. It was, as he feared, a typical small Ohio town. From the pages of its weekly newspaper of the 1920s there emerges the image of a confident and proud, even smugly satisfied community, one that seemed to be adapting well to the challenges of this dynamic decade. With every passing year, it is evident that the layers of isolation in which the town had been enshrouded were being inexorably peeled away. The main line of the Pennsylvania Railroad, connecting Cincinnati and Chicago, ran along the eastern edge of town, hard by the Seven Mile Creek, providing the community with its major connection to the wider world. Nearly half of the families now owned an automobile. The recently graveled U.S. Highway 127 cut through the center of town, bringing an increasing number of tourists, who sometimes stopped for gasoline, a bite to eat, perhaps a few sundries on their way between Cincinnati, Toledo, and Detroit. The Dover Theater offered Hollywood's latest hits, and "of an evening," as the local colloquialism went, residents tuned into the world via the powerful signal of radio station WLW in Cincinnati. Machine technology had also modified the way farmers spent their time; few of them anymore went into their fields to plant and harvest by hand, for they had long since adopted the most modern of field implements. Tractors were now replacing the once prized enormous draft horses.

The Census of 1920 reported that Camden, its townsite now a century old, was nearing a population of a thousand. It was located in the south-central part of Preble County in Somers Township, forty miles north of Cincinnati and thirty-five miles southwest of Dayton. The Indiana border lay just twelve miles to the west, and a dirt highway leading to the Hoosier town of Liberty ran through some of Ohio's richest farm land. Just as Sherwood Anderson had dreamed, Camden lay nestled in a small valley harboring the usually sluggish Seven Mile Creek. Large hills to the east and west overlooked the valley, and beyond them, as far as the eye could see, lay the economic foundation for the community, a seemingly endless stretch of fertile farmland. Most family farms ranged between 160 and 600 acres in size, although many smaller ones were squeezed in among the larger operations. The gently rolling fields each year yielded large harvests of alfalfa, corn, oats, and wheat. The oats and wheat were shipped to market, but much of the alfalfa hay was used to feed the large Holstein and Jersey milking herds that roamed the lush pastures; the large yellow ears of field corn were used to fatten hogs and beef cattle for market. It was from this panorama of bountiful green and golden fields, from the red barns and the sturdy white frame farmhouses, that the town of Camden derived its livelihood. It was a typical midwestern small town, and nothing like the village that existed in Sherwood Anderson's escapist daydreams.

~

The first white settlers arrived in the area in 1803, the same year that Ohio was admitted to the Union as the seventeenth state. Settlement on the future site of Camden occurred in the wake of the removal of the several Indian tribes that had long inhabited the area. The Miami was the dominant tribe in southwestern Ohio, although their largest numbers were located in permanent villages about a hundred miles to the north. At those sites the Miami grew corn and other crops to supplement their hunting and fishing. The Shawnee occasionally slipped into

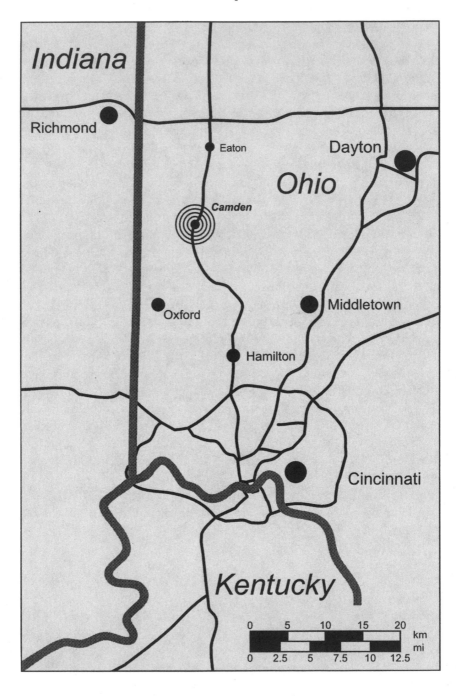

Indiana

Richmond

Eaton

Dayton

Ohio

Camden

Oxford

Middletown

Hamilton

Cincinnati

Kentucky

0	5	10	15	20	
					km
					mi
0	2.5	5	7.5	10	12.5

the Seven Mile Valley on hunting expeditions originating from their base in south central Ohio near what is now Chillicothe.[10]

Much of the Indian movements took place along the stream that General "Mad" Anthony Wayne had called Seven Mile Creek on his hand-drawn maps because it entered the Miami River seven miles north of Fort Hamilton. This creek ran year-round, and every twenty years or so it became a formidable raging body of water capable of flooding substantial parts of the narrow valley, including the southeastern parts of town. Its headwaters lie twenty-two miles to the northwest near the southern border of Darke County. It is fed all along its forty-mile length by innumerable small streams and flows into the Great Miami River sixteen miles to the south. One of five major rivers that drain the state of Ohio, the Great Miami's headwaters lie in north central Ohio; it flows into the Ohio River ten miles west of Cincinnati. As white settlement in southwestern Ohio grew early in the nineteenth century, such future cities as Hamilton, Middletown, Dayton, Piqua, Troy, and Sidney were established along the Miami's banks.

Before the arrival of the whites, the area had changed little for many centuries. Except for a few primitive trails and permanent camps, the relatively few number of Indians who traversed the area (estimated to be just 20,000 for the entire area of Ohio in 1790) had scarcely altered the natural environment. An incredible diversity of wild life flourished. Early white visitors to the area reported observing many bear and a great number of deer. In addition, there were large populations of raccoon, muskrat, otter, opossum, mink, beaver, wolves, weasel, and red fox. The hardwood forests were alive with grey and fox squirrel and also provided a lush habitat for a colorful array of bird life that included nearly three hundred species, the most prominent being the robin, cardinal, sparrow, blue jay, crow, finch, owl, and hawk. Early explorers also reported enormous flocks of wild turkey. Birds and animals thrived on the wide variety of abundant nuts, wild grains, and berries. Even occasional sightings of bald eagles—which preferred Lake Erie habitats 150 miles to the north—were reported. The fresh and unspoiled waters of creeks and rivers were heavily laden with many species of fish, including perch, bass, carp, blue gill, crappie, and catfish. The region was also heavily populated by snakes, with water moccasins, copperheads, and timber rattlesnakes being the most feared.[11]

Ohio's settlers were "a profit-minded people" who were drawn by descriptions of the Ohio country as "the garden of the world."[12] The first whites to come into the area were particularly alert to securing for themselves the most promising farmland. Those who first explored the Seven Mile Creek valley were drawn to the lush grasslands located atop the hills to both the east and west. This westernmost extension of the Till Plains provided the first inkling of the vast prairies lying further to the west. These expanses of grassland were relatively few, but they were inviting to settlers because they could plant crops without first undertaking the arduous task of clearing mature forests. However, it was the enormous stretches of virgin forests covering much of the region that demanded attention. These forests, heretofore untouched by ax or saw, stretched as far as the eye could see.

The incredible stands of mature trees were viewed by the new arrivals as major obstacles to the establishment of productive farms. White settlers knew that if they were to survive, they would have to clear the land for planting and to permit sunlight to reach their crops. These forests must have seemed overwhelming to the newcomers. They were made up of maple, elm, hickory, ash, cherry, beech, oak, buckeye, walnut, and sycamore. Huge conifers—cedar and spruce primarily—tended to cluster among rocky outcroppings and in dark ravines. Beneath the trees grew an almost impenetrable thick underbrush, which included many varieties of ferns, grasses, weeds, and wildflowers; huge stands of thorny raspberry and blackberry bushes; a maze of vines; and many years' accumulation of dead leaves. During the spring and summer months, a canopy of green leaves shut out much of the sunlight, creating a dark and eerie atmosphere that undoubtedly produced a feeling of loneliness and isolation among pioneers who had to move through these forests before clear trails and primitive roads were cut into the terrain. The initial reaction of an explorer in nearby Illinois is illustrative: "When the traveller enters the depths of these dark old woods a cool chill runs over his frame, and he feels as if he were entering the sepulcher."[13] These intimidating forests were the natural product of a temperate climate that provided about 180 growing days and forty inches of rainfall per year, and deep and fertile soil.

Occasionally the early traveler came across impressive outcroppings of limestone, intricately layered and containing a treasure of fossils that would attract future armies of paleontologists and historical geologists. Some 125,000 years earlier, the Wisconsin Glacier, the last of a series of enormous ice sheets to visit Ohio, had pushed southward out of the Arctic, eventually covering three-fourths of the area of Ohio—19,728 square miles in total. It covered all but southeastern Ohio along an elliptical line extending from northern Hamilton County to lower Columbiana County. It reshaped the once rugged terrain, pushing, twisting, churning, and grinding at the topography for some hundred thousand years before it slowly receded. Around Lake Erie the glacier reached depths estimated at an incredible eight thousand feet, tapering off to about a thousand feet along its southernmost reaches in Hamilton, Clinton, and Ross Counties. This icy monster flattened and smoothed the land, producing the gently rolling countryside of contemporary Ohio. The geologist Arthur Harper notes that as the glacier receded, it was replaced by a "magnificent hardwood forest" that covered 95 percent of present-day Ohio. The Great Miami River and the Seven Mile Creek were products of this powerful visitor from the north.

As it slowly receded, the glacier left some four hundred feet of fill in what is now the Great Miami Valley, including incredibly rich deposits of rock, sand, gravel, and other terminal debris. The village of Camden is located near the terminal moraine deposited by that great glacier. It also sits on the ancient bed of the Hamilton River, which geologists es timate drained southwestern Ohio some five hundred thousand years ago; this gigantic river also left tremendous deposits of prime sand and gravel. The deposit is some 180 feet deep and extends the one mile width of the narrow Seven Mile Creek valley in which Camden is located. Nearly two hundred years of exploiting the Miami Valley for construction and industrial purposes has barely scratched the surface of this mineral reserve.[14]

Once Congress established policies to govern land sales and surveyors had mapped the region, the area was opened to white settlers early in the nineteenth century. This was accomplished in the wake of the military victory by General "Mad" Anthony Wayne over the Indians at the Battle of Fallen Timbers near present-day Toledo in August of 1794. The flamboyant Wayne's triumph had reversed several years of inept American military efforts to subdue the several tribes that had banded together to protect their lands. Two months of negotiations the following summer between Wayne and tribal leaders produced the Treaty of Greene Ville, which led to the removal of all Indian tribes to a line drawn across the north central part of Ohio. That line proved to be temporary, for within a few decades the removal of Indians from Ohio was complete.[15]

The Treaty of Green Ville ended the threat of Indian attack in the Miami Valley. After the federal government opened the area for land sales with passage of the Land Act of 1800, active immigration into the

Ohio Territory ensued. The Land Act encouraged settlers by holding the price of land to just $2.00 per acre. It permitted settlers to purchase parcels as small as 320 acres, and generous credit terms in the Act strongly encouraged families of modest means to participate. By 1803, when Ohio became the seventeenth state, more than 937,000 acres had been sold. As word spread back east about the fertile land and abundant wild life, a veritable flood tide of settlers descended upon the state.

∿

The settlers who established themselves on the future site of Camden in 1803 were part of that influx of pioneers that poured into southwestern Ohio. Most of them came down the Ohio River to Cincinnati in primitive flatboats and then moved inland via the Great Miami River. This trans-Appalachian migration was of epic proportions and pushed Ohio's population to 222,000 by 1810, and 581,000 in 1820. By 1821 more than seven million acres had been sold to settlers and land speculators. Those who settled in the Camden area came primarily from the middle and southern states, especially Pennsylvania, New Jersey, Maryland, Virginia, and South Carolina.[16]

The first family to settle along the west side of the Seven Mile Creek on the flood plain that what would become the village of Camden was that of David Hendricks, a former scout for General Wayne. A native of New Jersey, Hendricks had served in the Revolutionary Army as a teenager and later participated in campaigns against the Indians in Ohio under Generals Josiah Harmer, Arthur St. Clair, and Wayne. He became familiar with southwestern Ohio while traversing the seventy-mile route between Fort Washington on the Ohio River and Fort Green Ville during Wayne's campaign to break Indian control of the region in 1793–94. When the land along the Seven Mile was made available for sale, Hendricks purchased 480 acres. On October 3, 1805, his son George was the first white child to be born in newly designated Preble County. The following year Camden's founding family moved to the county seat of Eaton, next to Fort St. Clair, nine miles to the north. George Hendricks became a prominent local political figure and proved to be of hearty pioneer stock: he lived to the eve of the next century, dying in 1900 at the age of 95.[17]

∿

A steady stream of settlers followed David Hendricks into southern Preble County, among the first being several branches of the Pottenger

family that moved from northern Kentucky. The Pottengers were attracted by reports of fertile soil and abundant wildlife. John Pottenger
put his eleven children to work clearing their family's quarter section of
land and soon had field corn, flax, and vegetables planted around decay-
ing but stubborn tree stumps. His two brothers, Dennis and Robert, also
accompanied by large families, established farms nearby. John Pottenger
not only farmed but also manufactured gunpowder, operated a small
grist mill, and traded in smoked and salted pork. His gunpowder was
undoubtedly used by him and his neighbors to begin the decimation of
the wildlife population. An oral history by one of Pottenger's children
recorded in 1875 paints a clear picture: "When the Pottengers moved
into this part of the country, wolves, deer, opossums, foxes, and otter
abounded in great numbers; as many as eleven otter were killed in one
night. Deer were so tame that after cutting down a hackberry tree, while
the men would be working on the trunk the deer would be browsing on
the top." Late in his life John Pottenger was quoted as recalling that deer
"were as plentiful as cattle are now." [18]

The relentless slaughter of wildlife produced meat for consumption
and furs for sale to traders. As the historian John Mack Faragher has
pointed out, the presence of ample supplies of wildlife was a major cri-
terion in the selection of places of settlement on the trans-Appalachian
frontier. Especially in the late autumn, after the crops had been harvested, men took to the woods in search of game, hoping to provide
sufficient meat to last the winter. Hunting provided more than food: as
the historian Richard Slotkin has noted, the ability to hunt successfully
was a primary means of male self-validation along the frontier. Such
psychological needs meshed with the settlers' outlook toward wild animals. They viewed such predators as wolves and fox as enemies of their
livestock, and deer, rabbit, squirrel, and turkey as food for their tables.
Locked in what they considered to be a struggle for survival in an unfor-
giving environment, they were not concerned about the preservation of
native wildlife. The shooting of wildlife not only produced food but also
attested to the sure aim of the hunter. Conservationists these new Ohio
residents definitely were not. [19]

The settlers also assaulted the virgin forests. Timber provided lumber
to build their primitive houses and sheds, and also essential tools and
equipment, including anything from hoes and shovels to wagons. Trees
were also the major source of fuel and continued to be so until the introduction of bituminous coal from eastern Ohio and Kentucky almost a
century later. Rather than viewing the mature stands of enormous trees

as precious commodities to be preserved, or at least conserved, the settlers considered them major obstacles to be removed. The new residents of the valley were farmers who never doubted for a moment that the trees had to be removed to create clear, unshaded fields for planting.

Thus the trees in these magnificent forests were systematically girdled, felled, clear cut, burned, uprooted, and otherwise destroyed. For years a constant pall of smoke hung over the valley as centuries-old mature forests were burned to make way for the planting of corn, flax, oats, barley, and wheat. The initial crops were grown among the tree stumps, but over the years farmers used their powerful oxen—the animal of choice for the first few generations of farmers—to pull out the deeply rooted stumps. By mid-century the magnificent stretch of forest that had covered the Seven Mile Valley was gone, its heritage forever reserved to small patches of woods that dotted the dramatically transformed countryside. Gone too was most of the bountiful wildlife that had once roamed the area.[20]

～

By 1820 some 250 white settlers had established permanent residence in the immediate vicinity of the flood plain on the west side of the Seven Mile Creek, erecting crude houses and sheds near their stump-pocked clearings. The first brick house—a symbol of permanence and prosperity—would not be constructed until 1832. Wiry pigs, which had been brought by the earliest settlers, roamed the nearby woods, surviving on acorns, walnuts, hickory nuts, and roots. Come late autumn the unlucky ones would be butchered, and the pork smoked and salted. The early settlers usually owned a milk cow or two, occasionally a few beef cattle. They grew their own fruit and vegetables, and their expanding fields of wheat provided flour for making bread.

By 1810 several small gristmills were in operation along the Seven Mile. North of the settlement the creek developed a few small rapids with sufficient force to turn grist stones. Although farmers occasionally used homemade flails to separate grain from chaff, they preferred the less coarse flour produced by the mills, so they tended to bring their grain to the one of the small mills for processing. In the early years most of the flour was consumed by the farmers who grew the grain, but as production increased, the surplus was sold to traders who shipped it to Hamilton along the dirt road that now paralleled the creek.[21]

In 1818 three enterprising landowners decided to capitalize on the valley's prospects. They subdivided their lands and began to sell parcels for housing and commercial sites, envisioning the creation of a permanent town to serve as the hub of the growing farming population. The petition by James William Moore, Isaac Sutton, and James Black to the Preble County commissioners included forty lots located along the Hamilton-Eaton road running through the flat portion of the valley on the west side of the Seven Mile Creek. Their plan included two side streets and four alleys, with the center of the townsite located at the spot where the dirt road made a thirty-degree correction to the north. Their petition to the county commissioners specified that the streets were to be "three rods wide" and that the lots were to be "four rods in front extending back eight rods." Thus these three developers imposed for-ever upon the future town the standard size of private lots measuring 66 x 132 feet with streets being 50 feet wide. For reasons not quite clear, but most likely in tribute to some local family origins in England, the commissioners decreed, "The town shall be known and called by the name of Dover."[22]

Dover did not flourish. In fact, it languished. Lot sales were slow, although things were looking up in terms of the number of family farms being cleared. It was not until 1824 that a small post office was estab-lished in the home of postmaster Ira Place, but it turned out that the name Dover had already been appropriated by a town in the northeast-ern part of the state. Local politics apparently dictated that the town be renamed Newcomb in honor of the state senator serving the area, George Newcomb of Dayton. The Census of 1830 reported a population of 327 in Somers Township, and on February 10, 1831, the Ohio legis-lature passed enabling legislation incorporating the town of Newcomb. In 1835, for reasons not recorded for future historians but most likely related to the declining political fortunes of Senator Newcomb, the new village council voted to change the name of the community again. Sev-eral residents who had emigrated from South Carolina recommended the name Camden, after the town near where on August 16, 1780, American patriots had fought bravely, but unsuccessfully, under General Horatio Gates against a much larger and better outfitted British force commanded by General Charles Cornwallis.[23]

The incorporation papers established for Camden a typical village government of an elected mayor and five councilmen (a structure essen-tially unchanged to this day). In the early years, local elections seldom elicited much excitement because contested elections occurred only in-frequently. Rather, leading male merchants, professionals, and large property owners usually consented to run for office, they said, out of a sense of public responsibility. This paternalistic system of male estab-lishment leadership ensured that decisions affecting taxes, community

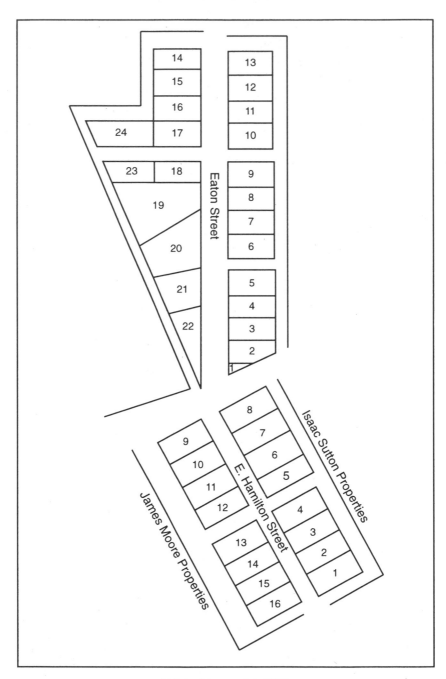

Original town plat, 1818.

improvements, business regulations, and major capital acquisitions would be in the hands of those whose financial interests were most heavily affected.

∽

Possessing a permanent name, populated by a group of determined residents, and equipped with a functional form of government, the village grew steadily if not spectacularly. It made the transition from frontier to organized community, being swept along by the rapid economic development of southwestern Ohio. From its inception, Dover-Newcomb-Camden was dominated by the economic powerhouse emerging forty miles to the south, Cincinnati. Built on a flood plain of the Ohio River fifteen miles east of the Indiana border near the site of Ft. Washington, Cincinnati established itself as the central market for the expanding agricultural economy of southwestern Ohio, southeastern Indiana, and northern Kentucky—what is known today as the "Tri-State Area." It also became the jumping-off place for families moving into the region. Calling their promising community the "Queen City of the West," energetic businessmen took advantage of a prime location approximately midway along the Ohio's route from its headwaters at Pittsburgh to Cairo, Illinois, where it flows into the Mississippi.[24]

By the third decade of the century Cincinnati had become the center of banking and commerce in the region. The major products of the city and its surrounding farmlands—processed pork and beef, corn whiskey, flour, and raw grain—were sent downriver to New Orleans on flatboats. Following the introduction of steam-powered ships on the Ohio River in 1811, it became feasible to ship goods upstream as well, although it was well into the third decade of the nineteenth century before this became common. By 1820 Cincinnati's entrepreneurs were reaping high profit margins from a flourishing flour milling and shipping business.

The flour trade was soon eclipsed by meat packing during the 1820s. Enterprising meat packers introduced new technologies in order to take advantage of the rapidly increasing demand for their products. The historian Daniel Aaron, quoting from a contemporary description, ruefully comments that within less than an hour, "the fated porker that was but one minute before grunting in the full enjoyment of bustling hoghood" would be reduced by "mallet—the knife—the axe—the boiling cauldron—the remorseless scraping iron" to nothing more than a "stark and naked effigy among his immolated brethren." Within hours, the remaining two hundred pounds of pork had been placed in a sealed barrel of brine, ready for shipment.[25]

By the 1830s Cincinnati's aggressive packers had introduced steam-driven conveyor belts to move pig and beef carcasses efficiently from one work station to the next. It was truly an efficient "dis-assembly" plant as the animals were slaughtered, cleaned, cut, smoked, sugar cured, pickled, packaged in wooden crates, and shipped. Cincinnati's meat packers provided one of the first large-scale examples of mass production in the United States. They not only produced quality pork and beef for national and international markets but also found ways to use animal by-products. It was during the 1840s that a pair of German immigrants, the Lever brothers, began manufacturing soaps, candles, and lotions; and other businesses produced leather products. As one observer commented, everything but the pig's squeal was turned into a marketable commodity. The Queen City now earned a much more accurate, if less flattering, nickname. By mid-century five hundred thousand animals a year met their fate in the city locals now called "Porkopolis." In an age before zoning and environmental laws, travelers to Porkopolis often remarked that they could anticipate the city well before it came into view from the aroma that filled the river valley. The English writer Frances Trollope, who visited in 1828, complained that it was impossible to cross a Cincinnati street without "brushing by a snout," and about "ordours that I will not describe, and which I heartily hope my readers cannot imagine."[26]

As they made the transition from subsistence to commercial agriculture, farmers throughout the Miami Valley rushed to increase pork production to feed the seemingly insatiable demand coming from Cincinnati. Although the quality of the wiry and semiwild pigs grown on the frontier was initially inferior—they were variously called "razorbacks," "alligators," and "prairie rooters"—farmers in nearby Warren County developed a new breed, the Poland China, whose popularity spread across the valley during the middle of the century. This animal was hearty, grew rapidly, and produced high quality pork. The emergence of southwestern Ohio as a major center for pork and, to a somewhat lesser extent, beef production resulted from the combination of temperature, rainfall, and soil which made the area a prime location for growing corn. What corn was not consumed by pigs or cattle was ground into flour or distilled into whiskey.[27]

∼

Livestock production grew so rapidly in the Seven Mile Valley that as early as the 1820s livestock traders in Camden had constructed holding pens near the creek along Cross (later renamed Central) Avenue, the village's primary east-west thoroughfare. While these traders often drove their livestock to market down the Hamilton-Eaton highway, they also experimented with stave-sided wagons that were pulled by oxen. Sheep were also raised, but in smaller quantities. Local appetites did not readily take to lamb and mutton, and the animals were raised primarily for their wool.[28]

Like the thousands of frontier farmers spreading across the trans-Appalachian west, those who settled along the Seven Mile Creek made the transition from self-sufficiency to commercial farming over a period lasting many decades. This process extended well into the twentieth century, but it began with the first generation of settlers who shipped their surplus production to Cincinnati. As new technologies made it possible to improve production per acre, farmers increasingly emphasized production for market. The first two or three generations relied heavily on human labor; large families were needed to provide sufficient "hands" to clear the land, tend the crops, and care for livestock. Families with six or more children were the norm, and many families had in excess of ten offspring. When they first took to the fields, their implements were crude, often handmade, and very basic: hoe, shovel, scythe, sickle, and rake. Those who used oxen for plowing employed a yoke, plow, and harrow, all handmade from local woods.[29]

Well into the later decades of the nineteenth century, oxen provided the primary source of power, but they were slowly replaced by improved technology. As new farm machinery revolutionized farming—John Deere steel plows, harvesters, threshing machines, discs—farmers converted to the more sophisticated and much faster draft horse and, to a lesser extent, the mule. By the 1850s wheat farmers were using horse-drawn McCormick reapers and steam-powered threshers, but change came slowly, and it was not all that unusual well into the twentieth century to see farmers who lacked adequate capital cutting wheat by hand with the same type of large wooden cradles that had been introduced in the 1830s.[30]

～

Camden's first tradesmen operated small gristmills and general stores. As early as 1810 two small "corn cracker" mills were in operation. Not only did corn help feed the growing hog and cattle population, but settlers learned to rely on this essential crop for such daily staples as cornbread, mush, and hominy. Early on, John Stubbs demonstrated the possibilities of economic diversification when he expanded his services by adding a sawmill and a wool-carding machine to his gristmill along

Barnet's Mill was constructed along the Seven Mile Creek a mile north of town in 1862. A hub of activity throughout the late nineteenth century, the mill was abandoned about 1900 and eventually razed shortly after World War II. This picture, taken about 1930, first appeared in the *Preble County News*. Courtesy Camden Archives.

the creek. Expanding wheat crops prompted Stubbs to build a larger facility in 1832, complete with three buhrstone runs. The business was later purchased and expanded by James Barnet and William Whitesides. After a fire destroyed the facility in 1862, Barnet and Whitesides constructed a three-story storage elevator and modern facility with an enormous investment of $45,000.[31]

In addition to the mills, several small cooperage shops opened to turn out the many sizes and shapes of wooden tubs, casks, barrels, and hogsheads required for processing, storing, and shipping agricultural produce. Although several small one-man operations were set up in backyards in town, the growing enterprise of Barnet and Whitesides employed several coopers to produce barrels for shipping their flour to market. Local distillers used barrels to age and ship their corn whiskey, although the production of whisky or beer never grew beyond the size of a cottage industry. Most of what was produced locally was apparently consumed locally.[32]

In 1820 real estate promoter and town founder James Moore was operating the only store in Camden, a combination general store and tavern located on the corner of what would become the town's main intersection of Cross Avenue and Main Street. As the town grew, so did the number of merchants. By 1850, when the town had reached a population of 400 with approximately 750 persons living on the surrounding farmland, Camden had a substantial number of merchants. With increased consumer demand came economic diversification. The Census of 1850 reported male occupations of carpenter, stone mason, huckster, minister, cooper, miller, laborer, basket maker, painter, plasterer, shoemaker, schoolmaster, wagon maker, shingle maker, lawyer, butcher, carriage maker, tavern keeper, grocer, tinsmith, carder, clerk, hatter, chandler, saddler, brick maker, teacher, cabinet maker, weaver, and teamster. And, interestingly enough, one Troilus Brown listed his occupation as "phrenologist." The local population now supported several taverns, a bakery, two livery stables, a butcher shop, a grocery store, a tin shop, a drug store, a dry goods and notions store, several blacksmith and harness shops, and two men's clothing stores.[33]

The most prominent of Camden's growing business establishments was a large general store operated by Clinton Chadwick and William Pottenger which offered a wide assortment of goods, including clothing, carpets, housewares, hardware, boots and shoes, linens, cast-iron stoves, and groceries. The county seat newspaper, the *Eaton Weekly Register,* took due note of the Chadwick-Pottenger enterprise, commenting upon the "commodious brick edifice, deep one way and broad the other, spacious between floors, and so much of its space as is not required by the proprietors for their extensive and unrivaled stock of merchandise is daily thronged with eager customers, intent upon procuring good wares and bargains."[34]

Pottenger and Chadwick also traded in farm commodities; in 1855 they advertised that they had an immediate market for "20,000 bushels of corn, 20,000 pounds of wool, 8,000 bushels of oats, and all the flaxseed we can get, for which the highest price will be paid in cash." But their economic base was general merchandise, which they procured from wholesalers in Cincinnati. "That the people in the vicinity know how to appreciate such an establishment at a point so convenient, is evidenced in the rapid extension of its business and the prosperity of the proprietors," the *Eaton Weekly Register* reported in approving fashion.[35]

With growth and the passage of time came a sense of permanence. The raw and crude appearance of a frontier community slowly disappeared. Prosperous families now constructed houses out of locally made brick. Several two- and three-story brick commercial buildings appeared along Main Street, a sure sign of community progress and the prosperity of their owners. The brick came from a small brickyard that had been opened just east of the Seven Mile Creek where a concentration of high quality clay was discovered, a resource deposited by the Great Wisconsin Glacier. On the southwestern corner of the intersection of Main and Cross stood the town's pride and joy, the imposing three-story brick edifice the Preble House. Built in 1846, the inn and tavern provided food, drink, and shelter for those traveling the Hamilton-Eaton highway by horseback or in the local stagecoach. The Preble House was owned and operated by William Pottenger and Stephen Payne.[36]

Signs of stability and expansion were evident elsewhere. The town's first physician and general surgeon, Dr. Lurton Dunham, hung out his shingle in 1832. In 1852 the population had reached the point where two physicians were kept busy. Their services were complemented by Bohn's Apothecary, which dispensed drugs, patent medicines, elixirs, and tonics. Camden even had a barber, who touted himself as a "tonsorial artist." His shop was complete with a prominent red, white, and blue barber pole out front, and he announced that he accepted both male and female customers, promising to cut hair "in any style," even offering "hair dying" as a house specialty. The local undertaker conducted a steady business, burying the recently departed in Fairview Cemetery, north of town.[37]

≈

Until the 1850s the dirt road (ambitiously called a "highway") that connected Hamilton and Eaton provided the town's lifeline to the outside world. Camden was only indirectly affected by the spectacular (and speculative) canal era that swept Ohio to the forefront of the nation's economic expansion during the 1820s and 1830s. The Erie Canal spurred an enormous frenzy of canal building in Ohio in the 1820s, led by Governor Ethan Allen Brown. State politicians and urban promoters knew that the stakes were high, and eventually the Ohio Board of Canal Commissioners approved three major north-south routes to link the Ohio River to Lake Erie, thereby connecting the entire state to the Erie Canal and the rapidly growing port of New York City. Southern terminuses were established at Marietta and Portsmouth, and by the mid-1830s these canals carried freight and passengers to Cleveland via Zanesville and Columbus.

In western Ohio the board of commissioners approved construction of the Great Miami and Erie Canal, which was built in stages depending upon available financing. The Cincinnati to Middletown section opened in 1828 and was extended to Toledo after the economic crisis of 1837. Unfortunately for Camden, the canal was constructed some twenty-five miles to the east. Consequently, this important artificial waterway had only minimal impact on the town's economy. It did, however, stimulate substantial economic development in Hamilton, Middletown, Franklin, Cincinnati, and Dayton, thereby creating an urban network in which Camden would later have to compete. Left high and dry by the canal planners, Camden's farmers and merchants still had to rely on the Hamilton-Eaton highway.[38]

When the railroad era opened, local leaders were determined that this time Camden would not be forgotten. Although much of the state's canal complex had not yet been completed, by the late 1820s Ohio's political and business leaders found themselves enmeshed in a new frenzy of chicanery and speculation. The high-powered politicking and deal making that had determined the location of canal routes paled in comparison to the orgy of speculation and crass politics that accompanied Ohio's entrance into the railroad era.

It did not take a perceptive futurist to recognize that the railroads would quickly eclipse the canals, in terms of both reliability and speed. It was equally apparent that good rail connections to major markets held the key to any community's economic future. The legislature approved its first railroad charter in 1832 for the stillborn Ohio and Steubenville Railroad; like many other railroad speculations, it was never built. The legislature approved 68 other charters in the same decade despite the economic downturn of 1837, another 76 companies in the 1840s, and before the Panic of 1857 brought at least a temporary modicum of sanity and financial reality to the process, 140 in the 1850s. Typically, these were short lines, financed largely by local investors, although sometimes state funds were made available to provide construction capital if lobbyists could convince pliable legislators. Despite many a failure and scandal, by 1851 trains ran regularly from Cleveland to Cincinnati, and along many shorter connecting routes as well.[39]

It was in the middle of this frenetic period of railroad construction that Camden's commercial elite, led by Dr. Dunham and the mill owner David Barnet, joined with leaders in the county seat of Eaton to secure investor support for the Hamilton and Eaton Railroad. The best route lay along the Seven Mile Creek bed. Construction started in 1849, and for three years locals buzzed with news about the progress being made by construction workers. In May of 1852 the first wood-burning traction

For nearly a century the railroad depot located on the east side of town was a focal point of passenger travel and freight transport. The first depot, built in 1867, was replaced with this facility in 1896. The depot was torn down in 1972, ten years after freight service and twenty-one years after passenger service was terminated. Courtesy Camden Archives.

engine hissed and steamed its way into Camden, sparks flying dangerously and setting a few small fires along the track bed. It was greeted by an enthusiastic crowd at the future site of the depot on Cross Avenue. Curiosity undoubtedly lured most of the throng who gathered alongside the creek, but also the prospect of winning the raffle prize, a free round-trip ticket to Hamilton. Not all locals were enthralled, however: teenager Benjamin Lamm proclaimed the iron horse to be "the work of the devil" and took an errant potshot at it with a squirrel rifle. In 1863 the local company sold out to the Cincinnati, Richmond, and Chicago line, which in turn was swallowed up by the Pennsylvania system in 1890.[40]

By the end of the Civil War, the Cincinnati, Richmond, and Chicago Railroad provided daily passenger and freight service for Camden. A wooden depot was constructed along the siding in 1867 and soon became a popular hangout for local men, who shared gossip, argued baseball and politics, swapped lies and jokes, complained about the weather, and chewed tobacco around the pot-bellied stove strategically located in the middle of the stationmaster's office. The mail came and left through the depot, and the stationmaster also controlled the key to the Western Union telegraph service. Farmers shipped their grain and livestock to market from this siding, and business grew so great that a fenced stockyard had to be constructed to maintain order. In 1877 an estimated $250,000 worth of livestock went to market from this location.[41]

Although the most modern of transportation technologies was now firmly established, the town did not grow at a more rapid pace than it had before 1850. The promise of a railroad connection often proved greater than its performance; like many other small communities that had anticipated a period of growth after acquiring railroad service, Camden saw little economic change.[42] Access to the railroad insured that the town would become a more convenient and efficient market for local farmers, and Camden continued to grow, but at the same sluggish pace as before. Each decade the federal census reported a hundred or so new residents. Natural growth, supplemented by a few new residents, produced modest population increases. The same familiar family names appear on local records year after year—McCord, Danser, Pottenger, Newton, Moore, Ferguson, Roberts, Jones, Marsh, Patterson, Craig, Mann, White, Fornshell. For the next fifty years the village maintained its slow growth rate, which produced social stability, confidence in the future, even a degree of smugness.

∽

As the town matured, it saw the establishment of institutions and businesses essential to the functioning of an organized community. Early records indicate that the first school classes were held in 1818 under the guidance of a teacher paid directly by parents of the few students. In 1825, under Ohio law, a board of directors for the local school was established by Somers Township officials so that a modest property tax could be collected to support public education. In 1838 a small school was constructed on West Cross Avenue which served its purpose until a four-room brick building replaced it on the same site in 1853 at a cost of $4,000. Students studied in consolidated classes to the equivalent of the eighth grade.[43]

Fragmentary records indicate that the local educational enterprise suffered from the usual problems of discipline, truancy, and teacher turnover. Passage of a compulsory attendance law in 1877 by the Ohio

This school building, constructed in 1853, was torn down in 1904 to make room for a larger building. This picture was taken around 1875. Courtesy Camden Archives.

legislature, made effective by the prospect of the loss of state funds for noncompliance, led to the employment of a part-time truant officer. In 1881 local records show an enrollment of 108 students served by three female teachers, whose salaries ranged from $33 to $40 per month. The principal, Oscar Corson, earned $62. In 1890 the first high school graduating class of three received diplomas.[44]

In 1903 state building inspectors condemned the half-century old wooden school, and taxpayers approved a $15,000 twenty-year bond issue to construct a two-story, nine-room brick building on the same site. The highlight of the dedication ceremony in 1904 was the presentation by the local chapter of the Women's Christian Temperance Union of a photograph of Frances Willard that was hung in the main lobby. In 1909 the high school class graduated nine students. Enrollment increased in 1915 when the voters approved funding to consolidate the Camden school with the few one-room rural schools being operated by the Somers Township trustees, requiring the purchase of ten horse-drawn wagons to transport students to school.[45]

A major milestone for any community in its march toward respectability is the establishment of a public library. In Camden, the push for a library coincided with the community's efforts to improve its public school system. The library began as a service project of the Philomathean Club, a women's literary society that had its roots in the post-Civil War years. The leaders were wives of some of Camden's prominent businessmen and professionals: Lora Shuey, wife of the only attorney in town and one of its most serious Republicans; Ola McChristie, wife of the owner of a printing and photography shop; and Amy Danser, wife of the town's jeweler. Society members sold raffle tickets to raise monies to purchase a core collection of several hundred books, and solicited donations of used books from townspeople. They secured space in the small office of the Camden Building and Loan, even getting its director to serve as an ad hoc librarian. In 1906 the city council granted a modest sum to pay for the rental of rooms, and the board of education formally accepted responsibility for its operation; in 1913 a more spacious area was rented on the ground floor of the new Masonic Hall on South Main Street, where the library remains to this day. In 1931 the library reported a collection of over three thousand books, and an

Constructed in 1904 at a cost of $15,000, this nine-room school building still stands. It served as an elementary school until 1958 and today houses a small antique store in what was once the second grade classroom. Courtesy Camden Archives.

astonishing circulation of fifteen thousand. The Philomathean Club's service project was but one example of a nationwide reform effort spearheaded by women's service groups to improve their communities.[46]

～

In addition to improving public education and advancing literacy, Camden also embraced new technology. In 1881 the Hamilton, Camden, and Eaton Telephone Company installed a primitive system, and a journalist optimistically reported, "A telephone line extends to West Elkton, and from there to Camden, affording easy communication from the outside world." Wooden poles to carry the lines sprouted up along the dirt highway from Hamilton to Eaton, sure signs of progress. For the first fifteen years of its participation in the telephone era, Camden had one solitary telephone, located in Lee Danser's jewelry store. In 1900 businessman Samuel Morton and a few associates received authorization from the village council to provide local service, and they set about installing poles, lines, and a switchboard. The Camden Telephone Company initiated service to its 25 customers in the fall of 1901, charging businesses $2 per month and residences $1. Within two years, lines had been strung to nearby towns, and the number of subscribers exceeded 250, with more than 50 others on a waiting list.[47]

Telephone service arrived a few years ahead of electricity. As early as 1870 the council had authorized the installation of two gasoline lights to illuminate the corner of Main and Cross. Street lighting was a symbol of an up-to-date town, although considerable debate ensued before the parsimonious council voted to appropriate $33.75 for the purchase and installation of two light poles; included in this appropriation was authorization to acquire a tin can and an initial supply of five gallons of fuel. Public reaction to street illumination was so positive that six more lights were installed down South Main Street later that year.[48]

This modest improvement helped prepare the town for electricity. In 1883, amid a flurry of publicity, the city of Dayton installed electric street lights, and the Dayton Electric Company began extending service to businesses and residences. It was not until 1898 that a group of Camden investors were ready to take the plunge. The village council authorized the recently formed Camden Electric Company to build a generating facility and extend lines throughout the community. Service proved spotty and profits skimpy, and the company went through several owners and management reorganizations before it was purchased by the Liberty (Indiana) Light and Power Company in 1915. By this time Camdenites

The communications center of American small towns was the local telephone switchboard. It remained part of Camden's life until the installation of modern switching equipment in 1959. The women who commanded Camden's switchboard posed for this picture in 1948. Courtesy Camden Archives.

had incorporated electricity into their daily lives, but farms were still without service—a major disparity between town and country.[49]

With the publication of its first weekly newspaper, Camden took another major step toward establishing its identity as a town of substance. On June 2, 1877, the *Camden Herald,* edited by Will Hartpence, made its appearance. Until this time residents had relied upon the *Eaton Weekly Register* or the *Eaton Democrat.* Those eager to keep abreast of national news purchased one of the several competing daily Cincinnati newspapers that were tossed off at the depot from slow-moving trains. Hartpence had a short but fiery run. The new editor was a dedicated temperance zealot and not reticent about speaking his mind on community issues. He took special delight in embarrassing local men whose personal behavior did not conform to his view of proper decorum. Freedom of the press sometimes has its costs. When Hartpence shut down in late 1879 only two merchants were still regularly purchasing advertising. He sold the *Herald*'s Linotype and press to local investors and decamped for Indiana. Shortly thereafter the much less abrasive *Camden Gazette* filled the void.[50]

This picture, taken in 1893, shows a covered brick walk on the northeastern corner of Central and Main. The building still stands and was for more than fifty years the location of the local telephone company's switchboard.

In 1902 the owners changed the weekly's name to the *Preble County News,* and it would appear every Thursday morning for the next eighty-six years, its masthead and four-page format seldom changing. Front-page stories featured a special event or elections and obituaries of prominent locals who had been "called." Extensive discussions of the weather, press releases from Ohio State University's agricultural extension service, local sports results, and the all-important "personals" column vied for front-page treatment. The inside pages were devoted to advertising, filler from national newspaper services, legal notices, county budget detail, and school lunch menus. Subsequent editors learned a lesson from the speedy demise of Will Hartpence and assiduously attempted to avoid controversial issues. When it became absolutely necessary to report on topics that divided the community, the editor used such vague and murky language that only those who already knew the details of the story could fully understand what was at issue. Always Republican in tenor, the *News* seldom bothered to endorse candidates; it merely ignored Democrats whenever possible. The boldest editorial positions ever taken were to endorse school or village bond issues in the name of "progress."

∿

The local newspaper's Republican perspective met with the widespread approval of the local readership. Camden's voters had a strong Whig inclination before the Civil War and early on embraced the Republican Party and never let go. While the Civil War provided an emotional tie to the Grand Old Party, the attraction to the Republican Party was primarily economic and social. Like the majority of Ohio voters, Camden's (male) voters tended to vote the way they had shot during the war; but even more fundamental, this was a community of dedicated small capitalists attracted to standard Republican policies favoring high tariffs, low taxes, and maintenance of the gold standard. The Republican proclivity to view labor unions with considerable skepticism also meshed well with local views, molded by the dominant agricultural economy. Camden voters had nothing in common with the socialists and union radicals who occasionally raised a ruckus in Cincinnati and Cleveland, and they certainly had no sympathy for the hell-raising Populists out on the Great Plains. They perceived the Republican Party as their party: middle class, probusiness, antiradical, cautious about immigration, fiercely patriotic, instinctively opposed to taxes, and strongly resistant to government interference with property rights.

Camden's voters routinely supported most any Republican in national, state, and county elections. Although the Republicans generally controlled Preble County offices, upon occasion strong Democratic candidates could and did win; but they had to get their majorities elsewhere in the county. Camden's voters proudly supported fellow Buckeyes Ulysses S. Grant, Rutherford B. Hayes, James Garfield, William McKinley, William Howard Taft, and Warren Gamaliel Harding. To be born a white male in small-town Ohio after the Civil War, a biographer of Harding once commented, was to be born a potential future president. Perhaps, but such a young man also had a great likelihood of becoming a staunch Republican.[51]

The pivotal presidential elections of 1896 and 1900 are especially instructive. In those years tensions rose to a fever pitch as the two national candidates debated fundamental issues from radically different perspectives. Camden's Republicans apparently feared the Apocalypse should the Great Commoner, William Jennings Bryan, seize control of the federal government with his free silver heresies. M. E. Fornshell, editor of the *Camden Gazette,* undoubtedly summarized the views of most Camden voters when he denounced Bryan as an "evil example of a presidential candidate." Calling for a "rebuke by the voters with crushing emphasis," Fornshell concluded, "Dangerous as are the polices that he avows, far more dangerous is the spirit of envy, and malice, and discontent . . . and all that brood of evil passions to which he constantly appeals."[52]

During the election of 1896, loyal Camden Republicans attended

Camden's faithful Republicans turned out in full force on October 20, 1902, to welcome Cleveland political giant Mark Hanna. Main Street looking south from the intersection with Central Avenue. Courtesy Camden Archives.

local rallies, imported anti-Bryan speakers from Cincinnati, erected a "McKinley pole," marched in parades on Main Street, and even traveled to nearby towns to spread the gospel. Bryan's agrarian radicalism had no appeal to local farmers either.[53] They had periodically felt the sting of depressed commodity markets, but they were fortunate to have opportunities to diversify their products. Unlike the southern cotton or Great Plains wheat farmers, and thanks to the weather they often cursed and the fertile soil they plowed, Camden's farmers were not dependent upon a primary crop. Their income came from many sources—corn, wheat, oats, barley, flax, eggs, soybeans, milk, beef, pork, poultry, and wool. Even those farmers who had invested heavily in commercial farming still grew much of their own family's food. Farmers from the smallest to the largest operations supplemented their cash crop incomes by selling on the local markets the surplus from the large gardens tended by their wives and children. Thus their cash flow benefited from the sale of such easily grown items as tomatoes, potatoes, sweet corn, beans, peas, carrots, walnuts, apples, peaches, lettuce, cabbage, radishes, popping corn, beets, onions, and spinach. Those who tilled the soil in Somers Township had little in common with the agrarian radicals out beyond the Missouri River. On election day in 1896 they and like-minded men in Camden voted by more than 2–1 for McKinley and sanity. The *Gazette* proclaimed McKinley's victory with a banner headline, "Victory! Ohio's Noble Son, Our Next President."[54] Four years later, they reaffirmed their strong distaste for Bryan.

On October 20, 1902, Camden enthusiastically welcomed a visit by McKinley's shrewd campaign manager and major benefactor, the Cleveland iron and shipping magnate Mark Hanna. Main Street was festooned with patriotic banners and flags and lined with cheering crowds of thankful Republicans who had come to express their gratitude for his having helped save the Union from the radical from Nebraska. Hanna's visit would long be remembered as a high point in the town's political history.[55]

Even in 1932, when heavily Republican Preble County gave Franklin Roosevelt a 6,210–5,205 margin, Camden voters went for Herbert Hoover by a few votes. Even the worst of the Great Depression was not enough to prompt a temporary abandonment of the Grand Old Party. Nonetheless, there were some prominent residents who persisted in their loyalty to the Democratic Party. They were proud, defiant, and outspoken, but invariably outnumbered. At times, as in 1932, they could stir things up, but locals viewed the Republican Party as the unquestioned tribune of American capitalism. Through such agonies as free

This rare picture, taken about 1880 from the hill on the west side of town called Mt. Auburn, shows the decentralized nature of the placement of houses and outbuildings. The steeple of the Methodist Church can be seen on the right side of Hendrix Street. Courtesy Camden Archives.

silver and New Deals, cold wars and shooting wars, New Frontiers and Great Societies, even Watergate, the Republicans held the allegiance of Camden voters as if in a vise.

～

As the village of Camden moved into the twentieth century, it had established a mercantile economy that served the needs of local agriculture. Conservative in their politics and prudent in their finances, generally satisfied with the status quo, the town's leadership had fallen into a pattern of responding to community needs only when absolutely required to do so. This hesitancy to respond quickly to challenges became a community mind-set that would change little in the decades ahead. Even the most perceptive of citizens, however, could not have anticipated the tumultuous impact that outside economic and cultural forces would have on the community in the new century.

2

Winesburg: Life along Main Street

Despite the fluctuations of economic cycles, America's small towns had good reason for optimism as the twentieth century dawned. The anguished cries of the farm radicals of the 1890s faded as farmers used new technologies and scientific advances to increase production and as national and international markets grew. Although this expansion sometimes led to depressed commodity prices due to market surplus, in the long run increased income trickled into local economies. All in all, life along the Main Streets of America was good. The future seemed promising.[1]

Little did town leaders realize that powerful external forces were poised to undercut their economies and ultimately remove their communities from their central place in American life. As the historian Murray Klein puts it, by early in the twentieth century technology had turned the towns into "sort of a national still life," making them "the shards and icons of a vanishing way of life."[2]

Residents and leaders of these communities did not foresee the changes that would cause political power, business, and ultimately people to flow from the towns to the cities. They did not anticipate the lure of the metropolis—indeed, most rural and small town residents held the growing cities in contempt—and the long reach of the corporations that would develop there. The residents who lived in or near small farming communities could not envision the eventual coming of the Age of Wal-Mart in the distant 1970s, a development that would essentially apply the coup de grâce to the once proud and independent

Main Street culture.[3] But by 1900 the inexorable process of consolidation and concentration had already been established.

~

Camden was one such town caught up in this cultural transformation. By the end of the nineteenth century, Camden was indistinguishable in appearance, form, and function from some ten thousand similar communities spread across the land. These farming towns remained comfortable "island communities," capable of existing in a relatively self-sufficient manner.[4] The further west they were, the closer they were tied physically and emotionally to the frontier. The midwestern towns in which Sinclair Lewis, Hamlin Garland, and Willa Cather grew up, in Minnesota, Wisconsin, and Nebraska, had existed for only a few decades and everywhere traces of the frontier were still evident.

These communities provided the vital economic and social hub for the surrounding farmland. There were so many scattered across the landscape because each had to be located within the reach of horse-drawn buggies and wagons. Each town provided the necessities: a bank, a weekly newspaper, a general store, perhaps a clothing emporium, a school, a barber, a physician or two, a lawyer to draw up wills and provide assistance for those who entered the county courts, several livery stables, harness makers and blacksmiths, a few taverns, an undertaker, and, of course, several churches.[5]

The passing of the seasons dominated life in these secure communities, a rhythm attuned to the peaks and valleys of activity on the farms they served. The arrival of spring meant an end to the tedium of winter and the start of the long and arduous, but optimistic, days of planting. Summer meant searing heat and oppressive humidity as endless hours were spent tending fields and livestock. The harvest days of autumn brought with them a much anticipated climax to the growing season — with luck a reward when crops were sold to market — and then a slowing of the work cycle and anticipation of winter. Life on the farm and in the nearby towns ebbed and flowed with the passing of the seasons.

America's small towns of the late nineteenth century were tightly knit social organisms built around shared cultural and social values. With some notable exceptions, these towns were overwhelmingly Protestant; the doctrines of the Baptists, Methodists, Presbyterians, and Lutherans generally set the tone, although in certain areas, such as northwestern Ohio, there were strong pockets of Catholicism. The churches provided the major social outlet for the residents, a role that they reluctantly yielded to the public schools as the twentieth century unfolded.

Everyone in these communities knew their place and role. Men were, indeed, the head of their families, providing for material needs with their labor, presiding at the dinner table, handing out the more physical forms of discipline to the children. But man's domain was largely outside the home, in the world of business or physical labor. For young children, the home was a special preserve of security, supervised by their mother. "I lived in my mother's world, not my father's," a man recalled of his childhood in a small New York town at the turn of the twentieth century. "My mother fed me, clothed me, taught me, and entertained me. She made the rules and set the tenor of the household. Her ideas, not my fathers, became my ideas."[6] This period was, of course, the heyday of Victorianism, when the widely accepted rules of domesticity restricted women to the home. This was especially true in the small town. Women were responsible for running the household, nurturing the young, and participating in church activities. They were expected to be discreet in their dress and behavior, deferential to their husbands, obedient, and, at least publicly, subservient.[7]

Viewed from a distance, life in America's small towns seems to have flown naturally from a fount of shared assumptions and values. The basic institutions of the church, the school, and the home all contributed to the unchallenged moral code that controlled thought and action. The essential truths of the Bible were accepted without question, and a code of conduct and moral behavior was central to the moralistic teachings that pervaded the *McGuffey Readers* in the primary school. The centrality of these ideas was reinforced in Sunday school, from the pulpit, and around the family dinner table.[8]

William Holmes McGuffey's elementary school readers addressed what he considered to be a classless society. But the values that he laced throughout his readings were those of the white middle class. His was a world of order, discipline, reverence, sacrifice, work, sobriety, obedience, and deference to established authority. His teachings not only meshed with the assumptions of small-town Americans but also continually reinforced them as year after year the dog-eared readers were passed on from one class to another. Although most residents considered themselves to be middle class, careful observation would have revealed the existence of many small but important nuances indicating gradients in social standing depending largely upon income, education, occupation, and religious faith. Certain behavioral characteristics were expected of those enjoying substantial social standing; sobriety, diligence, probity, reliability, and a responsible work ethic went a long way toward determining one's standing in the community. Residents believed in the inevitability of Progress, a benevolent but demanding God, and the American Dream. They were unquestionably patriotic. Day laborers were respected for their diligence and industry but did not enjoy the status of the town doctor, banker, newspaper publisher, or businessman. Teachers and ministers found themselves in the ambivalent and sometimes awkward roles of being highly regarded but poorly paid. They helped maintain and protect community values but did not produce wealth, and they knew that their behavior was always under special scrutiny.[9]

These "island communities" shared something that was, at the time, considered by most residents to be very special. They provided an inclusive environment in which each resident—as long as he or she conformed to accepted patterns of thought and behavior—was considered to be part of an extended family. "In the nineteenth century," Lewis Atherton observes, "people were born into the small town as they once were born into the church. They 'belonged' by their very presence, and they had something larger than themselves to which to cling."[10]

This sense of belonging pervaded all aspects of life. Children at play could roam the streets of the town without fear. The cloak of protectiveness kept teenagers focused on wholesome activities; even the perpetrators of Halloween pranks were usually quickly identified and properly chastised if the transgression was serious enough. This communal spirit extended to the retired and even to the retarded. Sherwood Anderson wrote of Turk Smollett, an "old man with an absurdly childish mind," who took great delight pushing his wheelbarrow full of wood up Main Street because he attracted attention in the form of shouted greetings from amused townsfolk. It was Turk's way of affirming that he held a special position in Winesburg; he belonged.[11]

There was, of course, another side to this pervading sense of togetherness and belonging. The pressure to conform to community standards was intense, and those who were unable to adapt either left or retreated into a shell of isolation. There were always eyes watching the behavior of neighbors; gossip was endemic. Hamlin Garland described the "militant social democracy" that was both "comical and corrective" in the ongoing process of policing behavior. In commenting on the pervasive role of gossip, he said it "served as an information judge and jury, and it sat daily to pass on every individual in the town." Sherwood Anderson describes the plight of salesman Elmer Cowley, whose inability to adapt to the behavioral standards of Winesburg made him the incessant target of community criticism, from which he ultimately felt compelled to escape, ironically fleeing to Cleveland, the largest city in Ohio, to find solitude and inner peace.[12]

In a small town, everyone knew everyone else, and while that meant unacceptable or nontraditional behavior was quickly identified and powerful community sanctions imposed, it also meant that the protective cloak of the community was available in times of emergency or need. Criminal activity of any type was extremely rare. Although most towns had a local marshal, his was a part-time job, quite possibly a modest political sinecure. His most pressing duties entailed dealing with occasional public drunkenness or other disorderly behavior. Crimes of violence were almost unheard of.

The community also performed the function of helping the needy. When a family fell on hard times, neighbors discreetly came to their assistance with food, medical aid, clothing, and fuel. Each church operated its own charitable program, but often "neighborly" assistance spontaneously filled in when residents saw individuals or families in need. A death or serious illness produced an outpouring of casseroles, roasts, desserts, offers of help, and, of course, plenty of sympathy and consolation. Town doctors were legendary for their ability to forget to send a bill to those suffering from economic woes.

The organized social life of the American town in the late nineteenth century revolved around the church. The frequently tenuous status of ministers was always a staple of the gossip mill. Sunday was a day for rest and worship. Stores and taverns were closed, and church attendance offered the only meaningful opportunity for social outlet. Keeping the faith in America's villages was often an all-day event along Main Street, beginning with a Sunday school that provided religious instruction for all ages, followed by a lengthy formal service. The "Lord's Day" often culminated with an evening of "preaching" and hymn singing. On weekdays women attended aid society meetings, sewing circles, and Bible study classes. Men's and youth groups met during weekday evenings. Regular Wednesday evening services, which replicated those held on Sunday mornings, were not unusual. Frequent church fund-raisers, often called "fairs" or "bazaars," provided opportunities for socializing,

Camden residents apparently took their religious obligations seriously, if this un-smiling group of Methodists, who posed for a camera in 1899, is any indication. Courtesy Camden Archives.

as did the ubiquitous potluck supper. Religion provided a vital sense of social cohesion that reached throughout the town and into the adjacent farmlands.[13]

Secret lodges and societies complemented the influence of the church. The Masons, Odd Fellows, Moose, and Benevolent and Protective Order of Elks, among the more prominent, provided opportunities for businessmen, professional leaders, prosperous farmers, and landowners to socialize, supposedly in a nonalcoholic environment, complete with solemn, secret rituals. The lodges also facilitated the development of an exclusive male society conducive to the cutting of business and political deals. Although the several lodges and secret societies competed for membership, the most prominent by far was the Masonic Order. In Camden, as in so many places, any man who was anybody belonged to the Masons and spent many an hour memorizing his ritual lines before initiation ceremonies. The organization had its origins in the American Revolutionary era and provided a network that connected virtually every town throughout the United States. In nineteenth-century America, membership was almost a prerequisite for a man with serious political or business aspirations. The historian Arthur McClure accurately observes, "Masons were at the core of power and money." The Order usually held its secret meetings in a "lodge hall" located on the second floor of an important business building; Camden's lodge met above the post office in one of the town's most prominent brick buildings. Central to the teachings of the organization was a belief in God, charity, and patriotism. Great attention was paid to performance of the rituals, especially initiations, which required officers to recite extensive lines from memory. The Masonic Eastern Star was the women's auxiliary, complete with its own rituals, secrets, and social events.[14]

An active Masonic Order usually held several social events a year—banquets, balls, receptions, lectures—as well as contributing to the charitable needs of the community. Although the prestige of the Masons was unshakable, other rival fraternal organizations, such as the Elks, Odd Fellows, Redmen, and Woodmen of the World, also enjoyed popularity. It would not be until after World War I that a new wrinkle to patterns of male associations gained popularity, with the spread of the much less formal luncheon service clubs such as the Kiwanis, Lions, and Rotary.

Saturday evenings provided a special time for community activity. Camden's businessmen, many residents recall, seemed to make half of their sales on Saturday night. It was a time for farm families to mingle with town residents. The novelist Glenway Wescott recalled about his childhood in Wisconsin, "As the sun hurried west . . . everywhere men and women and children were made eager by the thoughts of the night. . . . For the night was Saturday night and they were going to town. And in Middle America, in the numberless small towns that serve the people of the farms, there is no more magical time. It is the sweet reward of the long week's labor; it is their opera, their trip to Zanzibar."[15]

On warm spring and summer Saturday evenings people crammed the streets. Men headed for their favorite barber shop for talk about the weather, commodity prices, and politics while enjoying the fragrances of witch hazel, bay rum, cigar smoke, and feeling the sensual pleasures of a close shave and hot towels. Farmers and townsfolk mingled at popular locations, perhaps on a bench in front of the bank or in a tavern or drugstore. While women did their shopping, children wandered the streets in groups with their friends.

1900 BAND.

The mark of a progressive town between the Civil War and World War I was a sprightly, uniformed town band. In 1907 the pride of Camden posed for a photographer. Courtesy Camden Archives.

On special occasions crowds gathered to hear the town band perform and enjoy homemade ice cream and lemonade sold by a church group. From the late nineteenth century until about World War II, a town had to have a band if it were to be considered up-to-date. The roguish hustler "Professor Harold Hill" depicted in Meredith Willson's *Music Man* played upon the sense of guilt and failure of River City's good citizens when he got them to pay for a youth band, complete with new uniforms and a tuba. Sherwood Anderson got it right when he commented, "What does a band mean to a town? Better to ask what is a town without a band?" All across the country, a community band was viewed as a primary community asset, the booster of spirit and patriotism at major holiday celebrations and a surefire attraction on sultry summer Saturday nights.[16]

~

These warm, human aspects of community life notwithstanding, the physical appearance of the turn-of-the-century small town was often less than inviting. In contrast to the trim and neat appearance of the long-established New England village, many towns west of the Appalachian

Mountains were only a few decades removed from the frontier and projected a raw image of stark functionalism. Willa Cather described Black Hawk in *My Ántonia* as a "bleak and desolate place." Its business district contained "two rows of new brick 'store' buildings, a brick school-house, the court-house, and four white churches."[17] When Carol Kennicott first arrives in Gopher Prairie in *Main Street,* she reacts with dismay as she surveys an unkempt Main Street "with its two-story brick shops, its story-and-a-half wooden residences, its muddy expanse from concrete walk to walk, its huddle of Fords and lumber wagons." There is no architecture of distinction, no lovely parks, no public squares like those she had appreciated in Chicago and the Twin Cities.[18]

In presenting this view of what became the prototypical American small town, Sinclair Lewis had merely used a vivid description of his hometown of Sauk Centre, Minnesota. "It was not only the unsparing unapologetic ugliness and the rigid straightness which overwhelmed her. It was the planlessness, the flimsy temporariness of the buildings, their faded unpleasant colors. The street was cluttered with electric-light poles, telephone poles, gasoline pumps for motor cars, boxes of goods. Each man had built with the most valiant disregard of all the others."[19] Despite many comments by locals about Camden's attractiveness, it too was a rough and unfinished place. Many vacant lots dotted the side streets. Its business district reflected a lack of planning, featuring slapdash wood frame buildings squeezed in among the prominent two- and three-story brick structures. Crude wooden walkways enabled pedestrians to remain above the mud (or dust) of Main Street. It was not until the 1920s that they were replaced by concrete walks. Early in the new century, ugly utility poles were imposed upon this already bleak scene.

Camden's appearance reflected the fact that America's towns were built by individual investors with little interest in aesthetic matters. Developers and businessmen had no zoning, planning, or environmental boards to mollify. Consequently, these creations of the free enterprise system naturally reflected a crude, capitalist imperative. The closer towns were to the frontier, the less pleasant they were to the discerning eye. At the time of the birth of its most famous son in 1885, Sinclair Lewis's biographer Mark Shorer writes, Sauk Centre was "ugly — raw and bare and gawky." It was scarcely thirty years old, and its crude appearance reflected its proximity to the frontier, "bleached and parched and sweltering in summer . . . gaunt and rutted and cruelly frozen in winter."[20] Not only did the business district exemplify the pragmatic, bottom-line imperatives that motivated local merchants, but so did the homes in which most residents lived.

~

Although larger towns tended to emulate the cities, with clearly identified neighborhoods related to class and status, smaller ones more commonly gave expression to the widespread sense that the great majority of residents belonged to an all-encompassing middle class. Houses were located on spacious lots set relatively close to the streets with ample backyards to allow for clotheslines, a vegetable garden, a horse barn, and a privy. The nearer to the East Coast a town was located, the closer the housing was placed to the street, a legacy of the English influence. Most residences were of wood frame construction, with brick often identifying the homes of the more affluent. Working-class families tended to live in simple, one-story, boxy structures that seldom exceeded eight hundred square feet. More-affluent residents occupied two-story structures that often featured a large front porch and substantial ornamental scrolled woodwork. Many featured turrets or bay windows, sometimes stained glass or black iron sculptures around the front door. Victorian standards gave builders and owners considerable leeway in constructing and decorating houses; each house was distinguished from its neighbors, but conventional tastes almost required that wood houses be painted white. Architectural diversity might have been restrained within conventional, sometimes gaudy Victorian boundaries, but at least housing styles did not exude the drab sameness that would characterize the tract developments built after World War II.[21]

The insides of the houses were strikingly similar. The small working-class houses featured a few cramped rooms cluttered with slapdash furniture and appointments. A small front porch contained a swing and a couple of chairs. More-affluent homes featured a larger front porch, but they were distinguished by the presence of a front parlor that was reserved for special occasions and contained the family's most expensive furniture and collectibles. "The parlor was a special room, different from all the utilitarian rooms of the rest of our house," William Eikenberry, the son of a prominent businessman, recalls of his youth spent in Camden. "All middle class homes had parlors. This room was not for reading or eating or sleeping. . . . It was furnished with an upright piano, keyboard always closed, uncomfortable overstuffed chairs, a somber colored floor carpet, and similar wall papers." Eikenberry recalls the walls hung with pictures of biblical scenes and unsmiling family portraits. "A

Unknown husband and wife pose in 1875 in front of their modest home located on South Second Street. The following year Sherwood Anderson was born in a similar cottage a few blocks away. Courtesy Camden Archives.

library table held the family Bible and a prominent fixture or two. In the room were held funerals and weddings and it was opened only for greeting guests of great importance."[22] It would not be until after World War I that the imposing parlor began to give way to the more comfortable "living room," a term that indicated funerals were now held outside the home in a "funeral parlor."

The typical house also contained a formal dining room, adjacent to a large kitchen dominated by a wood-burning cast-iron stove that helped heat the structure. During hot summer days a smaller stove was used to prepare meals on a screened back porch, which also contained the pump connected to the family's water supply, a well or cistern. A large entry hall led to the stairs to the second floor, where there were several bedrooms. Beneath the house, the cellar provided a depository where eggs, milk, butter, and smoked meats were stored in the cool, damp atmosphere. Bins contained the produce of the backyard garden and fruit trees—potatoes, onions, pears, peaches, apples—and along the walls wooden shelves bent under the weight of home-canned fruits, jellies, sauces, and vegetables. More-perishable items were stored in the wooden ice cabinets on the back porch, their contents cooled by blocks of ice that had been cut from local ponds and stored in heavily insulated buildings under blankets of sawdust.[23]

The spatial relationships of contemporary American communities had not yet fully taken shape a century ago. The poor tended to live on the outskirts of town, sometimes in a segregated "shantytown," often situated across a river or "on the other side of the tracks." The most prestigious homes were often centrally located on the edge of the business section, or on the town square if a New England village pattern was employed. The larger the town, the more its neighborhoods reflected status and the tacit social segregation that such attitudes produced. Even then it would not be unusual for the most prestigious houses in town to be located next to quite modest structures. Many merchants, especially the less prosperous, lived above their shops or in living quarters attached at the rear.

Although those who laid out the towns often had to adapt their plan to a meandering creek or river, they earnestly sought to impose a sense of order upon the wilderness with the familiar grid street pattern. The primary thoroughfare that penetrated the business district was frequently named Main Street, with other streets being given the names of historical figures (Washington, Lincoln, Jackson, Grant), or trees (Elm, Maple, Ash, Walnut), or prominent local pioneers. If the patriotic, environmental, or nostalgic impulse did not inspire, the streets were efficiently marked by letters of the alphabet or numbers. In many very small towns officials did not even bother to assign house numbers because everyone in town knew who lived in each residence anyway.[24]

Whatever their name, the streets were generally unpaved. During the dry summer months the town council might appropriate funds to oil the streets to keep the dust level tolerable, but rain and snow produced muck and mire that plagued every community. Whenever community spirit and available funds reached a sufficient level, major thoroughfares were paved with brick or stone; earlier street improvement efforts had featured wood planking. No matter the season or condition of the streets, the substantial deposits of manure and urine left by the fleet of horses treading the town streets produced not only logistical problems for pedestrians but also a fetid stench that endured until the automobile culture drove the horses from the streets.[25]

When Carol Kennicott moved with her new physician husband to Gopher Prairie about the time of World War I, the automobile had already prodded America's town officials to begin the expensive process of paving. It was not until 1924 that Sauk Centre paved its major thoroughfares, in a concession to the new age of automobility. In that same year Camden's frugal village council authorized a similar upgrading of

The Eikenberry Seed Store was one of several Camden businesses and homes ravaged by a rampaging Seven Mile Creek during the famous flood of 1913. This photograph shows an inundated East Hendrix Street some five hundred yards from the bed of the normally placid creek. William Eikenberry, who grew up in the house on the right, later recalled counting more than twenty dead cows in the field behind his home when the waters receded. Courtesy Camden Archives.

the town's infrastructure. The ascendancy of the automobile meant that the aromas of the horse era began to fade. Although the automobile culture produced an ugliness and major irritations of its own, it was generally welcomed as a major environmental advance over the horse. The automobile also provided an important impetus to the local economy. Service stations, repair shops, and automobile dealerships took their place in the local business system as livery stables, harness makers, and blacksmith shops receded into memory.[26]

∾

At the onset of the twentieth century, America's Main Streets remained a premier outpost of the nation's capitalist system. The small town was founded, designed, and operated as a commercial center for the region it served. It provided a convenient place for local moneymakers to operate, and its leaders held most dear to their hearts the preservation of and increase in property values. Thus the center of town featured the offices of the locally owned bank, the general store, the newspaper office, and, if it were designated as the county seat, the court house, usually constructed in classic Greek Revival grandeur. Extending outward from this cluster of primary buildings was an eclectic assortment of small businesses and professional shops. Churches held strategic locations, usually on the edge of the business district, as did the public school building. Along Main Street, capitalism reigned supreme.

It was, in fact, the unapologetic embrace of the verities of the emerging capitalist order that helped provoke the sustained outburst of criticism from urban intellectual circles during the 1920s. As the American economy entered the industrial, corporate phase of its development in the post–Civil War years, town merchants and other leading citizens enthusiastically embraced the new capitalist ethic. "The day of the hustlers is at hand," Sherwood Anderson wrote disparagingly about his hometown of Clyde. Traditional small-town mores had placed great emphasis on self-denial, neighborliness, and character, but those values now tended to give way to the crass, bottom-line aggressiveness of the Gilded Age. The tenets of the Protestant Ethic dominated the towns of America. The quest for "Acres of Diamonds" took place in towns large and small and needed little prompting by the famous Presbyterian minister Russell Conwell. This new ethic captured the hearts of Main Street merchants and swept aside any doubts about the virtue of acquiring wealth. Would-be Rockefellers now took their place on Main Street, with their values of rugged competition, the driving of hard bargains, and self-interest. Critics complained that the values of the city had seduced small-town America.

All was not well, however, between the merchant and his primary customer, the farmer. Atherton demonstrates that merchants on the Middle Border (roughly Ohio to Missouri and north to Minnesota) worked hard to establish and maintain a mercantile monopoly, as can be seen quite vividly in their sustained efforts to keep out competition from nearby cities. Their pricing was usually at the high end, and farmers continually complained about the high cost of doing business in town. The antagonism reached a high pitch when mail order catalogs appeared in the late 1870s. Merchants saw only doom when Montgomery Ward and Company opened its mail-order service and published catalogs with the nonurban customer specifically in mind. External competition increased when the Chicago mercantile powerhouse of Sears, Roebuck entered the mail order fray in 1886. Merchants feared a loss of sales to these city marketing giants, who offered a much wider range of goods at lower prices, and groused especially about farmers demanding credit from them while willingly paying cash for mail orders.

The battle raged for several decades, with merchants often opposing, or at least not supporting, such innovations as rural free delivery and parcel post. Farmers naturally saw such innovations as a means of reducing their isolation and took a dim view of the intractable opposition put up by merchants.[27]

~

Tensions such as these undercut the more benevolent and inclusive image the small towns wished to project. It is not surprising that during the second decade of the twentieth century the image of the small town as depicted in American letters changed. Up until this time the small town had been viewed as an ideal environment in which God-fearing people worked hard and raised their families the right way within the protective circle of a caring community. Harriet Beecher Stowe's 1869 novel, *Oldtown Folks*, described a New England village "as pretty as ever laid itself down to rest on the banks of a tranquil river." In Oldtown, life revolved around the post office and general store, where there took place "a general exchange of news, as the different farm-wagons stood hitched around the door, and their owners spent a leisure moment in discussing politics or theology from the top of codfish or mackerel barrels, while their wives and daughters were shopping among the dress goods and ribbons on the other side of the store."[28] Nathaniel Hawthorne and Mark Twain might have portrayed the darker side of human behavior in the small towns of New England and the Mississippi Valley, but their primary concern lay with the people who lived there and not the community itself. Their towns merely provided a place for them to explore the dark sides of human nature.[29]

The more serious of the early critics were Thorstein Veblen and Hamlin Garland, who had both been raised on farms in the upper Midwest during the post–Civil War era. It was as a young man growing up in rural Nebraska and Wisconsin that the iconoclastic Veblen developed the critical perspective that would become central to his critique of American capitalism. Veblen argued that the self-proclaimed virtues of neighborliness and friendliness disappeared when it came to solidarity between merchant and farmer, contending that "the country town of the American farming region is the perfect flower of self-help and cupidity" with its central mission to charge "what the traffic would bear."[30]

Hamlin Garland's realistic appraisal of the drab and hard life lived by midwestern farmers set a tone that would be repeated by many writers to follow. The prairie farmers he knew as a youth led lives characterized by hard work and low economic rewards. Their lives were seldom enlivened by social or intellectual outlets, since the necessary daily rituals of caring for animals and crops provided little opportunity for release from a never-ending tedium. Contrary to the many Jeffersonian prophets commanding the political and philosophical high ground, Garland could find little that was romantic or spiritually uplifting in the lives of the people he had known and·observed on the Middle Border. He also contended that the grim existence of farm families was essentially replicated in the towns that served them. In *Main-Travelled Roads* Garland wrote of a dusty country road that had "a dull town at one end and a home of toil at the other."[31]

The assault by intellectuals on the small town emanated from Chicago and New York, havens for America's literary elite. In many cases, those who took particular aim at the small town had themselves grown up there, and they often drew heavily on recollections of their own youth. From the pens of some of the nation's best writers flowed a steady stream of essays and novels portraying a seamy society in which intolerance and hypocrisy flourished in a provincial environment that discouraged intellectual curiosity and embraced a crass materialism.

For many decades the suspicious Jeffersonian view of the big city had dominated intellectual life, romanticizing the virtues of rural life. Now the tables turned. One of the unwritten assumptions of this new thrust was the corrupting influence of American capitalism. As intellectuals explored the corrosive features of one of modern capitalism's creations— the new middle class—they discovered that it was firmly rooted in the values of the small towns from which many of them had fled. Just as it became intellectually fashionable in the 1920s to denounce Babbittry and to look to the cities for social liberation and cultural uplift, it also seemed right and proper to place the blame for the distorted values of modern American capitalism upon the small town.

Thus Willa Cather, firmly ensconced on the East Coast, drew upon her childhood in Red Cloud, Nebraska, to describe such dreary and oppressive places as Black Hawk and Moonstone, where petty and often vicious individuals preyed upon the unsuspecting innocence of the pioneer immigrant farmers. Sherwood Anderson had left Clyde for Cleveland and the business world, which he in turn abandoned for the literary circles of Chicago to write about the "grotesques" of small-town Ohio, and even more pointedly about the destructive forces of capitalism upon a small town in *Poor White* (1920). In 1908 the novelist Zona Gale had depicted "my joy in living in this, my village," thanks to the nurturing atmosphere of its people. But by 1920 the euphoria of *Friendship Village Love Stories* had given way to a radically different small town, one overwhelmed by nastiness, cruelty, and selfishness, in her *Miss Lulu Betts*. Edgar Lee Master's *Spoon River Anthology* (1914) presented a series of individuals whose lives were twisted by the pressures of the day, and in *Domesday Book* (1920) he described a town "devoid of normally happy men and women," whose lives were "dominated by greed, grossness and cynicism." [32]

The assault reached its zenith with the enthusiastic reception given to Sinclair Lewis's *Main Street*. Lewis had no doubts that his Gopher Prairie exemplified small towns everywhere and that it captured the true spirit of American civilization itself, however mean and shallow it might be. Lewis probed what he had earlier identified as "the village virus," an affliction that produced dull-witted if not greedy merchants, shallow women, hypocritical ministers, and mindless boosters who had neither the will nor the intellect to consider the false assumptions and values upon which their lives and communities were based. [33]

Of all of the books and articles about country bumpkins and small-town hicks which streamed into print during this era, *Main Street* most forcefully called into question long accepted myths. Most critics were delighted, and the *New York Times* suggested that Lewis and other writers "have brought out some unconsidered facts which ought to impose a judicious silence on the writers who argue that God made Hickville Centre and the devil made New York." No longer was the city the foul center that destroyed lives and squeezed the goodness out of mankind. Americans now had to reexamine their heretofore uncritical views of rural and small town American life. [34]

Lewis's sometimes satirical, often jeremiadic dismissal of the small town was motivated by his belief that American society itself had been overwhelmed by the crass materialism and pompous boosterism of the new and rapidly expanding urban middle class. George F. Babbitt does not appear in *Main Street,* but his influence is evident on nearly every page. When *Babbitt* appeared in 1922, Lewis depicted his central character as a realtor possessed of dubious ethics and a frustrated social climber in a typical midwestern city of Zenith (apparently a composite city based on research visits to Kansas City, Cincinnati, and Indianapolis as well as on his familiarity with Minneapolis). Lewis's readers easily

Main Street U.S.A. This picture, taken about 1918, could have been snapped any-where in the United States. Five Camden residents are shown taking the sun in front of McCord's Hardware Store. Courtesy Camden Archives.

made the connection between *Babbitt* and *Main Street* and understood that Babbittry had turned the thousands of America's Gopher Prairies into communities of despair.[35]

≈

News about the "revolt from the villages" had little impact on the lives being lived along America's Main Streets. Although local libraries stocked the new books and sophisticated journals, most townspeople were too busy with the pace of their lives to pay much attention. As the United States emerged from World War I and its aftermath, life never seemed so good in Camden or Sauk Centre. Business was improving, and the automobile was reducing the sense of isolation, as were motion pictures and the radio. The introduction of electrical appliances was making the routine of daily life more tolerable. More important, the prosperity of the 1920s was elevating the living standards for a majority of residents. The people living along Main Street America were too busy and contented to worry much about the comments of disaffected intel-lectuals living in such fearful places as Chicago or New York City.

3

Camden: The Halcyon Days of the 1920s

It was a town not unlike many others, undistinguished in appearance, lacking in any special geographical or historical attribute that would attract tourists, a generic midwestern town. From time to time locals liked to mention that it was the birthplace of Cyrenia Van Gordon, a prominent, if somewhat cantankerous, soprano on the world opera circuit, and, of course, Sherwood Anderson. After what Anderson had to say about small towns, however, many locals were uncertain whether that was a fact they wanted to advertise. By the late 1920s Camden had taken on a mature, ordered, and reasonably prosperous appearance. New houses had filled in most vacant lots, and newly paved streets had acquired a peaceful, even stately appearance from the maple and elm trees that provided a natural canopy from April until October. Prominent businesses were located in well-appointed brick buildings that had been built during the nineteenth century, their well-maintained exteriors giving the impression of stability and prosperity. Neatly trimmed residential yards and flower beds reflected pride of ownership, while many backyards contained gardens that overflowed during summer months with vegetable crops. Solid . . . prosperous . . . conservative . . . cautious . . . but quietly confident, Camden reflected the economic expansion and resulting smug confidence that swept across the United States during the economic boom of the 1920s.

Camden could have been located elsewhere in the Midwest or, for that matter, most anywhere in the country. Indeed, Sinclair Lewis could just have easily placed his novel *Main Street* there. Camden had grown to maturity along its own Main Street. After the street crossed the Pennsylvania Railroad tracks at the south end of town, it proceeded northward into the center of the business district, where at Central Avenue it made a thirty-degree bend to the right and continued through several blocks of tree-lined residences. Once it left the town limits and passed the Fairview Cemetery, the highway wended its way north for nine miles through the Seven Mile Creek valley to the county seat of Eaton, and continued on in the direction of such distant cities as Toledo and Detroit.

~

Camden's life revolved around the intersection of Main and Central, already the site of several minor automobile accidents and innumerable near misses. Well into the 1930s the intersection was the scene of a contrast of technologies and lifestyles as automobiles darted around slower horse-drawn buggies and farm wagons.

Four commercial brick buildings guarded this busy intersection. On the northwest corner stood the imposing Dearth building, constructed in 1896 of brick and cut stone. Its first floor housed the town's drugstore with its popular soda fountain, magazine rack, and coffee shop; its upper two floors contained several offices and a few apartments. Bryson's Rexall Drug Store filled the prescriptions written by the two local physicians and supplemented them with a creative array of patent medicines, ointments, salves, lotions, and other mysterious potions. Bryson's was a venerable Camden institution, serving as the venue for the daily exchange of gossip and animated conversations that usually revolved around sports and politics. In the mornings its black-marbled counter and a few booths and tables provided a regular meeting place for businessmen seeking a cup of coffee and conversation; in midafternoon, when the high school let out, the adults retreated, their seats taken by energetic teenagers who took over the place to drink sodas and flirt.[1]

Across Central Avenue stood another three-story building, originally the Preble House of the pre–Civil War period. Its ground floor was now occupied by the Camden Hardware Store, and its upper levels were the province of the Independent Order of Odd Fellows. The larger of two such stores that geared their stock toward area farmers, Camden Hardware offered the usual assortment of hand tools, small appliances, replacement parts, and nuts and bolts.

Located on the northeast corner was a much less impressive structure that contained a small general store and, in the back room, the local telephone exchange, where a single operator switched calls for the Camden Telephone Company by hand, plugging and unplugging the wires of shared party lines. By the mid-1920s a majority of residents had telephone service. Everyone knew that their party lines were vulnerable to surreptitious listening, even from the operators when things at the switchboard got slow. Prudence and caution governed the free flow of information along the telephone lines. Atop the nearby Town Hall, hidden in a turret, was the electronic fire siren, audible for miles outside town when atmospheric conditions were right. Senior switchboard operator Orma Witherby or one of her associates would activate the siren whenever an emergency call came across the lines. Within seconds after the alarm began its wail, the switchboard would light up with a stream of calls from the curious wanting to know where to go to watch the volunteer firefighters perform.[2]

On the southeast corner was the town's most important enterprise, the First National Bank in Camden. The source of considerable local pride, it had been opened in 1906 with a capitalization of $50,000 and in 1926 boasted of assets of $550,000. The bank was operated by cautious officers who were carefully monitored by a board of directors reflective of the community's conservative elite. The ambience of the bank was that of a bleak jail. The tellers worked behind high bars—not surprisingly, the bank never endured a robbery attempt—peering over high marble counters that forced even average-sized adults to stand on their toes while making transactions.

This imposing, even intimidating environment did not prevent one of the town's biggest scandals. In 1931 cashier Fred Van Skiver, a thirty-seven-year-old local man and a bank employee for eight years, was arrested and charged with embezzling $20,000. Subsequent audits reduced that amount to less than $2,000, and the small loss was covered by a surety bond. When rumors about the theft entered the gossip mill, a run on the bank seemed imminent, but inflated fears of an impending collapse—undoubtedly intensified by the nation's sagging economy and gathering banking crisis—were quickly stilled by strong reassurances from bank officers. Van Skiver was convicted of embezzlement and spent eighteen months in the Chillicothe federal reformatory.[3] His caper shook the cautious citizenry to the core, however, and it took several years in a depression environment to restore full public faith in the town's primary financial institution.

The First National Bank in Camden was founded in 1906 and remained the heart of the town's economic life until it was absorbed by a chain banking firm in 1982. The bank prided itself on being able to weather the severe economic storm of the early 1930s. This picture was taken about 1940. Courtesy Camden Archives.

Camden's commercial enterprises radiated out in all four directions from its core intersection. A couple of doors down from the Camden Hardware Store on South Main Street was Shank's Variety Store. It had opened in 1911 and within a few years had become a community curiosity, its owners having early on lost any semblance of inventory control over the store's wide assortment of pins, thread, socks, toys, glassware, linens, dresses, curios, underwear, soap, lightbulbs, candy, pots and pans, shoes, comic books, dishes, and birthday and sympathy cards. These staples, as well as an eclectic assortment of other odds and ends, were hopelessly scattered about the store, with some items being buried under newer lines of merchandise for years. Over time a layer of dust steadily accumulated on the shelves and tables, adding a curious quality to the disheveled displays. Local customers had long since learned not to look for the item they wished to purchase, but to ask a member of one of the several generations of Shanks who might be tending the store. The clerks, family members all, could usually locate any item from the confusing pile of goods with a swiftness that mystified even their most regular customers.

The store's motto, emblazoned on its receipts and stationery, explained its modus operandi perfectly: "If you don't see what you want, just ask for it and we will find it." Often in their search for an elusive item the staff would have to move other goods, thereby adding to the chaotic appearance of the shelves and bins. The mounting clutter and confusion persisted until the family finally gave up in 1970, and the remaining inventory was sold in a public auction that understandably attracted an unusually large crowd of curious onlookers.[4]

Across Main Street from Shank's was Camden's oldest continuous business, Jacob Collett and Sons' Men's Clothiers. This staid enterprise had been located in the same dark and stuffy store since it began operations in 1855. Much of the merchandise was hidden from view (and touch) in heavy wooden drawers and behind wall partitions. The dim ceiling lighting often required a cautious purchaser of a suit to take it out to the front sidewalk to ascertain the precise color of the fabric. Further down Main Street were a couple of small restaurants whose ownerships seemingly turned over with the seasons, Jessie Roberts's fabric and sewing notions store, a furniture store, Lee Danser's Jewelry Store and Watch Repair, a pool hall featuring two aging green felt-topped tables, a barber shop with the *Police Gazette* providing the major reading matter for waiting customers, and Caskey's combined appliance, grocery store, and egg exchange. At the end of the long block, the small office of the United States Postal Service and the town library shared ground floor space in a spacious brick building that housed on its upper floors the Masonic Order and its ladies' auxiliary.

Anchoring the south end of the business district was the two-hundred-seat Dover Theater, which had introduced motion pictures to Camden in 1909 and remained a thriving business (open on weekends only) ever since. "The pictures being run at the Dover are in every way of the highest class," the *Preble County News* commented in 1911, urging readers to take in *A Country Cupid* and *Red Cloud's Secret*. A few years later the newspaper urged residents to see an unnamed film with the enticing promise, "If the great automobile scene does not thrill you—you are past thrilling." The Dover offered feature films on Friday and Saturday nights and matinees on Saturday and Sunday afternoons.

Main Street looking southward in 1939. Note the brick-paved street. Collett's Men Store is on the immediate left. The three-story building on the distant left housed the post office, the town library, and the Masonic Lodge. Courtesy Camden Archives.

Sometimes a film seemed a little too modern for local tastes. In 1927 some parents denied their children permission to see a hot new Hollywood release, *Love 'Em and Leave 'Em,* but had no concerns about a 1928 epic, *Blood Will Tell,* which featured Buck Jones in "a Western conflict of might and right."[5]

During the years that Irwin Anderson repaired harness at his shop on North Main Street he was but one of many artisans serving the needs of a society dependent on the horse. The arrival of the automobile and tractor meant the rapid demise of the once prominent livery stables, blacksmith shops, and harness shops. The first automobile appeared in Camden in 1903, and by the mid-1920s automobility had transformed both local transportation systems and businesses; it also had a major impact upon the way work was done on the farm. Young men adept at working on machinery now took jobs in the service stations and automobile repair shops that had sprung up to cater to the new trade. Mechanics who could keep the nation's first generation of Fordson, Farmall, and John Deere tractors and power-driven machinery in working order were in demand.

In 1907 local businessmen Robert Duvall and Edgar Fornshell opened an automobile dealership selling the ill-fated Lambert, a large two-seat, friction-drive vehicle powered by a two-cylinder motor. Prices ranged from $800 to $2,000, prohibitively expensive for most locals. Fornshell later sold Maxwells, which his advertisements dubbed "America's Wonder Car." On the eve of World War I, a Maxwell could be purchased for $695. Businesses that had served the needs of the horse-drawn era were forced to respond to the new technology. In 1914 Ernest Bertsch, long-time operator of a wagon and buggy sales, paint, and repair shop ("Fine Carriage Painting, Repairing of All Kinds Neatly Executed on Buggies, Phaetons, Carriages, Runabouts") announced that he was now offering automobile body repair and paint services. Other mechanically minded men began repair services in their backyard sheds, which had formerly sheltered the family horse. Merchants also responded to the increased automobile and truck traffic that came through town: Frank White opened a White Star service station at the south end of town in response to the growing tourist trade, and local restaurants began serving meals

Livery stables such as this one located on East Central Avenue were doomed by the arrival of the Automobile Age. This photograph was taken around 1885. Courtesy Camden Archives.

A town caught between two eras is dramatically pictured in this 1914 photograph of two internal combustion-propelled rural mail delivery vehicles and four horse-drawn carriages and their drivers. Courtesy Camden Archives.

to strangers passing through. A cluster of small tourist cabins, painted white with bright green roofs, opened for business on the north edge of town. Several families with homes along Main Street began renting upstairs rooms to motorists.[6]

The automobile of choice in Camden and its farming environs was the Tin Lizzy, the ubiquitous black Model T that Henry Ford sold for prices as low as $295 FOB Detroit. At first, residents had to travel to Eaton or Hamilton to purchase one, but in 1927 young William Matt moved to Camden from Cynthia, Kentucky, to establish a Ford dealership. Matt, who became one of Camden's leading citizens, offered competitive prices and a full range of repair services. The new Ford dealer became active in the local Presbyterian Church and the Masons, and he even joined the prestigious Eaton Rotary Club. Matt also ingratiated himself with the editor-publisher-owner of the *Preble County News* by purchasing large advertisements. Matt's sales grew as locals responded to such jingles as:

> If you're thinking of an Auto
> On which you can rely—
> Then get a demonstration
> In a new Ford before you buy.
> If you'll stop into our salesroom
> We can quickly show you why
> The new Ford is a real sensation
> And is the car you ought to buy.[7]

Grateful for such advertising, editor Ray Simpson featured Matt and his Ford agency in a news story on the front page, taking note of the agency's reputation for "the splendid service which Mr. Matt gives his patrons at all times." Located in a modern new facility on North Main Street, Simpson proclaimed, "is the headquarters for America's most popular low-priced car. We cannot fail to compliment Mr. Matt for the high standard he maintains in the conduct of his worthy enterprise and all who may have dealings with him will find him a gentleman whom it is a pleasure to know and do business with at all times."[8]

~

Despite the encroachments of modernity, when it came to essential services Camden in the 1920s remained relatively self-sufficient. The local labor force provided adequate numbers of plumbers, carpenters, tinsmiths, shoe repairmen, roofers, and electricians. Some men earned modest livings as handymen, doing yard work and general repairs, while women, often widowed, "took in" laundry and worked as day maids for some of the town's more affluent families. Four small grocery stores served their customers, as did one specialty meat market. Next door to Shank's Variety Store stood the curious but venerable general store operated by the reclusive Bailey brothers. Catering largely to lower income farm families, these two men sold newspapers, a few popular magazines, soda pop, candies, Red Man and Mail Pouch chewing tobacco, King Edward and R. G. Dunn cigars, Lucky Strike and Chesterfield cigarettes, fifty-pound cloth sacks of flour and sugar, and an eclectic assemblage of canned meats, sardines, fruits, and vegetables. In the back of their dimly lit shop could be found a modest selection of heavy-duty work shoes and the ever popular bib denim overalls and work caps, standard work attire for laborers and farmers.[9]

A block south of the Dover Theater near the end of South Main Street stood one of the town's most successful enterprises, the Eikenberry feed store and grain elevator. Owner Eby Eikenberry had carefully expanded the company since the turn of the century, adding coal and fuels to his business, even extending his enterprise to locations in Seven Mile, Hamilton, and Eaton. During the July threshing season, Eikenberry's towering eighty-foot grain elevator, located next to a railroad siding, became a center of twenty-four-hour activity as farmers brought their wheat to market. Eikenberry's son recalled the excitement of these days, especially the long lines of wagons stretching up Main Street: "The big

Taking newly harvested wheat to market along South Main Street in 1901. The large size of the new elevator built along the Pennsylvania tracks prompted locals to call it the "Jumbo Elevator." Courtesy Camden Archives.

draft horses pulling these heavy loads were a small boy's wonder." Although the threshing season was the highlight of the summer, the store and elevator remained busy throughout the year, purchasing and shipping hay, corn, oats, and barley and providing farmers with fertilizers, seed, fencing, small implements, and the new pesticide sprays that were beginning to come on the market.[10]

Not only was Eikenberry one of Camden's premier business leaders, but he also developed a parallel career in public service, becoming a leader in national associations of grain dealers, holding a lifetime appointment on the Board of Trustees of Ohio University, and serving several terms in the Ohio state assembly. A conservative Democrat, Eikenberry was an anomaly in Camden politics, a man whose stature as a community leader enabled him to overcome strong Republican loyalties to win and retain a seat in the legislature.[11]

Just north of Eikenberry's elevator were the low-slung buildings of Neff and Fry Company, the town's biggest employer. In 1916 two rural mail carriers, who had tired of fighting the mud and ruts of the unimproved country roads, founded a company to manufacture interlocking cement staves, which permitted the construction of a much improved farm silo. Theirs was truly an example of the American entrepreneurial spirit at work. Charles Neff and Merle Fry had conceived of their idea while talking to farmers on their mail delivery routes.

Area farmers had tired of absorbing financial losses caused by leakage in their wooden storage bins. Neff and Fry promised farmers that they could construct "the silo that will stand for centuries and give absolute perfect satisfaction every day it stands."[12] "The wood silo has served its time and purpose and must step aside for the march of time and progress for something better and more lasting," the *Preble County News* noted when the company commenced operations.[13] The development of this concrete construction business was facilitated by Camden's location on top of one of the nation's largest and most accessible deposits of high quality sand and gravel.

Within two years Neff and Fry had constructed more than three hundred silos on southwestern Ohio farms, including the talk of the area — a soaring sixty-nine-foot-high silo near West Elkton.[14] The entrepreneurial spirit burned brightly at company offices on South Main Street, and by 1930 the company had diversified into leak-proof burial vaults (discretely marketed as "surface sepulchers"), prefabricated chimneys, and large commercial storage bins. Neff and Fry Company provided steady employment for more than seventy-five men; some worked in the Camden plant while others traveled to distant sites to erect silos

Neff and Fry's small construction site in 1916, the year of the establishment of the firm. A short prototype of its cement silo is at the right, a supply of concrete stave components on the left. Courtesy Camden Archives.

and storage facilities. In 1925 tragedy struck when a laborer fell on an assembly site near Columbus and was killed instantly.[15]

~

Symbolizing the stability and confidence of the community was the towering red brick Town Hall. Located half a block west of the city's main intersection on Central Avenue, it had been constructed in 1889 at a cost of $15,000. This imposing Victorian structure loomed over the town like a protective uncle, housing the village council and Somers Township trustee meeting rooms and offices, a two-cell jail (which was rarely put to its intended use), public rest rooms, and the fire truck and equipment for the twenty-five members of the volunteer fire department. Upstairs was the "Opera House," a high-ceiling multipurpose hall that could hold an audience of four hundred for local talent shows or theatrical performances. The Opera House often featured performances of itinerant jugglers, magicians, ventriloquists, and musicians. Townspeople took pride in the hall's special features: a "magnificent 31 foot deep stage," elevated private seating boxes, and a small balcony. Most patrons sat in folding chairs on the main floor for performances, but on winter Friday nights the chairs were set aside and spectators sat on the stage to watch the high school basketball team perform on the main floor.[16]

The sturdy young men making up the 1916 Camden Cubs, floppy leather helmets and all. Boys' football lasted for only a few years; it was too difficult for such a small high school to field a viable team. Courtesy Camden Archives.

Located on the north edge of town, adjacent to fields of corn, alfalfa, and grazing cattle, stood the town's other symbol of community progress, the new, ultramodern two-story yellow brick school building completed in 1917 at a cost of $61,000. It had been built in response to threats by state education officials to shut down the local high school, which for years had held classes in rooms rented upstairs over a store.

During the 1920s local schools served about 425 students, the majority of whom were bused in from the farms each day. The new building served the needs of the upper six grades, while the elementary classes were held in the building on Central Avenue. Approximately forty students were enrolled in each of the first ten grades, but the size of the junior and senior classes dropped off to nearly half that number. To many teenagers and their parents, a high school diploma seemed of limited value. Few students aspired to attend college, and long-standing agricultural traditions prompted youngsters to function as adults at an early age. Many boys felt compelled to go to work by the time they became sixteen, while girls often opted for early marriage. The sixteenth birthday was that magic cut-off point when Ohio's compulsory school attendance law no longer applied if parental consent could be obtained.[17]

Curriculum in the elementary grades emphasized the four R's of readin', 'ritin', 'rithmetic, and rote memorization. The high school curriculum provided few electives and had not yet incorporated either vocational shop or agricultural courses, although basic classes in home economics were offered to aspiring homemakers. The most significant of the few electives available were Latin and music. Teachers' salaries remained low, and turnover among male teachers was high; faculty stability came primarily from talented local women.

Schoolteachers made up the majority of college graduates in Camden, although many of the elementary teachers lacked a college degree and held two-year certificates from a normal school. The high school teacher who held a master's degree was rare, and those individuals were accorded the dignified if unofficial title of "professor." The superintendent of schools was evaluated primarily on his ability to maintain discipline, keep the system operating within its parsimonious budget, and avoid controversy or scandal.

~

The town design followed a comfortable symmetry that emphasized the central corridor of Main Street. Two streets, Lafayette and Liberty, ran parallel to Main Street to the west and to two other residential streets,

Second Street and Depot, to the east. These streets were connected by three east-west streets to form a less-than-perfect grid. The Seven Mile Creek and the Pennsylvania Railroad established the town's eastern boundary; the crest of "Mt. Auburn"—actually a sloping hill that rose about three hundred feet to its crest—provided a point of demarcation to the west. Mature maple and elm trees lined the residential areas. The town's residents lived in some two hundred houses, the majority of which were of wood frame construction and inevitably painted white. With some notable exceptions, these houses were of limited aesthetic value, unimaginative, rectangular in shape, located toward the front of deep lots, their front entrances covered by large porches on which the adults were inclined to pass the evenings during the sweltering summer months.

Residential patterns reflected the middle-class status of nearly all of the town's residents. As was common in towns of this size, there was little outward evidence of class lines in housing patterns. No segregated shantytown lay on the town's edge. Modest cottages were scattered among larger, more pretentious dwellings, the most prominent of which were large two-story Victorian-style brick homes. Some status-conscious folk thought that the most prestigious residential locations lay along tree-lined North Main Street, but that was subject to debate. The dispersal of the finest houses throughout the community contributed to the sense that Camden lacked deep divisions over social class.

This appearance of a cohesive middle-class community was supported by the fact that the great majority of residents had western European origins. Most people could trace their family trees to Germany or Great Britain. Nonetheless, a definite class structure permeated Camden society. Most residents would have been baffled if questioned by a visiting sociologist about the criteria for defining social classes because no one discussed such an issue, but everyone knew their place in the pecking order and that of their neighbors. One's status not only controlled most social and economic relationships but also created expectations about one's behavior. Although the small size of the community led to considerable overlap, there were distinct upper middle, middle, and lower middle classes. The egalitarian spirit of the community precluded the recognition of a true upper class, and absence of the seriously impoverished meant that there was no genuine lower class.

Those who enjoyed the highest standing—membership in a distinct upper middle class—were the families of the men who provided the community's business and professional leadership. These individuals made up no more than 25 percent of the town's population. Over the years many of this elite group had invested in property and now owned rental houses and, in some instances, farmland. During the 1920s the upper middle class included such established businessmen such as grain dealer Eby Eikenberry, clothier Burdette Collett, furniture dealer Frank Eikenberry (no relationship to Eby), jeweler Lee Danser, auto dealer William Matt, bank president Howard Pattison, manufacturers Charles Neff and Merle Fry, publisher Ray Simpson, lawyer Frank Schuey, hardware store owner Robert Dusky, veterinarian Charles Otto, physicians Von Barnheiser and Jerrard Combs, gravel pit owner Frank White, mortician R. C. Nein, lumberyard owner Thomas Donahoe, and the superintendent of schools E. W. Schwing. As noted before, these men were overwhelmingly Republican in their politics (conservative Democrats Donahoe and Eby Eikenberry being the major exceptions). Some, but definitely not all, of this elite group held a college degree.

Members of this leadership elite interacted regularly in a variety of formal settings—as members of the Masonic Lodge, as members of a church (an overwhelming percentage belonged to the Presbyterian Church), as members of the boards of directors of the bank or the small savings and loan association. On most weekday mornings representative numbers of this elite could be seen discussing current issues over a cup of coffee at Bryson's drugstore. During the bleak depression years of the 1930s, it would be this group that provided the leadership in establishing the Progressive Club as a means of advancing community interests. Several took their turn on the Presbyterian board of deacons, the city council, the board of education, and the township board. Others felt no compulsion to serve on an elected body but probably participated in the informal process that identified candidates (who seldom faced opposition) for local office. These men and their families lived in the larger and well-appointed homes mostly clustered along North Main Street.

Their wives did not work outside the home and concentrated their time and energy on running a household, occasionally entertaining among their peer group, and raising children or helping with grandchildren. Upper middle class women tended to be active in the Order of the Eastern Star (the women's auxiliary of the Masons), the service sorority Delta Theta Tau, and the literary Philomathean Club. These women also belonged to the exclusive bridge groups that met on weekday afternoons for lunch and bridge. Acceptance into these groups was a closely guarded privilege; on occasion carefully selected middle-class women were invited to "sit in" as substitutes, but they were seldom invited to become permanent members. With the advent of reliable automobiles, these women expressed their social standing by doing much of their serious shopping in Dayton or Cincinnati, and their shopping excursions were often reported in the "Personals" column of the newspaper as a significant social event.

Located beneath this elite group was the middle class, approximately 50 percent of the community. Male members of this group tended to work for a salary or to be engaged in some form of service occupation that produced a modest annual income and lacked the professional status of the upper middle class. Prominent among this group were schoolteachers (including unmarried women teachers), bank cashiers, owners and operators of small, modestly capitalized businesses (family-operated grocery stores and meat markets, variety and notions stores, service stations), ministers, post office employees, Pennsylvania Railroad supervisory personnel, and tradesmen who engaged in small repair and service enterprises of which they were the sole owners and operators—tinsmiths, plumbers, auto mechanics, beauticians, barbers, electricians, roofers, shoe repairers, and carpenters.

These hardworking residents lacked the leadership qualities and, with the exception of the college-educated clergy and teachers, the more encompassing cultural-political outlook of the upper middle class. The determining factor of their status, however, was money; their disposable income was distinctly less than that of the upper middle class, and if they owned property it was usually restricted to their mortgaged homes or small businesses, some of which were operated out of their homes. Most members of this group, as aspiring capitalists, identified with the Republican Party. Although some of the more prominent members of the middle tier were selected to run for local office, they tended to be excluded from the informal nomination process. When it came to local politics, they were primarily followers and not policy makers. Many of this group found social outlet as members of the recently founded American Legion or the Independent Order of Odd Fellows, a secret male society that emulated but lacked the status of the Masons. Church membership gravitated toward the Methodist and Brethren Churches. With the exception of the poorly paid teachers and ministers, members of the middle group did not hold college degrees—many had not completed high school—and few had the funds or the inclination to send their children to college.

If the wives of this middle group belonged to an organization outside the home, it was most likely connected to their church membership. Some were active in the Daughters of the Western Star, an auxiliary tied to the Odd Fellows, or the American Legion auxiliary, and a select few

Patriotism was important in the 1920s, as evidenced by the uniforms of the seventh and eighth grade girls' drill team. Picture taken in 1924. Courtesy Camden Archives.

(such as women teachers) belonged to the Philomathean Club. Unlike most wives of the leadership group, they did not employ a weekly maid or hire out their family's washing and ironing. Some women of this class operated modest hairdressing businesses in their homes or worked as telephone operators or waitresses.

Although members of the leadership and middle groups did not overtly "look down on" the town's bottom social tier, neither did they associate with them in any meaningful fashion. Members of the lower middle class, about twenty-five percent of the population, were marked by a distinct lack of education or interest in cultural and political affairs. Many lived in small houses, duplexes, or apartments that were rented from members of the elite group. The men supported their families as unskilled laborers—at Neff and Fry, on nearby farms, as general handymen doing odd jobs. Some of their wives supplemented their familys' limited income by taking in laundry, working as maids, waiting on tables in local restaurants, or caring for children. Virtually no members of this class attended the Presbyterian Church and relatively few the Methodist; some found a "church home" when the Church of the Brethren was established in 1918, and later some would gravitate to the First Baptist Church, which opened its doors in 1945. Their own children tended to have little interest in school and often dropped out at the first opportunity to marry or take a job.

Another factor contributing to the sense that everyone belonged to an all-encompassing middle class was the fact that there were no black or brown faces to be seen anywhere in town. Nor was there any immigrant stock from eastern or southern Europe. There were no Italians, Irish, Greeks, Lithuanians, or Russians; no Jews, Asians, Hispanics, or blacks. Like so many of America's small towns that lay outside former slave states, there was a racial and ethic uniformity that everyone took for granted.

∽

Residents of this all-white town liked to pride themselves on their broad-minded approach to matters regarding race and discrimination. Students in the local schools were taught the legend (unsubstantiated) that several early settlers had come from the South because of their moral opposition to slavery. Students also learned local lore that insisted that Camden and its environs had been an important "station" on the Underground Railroad. In fact, whatever antislavery activity there was had been centered in a small colony of Quaker families who farmed near the crossroads of West Elkton, eight miles to the southeast.[18] Such self-proclaimed progressive racial attitudes did not attract blacks to the town, and if racial attitudes and customs evident throughout southwestern Ohio are any indication, it is doubtful that they would have been welcomed.

Racial and ethnic issues formed a dissonant background to American life during the 1920s, and Camden was not exempt. Public opinion divided in 1921 when a local branch of the Ku Klux Klan was formed; although no records of the Camden Klan remain, it is clear that the local organization enjoyed a healthy membership that probably approached seventy-five. In September of 1921 several community leaders reported that they had received unsigned threatening letters from Klansmen; ominously, the content of the typed letters indicated that the authors were local residents.[19] Newspaper editor Ray Simpson privately seethed over the Klan's appearance but elected not to denounce the group. Instead, he attempted to impose a news blackout on the organization. In 1923, however, the Klan conducted a series of parades and rallies that stirred the community to the point where he had to report the story.[20]

The Klan's emergence in the former Northwest Territory shocked many. The Kluxers became very powerful in neighboring Indiana, electing one of its members as governor in 1924. Southern Ohio became a haven for Klan activity as well, especially in the Dayton and Cincinnati areas. During the summer of 1923 a large cross was burned in a pasture east of Camden while an estimated fifty white-sheeted members milled about. Later that year the Klan received permission from the town council to hold a rally in the Opera House. This event precipitated considerable local interest and controversy, especially because it was preceded by a parade down Main Street, compete with burning cross, of an estimated sixty hooded members. Simpson, always on guard to protect the town's good name, reported that "apparently all participants came from out of town," although he knew better.[21]

Klan activity peaked in Camden in 1925, as it did nationwide. In that year local hooded patriots staged several rallies, with attendance at the most successful conclave estimated to approach 150 persons. One of the most vocal local Klan enthusiasts was apparently the pastor of the small Church of the Brethren, which had opened its doors only six years before. The public comments of the Reverend Charles G. Ronk in July of 1925, in particular those made during a special evening service designed to minister to the spiritual needs of visiting Klan members, drew substantial comment in the community. He even accepted a gift from visiting Klan leaders in the form of an American flag.[22] Although the Klan faded from view shortly thereafter—in Camden and across the Midwest—the controversy seems to have contributed to a sharp division within the church, and a few years later it was forced to close its doors for financial reasons.[23]

The demise of the Church of the Brethren—which proved to be temporary—left only two organized churches to compete for members. The Presbyterians met in a large white church on North Main Street, while the Methodists held services in a nineteenth-century brick building on South Lafayette Street. Both churches were established during the 1830s and had grown with the community. The few Catholics who lived in the area were forced to travel to Eaton or Oxford for services. In 1941, however, the Cincinnati diocese authorized acceptance of an anonymous $6,000 gift to start construction of a modest-sized building on the north edge of town.[24]

～

A quiet consensus pervaded local politics. It operated on a nonpartisan basis, although the majority of voters were registered Republicans. Seldom did serious competition occur for seats on the village council, township board of trustees, or board of education. Most local officeholders served out of a sense of community responsibility. The typical small-town politician, one scholar has observed, had no desire to disrupt the harmony of town life. He was concerned primarily with building a consensus rather than creating divisions, an approach that led to an avoidance of ideological issues and an emphasis on personalities.[25]

The tasks of local officials were relatively easy because divisive issues seldom roiled the local waters. Monthly village council meetings were usually informal with few if any observers. During the 1920s the most important issue was whether to pave the dirt streets. After considerable discussion, in 1925 the village council implemented a program to coat the secondary streets with "tarvia," an oil-based dust retardant, and to pave Main Street with brick. The new red brick street had a distinctive and attractive appearance, one that would disappear under a heavy coat of asphalt during the late 1940s in response to the toll taken by heavy through traffic.[26]

Keeping property taxes low was always the highest priority. More than one city leader ran for office promising to keep spending at an absolute minimum and business regulations equally minuscule. During the 1920s handyman Runky Roberts held the position of town marshal, for which he received $50 per annum to enforce the law on an as-needed basis.[27] The volunteer fire department's total budget—including salaries—did not reach $1,000 until after World War II. The crew of twenty-five volunteers was led by a fire chief appointed by the council. When the alarm on top of the Town Hall was sounded, many residents rushed to follow the firefighters to the scene of the blaze. The first crewman to arrive at the hall would fire up the boiler on the truck, which would be used to pump water from the several cisterns strategically located at each street intersection to collect rainwater. To be a fireman was very prestigious, and competition for the twenty-five slots was always rigorous.[28]

∼

It is doubtful that anyone bothered to consider the long-range implications that sunny May afternoon in 1903 when brothers Charles and Eby Eikenberry piloted their shiny new Oldsmobile down Main Street to the amazement and amusement of townsfolk.[29] It would be the descendants of that Oldsmobile, largely in the form of Mr. Ford's Model T, that would deliver the first telling blow to Camden's viability as a relatively self-sufficient community. Progress in the form of the horseless carriage was quick to come to Camden; the Eikenberrys took their triumphant cruise down Main Street just eight years after Henry Ford had guided his homemade quadricycle around his Detroit neighborhood. In 1905 Dr. Jerrard W. Combs fired up a one-cylinder International to make house calls in the countryside. By 1909 there were ten automobiles prowling the dusty (or muddy) streets of Camden, and four farmers had also purchased automobiles. Rural mail carrier Merle Fry became the talk of the town in 1909 when he purchased a Maxwell in which to make his rounds on Route 4. In 1914 nearly 50 automobiles were registered in Somers Township; by 1929 motor vehicle registrations in Preble County had reached 5,500.[30] The automobile had been transformed, within the span of two decades, from an expensive toy to a virtual necessity.

There was little opposition to the horseless carriage in Camden, or anywhere else in the country. However, newspaper editor M. E. Fornshell took note of an isolated case of resistance just a few months after the brothers Eikenberry introduced Camden to internal combustion transportation: "Farmers in the counties of northern Indiana are establishing an association, the object of which is to fight the automobile. . . . They declare the owners exercise absolutely no judgment, run them at a wild speed and show a criminal disregard for the welfare of persons driving horses. Many accidents have occurred, horses have been killed, and people injured. Organizations are at work in the rural districts."[31] Such concerns were heard during the early years of the automobile age, but they were soon stilled as the American people fervently embraced what its detractors liked to call the "devil wagon."

Nearly everyone longed for a more reliable, more durable, safer, and faster mode of transportation. Americans rationalized that if the automobile could rid the streets of the stench and residue left by the cantankerous hay burners it would be hailed as a major step forward in the history of mankind. The automobile was what America was all about: progress! As the automobile gained ascendancy during the 1920s, Ray Simpson frequently suggested as much. From time to time, however, he was moved to chastise local drivers for their lack of courtesy and for excessive speeds on town streets: "We've often wondered why it is that the average Camden motorist always has a sort of hostile feeling, the moment he seats himself at the wheel, toward the driver who is coming toward him or who is trying to pass him. Why is it that he harbors a suspicion that the other fellow isn't driving right or doesn't know how to drive, or ought not be allowed to drive?" And taking note of the increasing number of women drivers, Simpson wrote, "Even a pretty girl, charming everywhere else, arouses a certain suspicion when she gets back of a steering wheel."[32]

Simpson's newspaper reported a rising tide of injuries and a not infrequent number of deaths resulting from motoring accidents. In 1931

The popularity of the automobile increased the pressure on local government for paved streets. After much controversy, in 1925 the village council approved paving Main Street with brick. Workers are shown assembling their bricks at the corner of Main and Central. Courtesy Camden Archives.

the heroic action on a road north of town by the local railroad station agent, E. A. Bousman, was widely praised. He was a passenger in a roadster driven by popular local musician Dean Pottenger when the vehicle overturned and burst into flames. Bousman was thrown clear, but Pottenger was pinned beneath the car. Although suffering from severe bumps and bruises and quite possibly shock, Bousman was somehow able to lift the vehicle high enough to pull the unconscious driver to safety.[33] His incredible feat was the talk of the town for years.

By 1930 there was one automobile registered for every four Preble County residents. Farmers began converting to tractors. Motorists would still see a few teams working the fields in the years immediately following World War II, but by midcentury the powerful field horses had almost completely disappeared from the countryside.

Like many others, editor Ray Simpson believed that the automobile would make farm life much more tolerable. The motor car was, he proclaimed, "the greatest of advancements" because "it enables the farmer and his family to enjoy the things the town and city family enjoys, and to still remain on the farm. Farmers have reduced their hauling time by one-fourth through the use of autos, trucks and tractors, and more food is produced for the nation."[34] Nonetheless, the horse era did not end abruptly. In 1933 the village council voted unanimously to instruct the committee on streets and alleys to erect a large sign prohibiting automobiles from parking in front of the Main Street hitching rack.[35]

The automobile opened new vistas for their owners. The century-old dirt Hamilton-Eaton road was incorporated into the federal highway system under the Federal Highway Act of 1916. It now was known as U.S. 127 and by the mid-1930s had been paved from Cincinnati to Michigan. The historian John Rae points out that nearly 20 percent of all American roads were covered with asphalt or cement during the 1920s, and Ohio, with one of the nation's highest per capita automobile registrations, was a leader in the paving crusade.[36]

Paved highways encouraged longer trips. Camden area families now looked forward to day-long excursions to what were once considered to be relatively distant cities: Richmond, Indiana, (25 miles), Hamilton (20), Middletown (22), and especially Dayton (35). In particular, the automobile provided Camden shoppers many options beyond local merchants. Shoppers were naturally attracted by the excitement of a trip but also by the larger selections and lower prices they found in nearby cities. Unfortunately for Cincinnati, its downtown could be reached only after

The South Side Service and Comfort Station welcomed northbound tourists arriving on U.S. 127. This structure was typical of the roadside architecture that was transforming the appearance of America's Main Streets in the 1920s. This picture was taken about 1925. Courtesy Camden Archives.

navigating through several small towns, the city of Hamilton, and finally the congested residential and industrial areas of the city, which meant that the Queen City's shopping district lay a formidable two hours distant.

The result was that Dayton became the major shopping destination for Camden families. Located thirty-five miles to the northeast, this industrial city had become well known as the home of bicycle shop operators Orville and Wilbur Wright. Dayton was also the home of engineer and businessman Charles Kettering, the inventor of the much acclaimed electric starter and many other electrical devices. Kettering's company, the Dayton Electrical Laboratory Company (DELCO), was situated there, as were the modern factories of the Frigidaire home appliance company, National Cash Register, and a host of automobile and electrical parts manufacturers. With this industrial base, Dayton's population in 1930 had reached 201,000. Its attractive downtown shopping area featured a sparkling arcade with dozens of specialty shops and, in particular, the large and well-stocked Rike-Kumler Department Store. Dayton became a major attraction to shoppers throughout much of the Miami Valley.

By the late 1920s the gossipy Personals column in the *Preble County News* carried a standard item, with only the names changing from week to week: "Mr. and Mrs. Charles Neff and Mrs. Will Sebert were in Dayton one day last week." [37] The marketing department at Rike's was cognizant of the expanded market. In 1926 this enterprising retailer inserted an advertisement in the *Preble County News* praising Camden as "a fine agricultural center with 250 homes and 950 residents." The advertisement, undoubtedly appearing simultaneously in small-town weeklies all across the Miami Valley, then proceeded to invite residents of the town to do their shopping at Dayton's snazzy department store. [38]

The transformation of Camden's relationship with the surrounding region was a national phenomenon. In their study of Muncie, Indiana, the anthropologists Robert and Helen Lynd emphasized the changes wrought during the mid-1920s by the automobile in all phases of life. [39] In 1932 the anthropologist Albert Blumenthal noted that even an isolated mining town in remote Colorado had been equally changed: "Nothing has broken down Mineville's isolation as has the automobile. Connection with most of the principal towns in the region is maintained by daily bus service, and a freight truck makes daily deliveries to and from [the towns of] Gold and Smelters." [40]

Improvement of the highways also encouraged urban-based businesses to invade the outlying towns of the Great Miami Valley with delivery trucks. Soon grocery stores were stocking fresh breads that undercut the local bakery. Druley's Dairy in Eaton operated thrice-weekly home milk delivery, and Camden boys learned the basics of the free enterprise system by delivering to local residents copies of the *Dayton Daily News*, the *Richmond Palladium-Item*, the *Hamilton Journal*, and the *Cincinnati Times-Star*, whose advertisements provided additional incentives for launching out-of-town shopping expeditions.

The automobile also changed the perspectives and lifestyles of local residents. Families of even modest affluence now undertook summer vacations by automobile, with favorite destinations being the lakes of northern Michigan and the Great Smoky Mountains of Tennessee. "No Camden man 25 years ago thought that he'd ever be able to step in his own car and go anywhere his wife and children told him to go," Simpson informed his readers.[41] Many a Camden home now featured an ash tray or other souvenir that had been purchased in a distant roadside tourist shop. Status-conscious Camdenites also made certain that their vacation trip—the more distant the better—made the personals column.

In 1931 there appeared in the *Preble County News* an ironic juxtaposition of notices: "a well known local man," Harold Snider, announced the opening of a Chevrolet dealership on South Main Street, and a Richmond leather dealer announced a drastically reduced price of $4.50 for horse collars.[42]

≈

The automobile was just the most dramatic example of the ways in which life along this particular Main Street had changed. The feature films shown on weekends at the Dover Theater opened up a much larger, sometimes sensual and seductive world for those adults who could afford the twenty-five cents admission charge (ten cents for those under 12). Camden's barbering brothers, Cliff and Charles Dearth, had to stock pomade and learn how to trim long sideburns for those dashing young men who wanted their hair as sleek as Rudolph Valentino's. The radio quickly captured the attention of locals, with an estimated 60 percent of the homes now tuned in. They listened on Saturday nights to the latest hits broadcast directly from ballrooms in Chicago and New York City; raptly followed the Tuesday evening saga of the Harlem machinations of Madame Queen, the Kingfish and Andy; and tried to absorb the rapid-fire reporting of Floyd Gibbons. Noting that a major source of music had once been the parlor piano, an amazed Ray Simpson told his *Preble County News* readers, "Now we just grab our music out of the air."[43]

$\sim$

As the end of the 1920s neared, Camden residents had good reason to feel satisfied. For most, the quality of life had improved during the Roaring Twenties. The local economy seemed to be keeping pace with the expanding national economy. Neff and Fry had added an important new manufacturing dimension to the local economy, and farm income seemed good, if the activity at Eikenberry's elevator and feed store provided any indication. In 1928 Camden voters enthusiastically joined in the coronation of Herbert Hoover as the apostle of prosperity; like Americans everywhere, Camdenites fully anticipated that his expertise and experiences as an engineer, business executive, and government leader would enable him to lead the nation to a new level of prosperity. Significantly, the agricultural depression of the 1920s, which produced considerable grief on the Great Plains, had little impact on the diversified agricultural economy of southwestern Ohio. Consequently, Main Street was humming. Although business was good, some perceptive merchants had qualms about the erosion of consumer loyalty thanks to the steadily improving mobility of the local residents, but such fears were muted and not discussed publicly. Conversations tended to focus on the convenience of the new electric appliances, the mobility provided by the automobile, the new worlds opened up by radio and talking motion pictures, and the booming stock market. These signs of progress reinforced expectations that the future of Camden was bright.

To Camden's residents there wasn't much to complain about in the town. It might not be destined for major league status, and it seemed doomed to live in the shadow of the county seat of Eaton. But everyone agreed that it provided a pleasant, comfortable community, or as one resident of that period put it, "a nice place to raise a family and where everyone [is] friendly."[44] Camden boasted of an adequate school system with a modern new building, two established churches, virtually no crime, low taxes, lighted and paved streets, and no serious problems with bootleggers. Folks were even talking about replacing individual septic tanks and wells with a public water and sewage system sometime in the near future.

Masonic Lodge on the first and third Monday nights for the men . . . Philomathean Club for their ladies on the second Tuesday of each month . . . high school basketball on wintery Friday evenings . . . church every Sunday . . . good crops every summer . . . continuity and stability . . . Such was life in this small town as the 1920s came to an end. The farms provided a solid economic base, and Neff and Fry provided steady work for up to a hundred men. Stores buzzed with activity, especially on Saturday nights. Everywhere in this contented town there was evidence of Progress.

Given this environment, it is not surprising that a naive feeling of self-satisfaction bubbled up from Main Street. A visiting newspaper reporter picked up on this attitude in 1927: "Camden doesn't have a chamber of commerce, a commercial club or a civic boosting organization. It doesn't need one. Everyone who lives here sees to the matter of broadcasting the advantages of the town as a place to live and do business."[45] Times were good and the future seemed bright. With Herbert Hoover running things in Washington, what more could a person ask for?

~

Unfortunately for these confident Main Street Americans, the end of an era had arrived, an era that had begun during the mid-1850s and reached full flower by 1890, when the emergence of two hundred thousand miles of railroad lines had ineluctably pulled such isolated "island communities" as Camden into national and regional markets. Life in this small town had already been altered by the daily assault of urban newspapers, radio stations, delivery trucks, county agricultural agents, and a increasing flood of new products, services, and ideas. Farmers now followed the daily movement of prices on the Cincinnati livestock and commodities markets on Cincinnati station WLW. The automobile had freed farm families from the isolation of rural living and opened up new markets for selling their commodities as well as purchasing their children's school clothes. These disparate forces of modernism meant that Camden was now merely another bit player in a triumphant national economy.

In her sensitive and sympathetic photojournalistic treatment of American towns, Carole Rifkind suggests that by the end of the 1920s the new economic realities had already sealed the fate of the thousands of Main Streets across the nation: "With the automobile, the wide-circulation metropolitan news daily, radio, motion pictures, a faster-paced social life and the rise of white-collar occupations, long-independent small towns faced the harsh dilemma of stagnating or being swallowed by the spreading city. Now the city—not the farm or the town—dominated American life."[46] Like their small-town counterparts elsewhere, Camden's optimistic residents had not yet recognized that fact.

Then came the depression.

4

Depression: "The Worst of Times"

"These have been the worst of times," Ray Simpson commented in his weekly column in July of 1931. "Finances and industry have been under dark skies." What the country needed, this dedicated Republican concluded, was to "find a way to get back to normalcy."[1] Simpson was reluctant to say that the Great Depression had simply overwhelmed Camden's vulnerable economy, but that is in fact what happened. Although the unemployment and bread lines of the big cities captured the majority of the headlines, all across the United States small towns also faced economic crises of great magnitude. Plummeting agricultural prices cut the foundation out from beneath their economies, which resulted in a rash of farm mortgage foreclosures and layoffs of farm laborers. In the small towns that served them, local banks were forced into receivership, and the revenues of small-town merchants fell precipitously.

Up and down the Main Streets of America, the Great Depression was nothing short of a calamity. In confronting the cruel realities of the massive economic collapse, residents had to wrestle with the realization that many of the fundamental values upon which they based their lives were no longer viable. It was no longer possible to explain the existence of poverty as the result of laziness or personal failure. They now recognized that they did not have control of their own economic futures. As they signed up for a job with the WPA (Works Progress Administration), or sent their teenage sons off to a CCC (Civilian Conservation Corps) camp, or accepted Aid for Dependent Children, Camden residents understood that they were giving up their precious sense of independence and self-reliance. Recognizing that the origins of the economic collapse lay far outside the Seven Mile Valley, they perceived their vulnerability and interdependence with the world outside. An underlying tension persisted in Camden throughout the depression years as residents struggled with their desires to adhere to the beliefs they had long held dear while trying to survive. How were they to retain the values of the old culture even though it was evident that its foundations had crumbled?

∾

The stock market crash of October 1929 made few initial waves in Camden because relatively few residents invested in the market; those who had capital to invest tended to purchase farmland. It was the precipitous fall of agriculture commodity prices that captured the town's attention. Between 1930 and 1932 the price of grain fell by more than 40 percent; pork fell from $9.14 per hundred weight to just $3.62, and then again to $2.50 the following year. Corn went for just 15 cents per bushel, and wheat prices bottomed out at 25 cents. Wholesale eggs sank to 8 cents a dozen. By 1933 farm income stood at one-third of its 1929 level.[2] Farmers found themselves caught in a vicious squeeze because they had taken out mortgages and equipment loans based on the assumption that commodity prices would remain the same or increase. Their cash flow dwindled to almost zero because the cost of shipping crops and livestock to market became prohibitive given the low prices awaiting them in Cincinnati. Broken fences went untended and machinery was not repaired or replaced. In 1933 there were 298 mortgage foreclosures in Preble County. The farmer's predicament was succinctly summarized by Kansas journalist William Allen White: "Every farmer, whether his farm is under mortgage or not, knows that with farm products priced as they are today, sooner or later he must go down."[3]

The impact of falling farm prices on Camden's economy was devastating. The Eikenberry Seed and Grain Company was forced to liquidate in 1934; thirty-five years of success dealing in grain, seed, feed, and flour had come to naught. Merchants saw their sales fall precipitously. The Camden Loan and Building Association and the First National Bank struggled with a mounting number of loan delinquencies. Bank assets fell from $550,000 in 1929 to just $351,000 in 1933. Cautious management policies provided the necessary cushion to prevent failure, but many times its officers had to quell rumors about impending doom. Mortgage foreclosures and sheriff's sales became commonplace events; to give one example, the Camden Loan and Building Association foreclosed on a property owned by James Paxon, who could not make the weekly $2.50 payment on his outstanding $2,000 loan. Even sheriff's sales were no sure thing; on occasion the sale of a house appraised as low as $1,000 could not raise a single minimum bid.[4]

Everyone felt the pinch. With its silo construction business hurt by falling farm prices, Neff and Fry was forced to reduce its workforce by more than half; in early 1933 only twenty-three laborers remained on its payroll. Average pay at the town's premier manufacturer hovered between $6 and $10 for a sixty-hour workweek. The highest hourly wages topped out at about $15 per week. Farm workers were paid less than a dollar per day; some worked simply for room and meals. Families often doubled up, with two or more generations living in one house. When freight trains came into town, teenage boys risked injury by climbing onto moving open cars to heave chunks of coal onto the sidings, where members of their families waited to toss the pilfered fuel into burlap bags and hurry home to stoke the fire.[5] By 1934 the local newspaper reported that many "undernourished" students were receiving free meals at school, paid by funds received from the Civilian Works Administration. Local unemployment records do not exist, but in 1933 when the first federal work programs announced a handful of local jobs, nearly six hundred men from Camden and Somers Township applied.[6]

Families had to be resourceful to get by. Many farmers resorted to subsistence farming, and town families increased the size of their gardens. Bartering became commonplace. Workers were often paid in food or other tangible items. Housewives canned fruits and vegetables. As planting time approached in 1931, Ray Simpson devoted an editorial to urging residents to "plant a garden and use the food to tide the family over during these hard times."[7] Ivan Greenfill recalls that "there was always enough to eat" on his parents' small farm but "not many new clothes, but that was overlooked by all because no one had them." One woman remembers that her mother spent much of her time knitting and sewing clothing, and on those rare occasions when new clothes were purchased, they would be from Montgomery Ward sales catalogs. While wives sewed and "darned" stockings, their husbands became adept at repairing shoes, doing odd jobs, and cutting firewood. In June and July small armies of blackberry pickers roamed the woods and creek sides. For many families, hunting for small game in the fields and woods around town became much more than a sport; rabbit and squirrel provided meat for the table.[8]

Schoolteachers enjoyed steady employment, but salaries remained at very low levels—$500 to $800 annually. The school board froze and then reduced salaries and slashed operations budgets. In the spring of 1933 it was forced to close school a month early. In 1934 the twelve school districts in Preble County were $164,000 in debt. Camden's district was in deficit some $9,400, and some feared another closure. Teachers, however poorly compensated, were nonetheless paid in real dollars. They were acutely aware that their peers in some Preble County school districts were being paid in near worthless script. In 1935 the Monroe Township school had to close for several months. When one teacher landed a summer job in 1937 painting several barns for a local dairy farmer at twenty-five cents an hour, he was the envy of many of his peers. The coach at Verona High School got stuck for food and board expenses for his basketball team when the school board could not reimburse him. "A nice reward for winning the tournament," he later said.[9] The Camden village council, hard-pressed to collect its modest property tax assessment, cut costs to such an extent that it disconnected half of the street lights to save a few pennies a week.[10]

In 1931 the school board, under pressure to spread what few tax dollars there were to as many families as possible, instituted a policy requiring female teachers to resign their positions if they got married. Although the board did not require previously married women to forfeit their positions, it justified the policy by saying that a married woman's primary obligations were at home, which meant that she was "not in a position to give her undivided attention to the work, and for that reason cannot teach properly."[11] No one, of course, had the temerity to suggest that the policy should also to applied to newly married male teachers. This policy stimulated only modest public discussion, but it stirred deep resentment among women teachers. The policy remained in place until World War II created a severe shortage of qualified teachers of either sex, married or not.

At times the fight for survival led to brushes with the law. The news of the early 1930s was filled with reports from irate farmers about the stealthy work of chicken thieves. One farmer near Morning Sun made the news when he surprised a twenty-three-year-old thief at 1 A.M. one cold January morning. After Lorimer Charles had been robbed several times, he had rigged a simple alarm to the door of his chicken coop. When the confronted intruder pulled a small revolver, Charles blew his head off with a shotgun. Until repeal of the Eighteenth Amendment in 1933, the arrest of bootleggers was also a constant news item. Bootlegging, if one eluded the long arm of the law, was a profitable avocation. However, farmer Frank Statzer pushed his luck a little too far and after a second arrest was sentenced by the Preble County Common Pleas Court to spend "several months in the Cincinnati Work House to work off his time." [12]

In their study of the small city of Muncie, Indiana, during the 1930s, Robert and Helen Lynd reported that struggling families tended to keep their automobiles, even if it meant giving up their houses. They found that the automobile came before "marriages, divorces, new babies, clothing, jewelry, and most other measurable things both large and small." The fact that, as the Lynds concluded, the automobile was "one of the most depression-proof elements of the city's life" prompted humorist Will Rogers's comment that Americans were the first people to go to the poor house in an automobile. [13] This phenomenon apparently held true for Camden, because automobile registrations remained constant for the 1930s. Bill Matt sold fewer new Fords but kept his mechanics busy repairing aging ones; one federal government report indicated that the average vehicle on the roads was over five years of age. On a positive note, gasoline sold for just thirteen cents a gallon at Orville Wood's filling station on North Main Street. Still, many families did not have automobiles, and country roads and town streets alike were sprinkled with walkers. Those who did drive picked up local hitchhikers as a matter of course.

∽

Disaster often brings people together. In Camden, as across the country, the sense of community increased as people sought out activities in which they could share their lives with others in equally difficult circumstances. "Everyone was poor in money but rich in friends. People cared about each other and were willing to help." [14] The small library, with some 3,500 volumes, saw its circulation rate increase to the point that the number of annual book loans tripled the total library holdings. Card playing, always a favorite pastime, became even more popular, and, in an ironic twist, those who could afford to purchase it took to the popular new game "Monopoly." Church attendance and participation also increased. "All we had was the church and the school," one resident of the period recalls. [15]

Through their churches and in their neighborhoods, friends and neighbors looked after each other, especially during the most severe years of 1931 through 1934. "Everyone was friendly and helped each other out, and no one minded too much about not having a job because there were none to be had," one high school student of the early 1930s

This 1936 picture of a locally owned grocery store gives an idea of grocery prices during the depression years. Courtesy Camden Archives.

recalls.[16] Locals extended their protection to the hobos who passed through town. During cold winter months itinerant families were permitted to sleep in the jail cells in the Town Hall if they were otherwise unoccupied; at least it was warm. Locals would discreetly drop by the side door leading to the jail and provide these destitute persons with food; the next day the homeless would be on their way. Because of the railroad and the highway that cut through town, hobos were plentiful in Camden throughout the 1930s. The established ritual called upon them to knock on the back door if they were hungry, never the front. Negotiations sometimes involved an offer to do some yard work in return for a meal. Work or no, more often than not they were fed something, even if the kitchen shelves inside were almost bare. "I remember when a hobo would jump off the train and knock on our back door, Mom would always sit them in the shade on the back porch, and make them a meal with coffee or lemonade," Sue Silvers Knicker remembers. Some women, like her mother, were perhaps hedging their bets: "She never turned anyone away because 'one of them might be the Lord.'"[17]

Even the worst of times can sometimes produce economic opportunity. Such was the case with the motion picture business. In 1932–33 the Dover Theater temporarily closed, but in early 1934 it reopened with a special ten-cents admission charge for a Hoot Gibson western, *Local Bad Man*. In 1936 oil dealer and farmland investor Orville Wood—a young man possessed of entrepreneurial instincts and energies—purchased the Dover and remodeled its interior, increasing capacity to three hundred. At an announced cost of $4,000, Woods installed new seats and placed a sparkling neon marquee out front. Wood's promotions of free dishes and small cash drawings helped boost attendance. The movies provided a release from the pressures of the day and attendance remained steady. Camden residents were not alone in seeking refuge from the depression at the movies: an average of sixty million Americans a week attended a motion picture show during the 1930s. Improved sound technology made elaborate musicals a popular format, and Ginger Rogers and Fred Astaire sang and danced away the depression blues. Historical romances, such as all-time favorite *Gone With the Wind,* drew large audiences, as did Walt Disney's 1937 blockbuster, *Cinderella*. Local moviegoers also watched their share of western, gangster, and detective films in which the good guy always triumphed over the bad guys, truth and justice prevailed over evil, the striving poor hero eventually got rich (and sometimes the girl), and crooked politicians were flushed out of office. During the 1930s Hollywood became America's "dream factory," and those dreams and images of a better world helped pull Camden through the dark years of economic collapse.[18]

The motion picture business seemed so good that in November of 1934 barber Harold Dearth made the announcement that he planned to spend $10,000 to construct a new theater on North Main Street. The local newspaper headlined the news, emphasizing that the twenty-nine-year-old Dearth had contracted with Neff and Fry to build the concrete block facility and that only local men would be employed. In March the sparking new two-hundred-seat Majestic Theater opened with a special showing of *Kid Millions,* starring Eddie Cantor. Dearth boasted that he had installed the "newest and most scientific" RCA projection and sound equipment and that the seats were "the best available." This was an exciting development for a town that had been severely bludgeoned by the depression. Ray Simpson was quick to offer praise: "Camden maintains a pardonable pride in the opening of the new theatre as it is a home-owned, home-operated institution and has been designed and constructed by local industries and completed with Camden labor."

Dearth took out a large advertisement announcing that regular ticket prices would be twenty cents for adults and ten cents for children and that Clark Gable would appear in the next feature, *After Office Hours.* The following year Orville Wood, apparently a strong believer in the benefits to be derived from monopoly, bought out competitor Dearth and raised ticket prices to twenty-five cents.[19]

$\sim$

In his famous 1893 essay on the influence of the frontier on American history, Frederick Jackson Turner emphasized the role of cooperation among western settlers. He was merely repeating what the French journalist Alexis de Tocqueville had observed during his tour of the United States in the 1830s. It has long been recognized that in times of crisis Americans tend to band together to fend off whatever evil forces afflict them. This phenomenon was clearly manifest in Camden during the 1930s, most prominently in the creation of the Progressive Club in November of 1932. Nineteen local business and professional men—coming predominantly from the upper middle class—decided that a formal organization was needed to carry out important programs vital to the survival of the community. Similar organizations, often with the same name, invoking traditional American optimism and faith in the future, sprang up across the land. The anthropologist Carl Withers reported that local leaders in the Missouri town of "Plainville" also created a Progressive Club in the 1930s for the same reasons.[20]

The immediate need that prompted formation of the Camden Progressive Club was the run-down condition of the Town Hall. Erected in 1889, the building had been allowed to deteriorate over the years; reflecting public opinion, a parsimonious village council had not authorized sufficient funds for adequate preventative maintenance. The state of Ohio fire marshall's office had ordered the large second floor of the building closed to the public in 1929, citing a long list of safety problems. In particular, the inspector noted the absence of an external fire escape from the second floor, which contained the Opera House. The only access to the second level was via a wooden stairway and should it become blocked during a fire, a disaster was possible, even with the town's fire truck parked downstairs. During the 1920s use of the Opera House had declined as motion pictures had replaced traveling medicine shows and jugglers in popularity. Growing community interest in the boys' high school basketball team, however, sparked interest in remodeling the second floor to give the team a suitable place to play.[21] During the worst years of the depression, the condition of the Town Hall took on an important symbolic meaning to local residents, its condition becoming synonymous with the image of the community in general.

The Progressive Club sponsored a series of fund-raisers—Saturday night bingo games, a raffle, a fish fry—and extracted small donations of money and equipment from the unwary. Within a few months the substantial sum of $4,000 was raised to purchase building materials. Club members and other interested individuals provided volunteer labor—some had no other job anyway—tearing out the large but outmoded stage, laying a new hardwood floor for basketball, building two rows of seating around the floor (all that the cramped space allowed), refurbishing the small balcony, and, finally, installing new, freshly painted wooden backboards and an electric scoreboard on the north wall. On a much anticipated Saturday night in March of 1933 the efforts of the club were rewarded when the facility was opened. More than four hundred persons crowded up the wooden stairs to a free community dance on the new maple floor. At a time when the depression had reached its nadir, the residents of Camden had something to cheer their spirits. More than fifty years later, several individuals recalled that particular event as being something special in their lives. The city council, always alert to new sources of revenue, soon placed a $5.25 rental fee per game on the school board.[22]

Following this initial success, the Progressive Club took on a series of community projects. Within the community it assumed the roles of a service club, a chamber of commerce, and an all-male lodge. Membership in the Progressive Club indicated high community standing, and its meeting room on Main Street became a place for members to hang out, play cards, and engage in serious discussions about politics, the fortunes of the high school basketball team, and other matters of great import. A monthly fish fry—always a stag affair—was a popular social event for members.

Most community-wide activities for the next quarter century revolved around the depression-born Progressive Club, and membership was considered essential for anyone aspiring to a position of business and professional leadership. Membership soon grew to about fifty, where it stabilized. On the occasion of the club's eighteenth election of officers in 1950, the *Eaton Register-Herald* described the club as "a hard-working, go-getting, non-profit organization" that could be depended upon "to get the job done on any issue confronting them." From the membership came mayors, village council and school board members, bank board members, and business and professional leaders. Membership of women never became an issue. In the parlance of the 1990s, the club provided a venue for male bonding and networking.[23]

Following the renovation of the Town Hall, the Progressive Club decided to sponsor a celebration commemorating the town's hundredth anniversary as an incorporated village. In August of 1933, the worst year of the Great Depression, a week-long street carnival was held on Central Avenue in front of the Town Hall. Attendance was high, drawing visitors from many miles away and reaching an estimated four thousand on Saturday night, although few attendees had much money to spend on carnival rides and games of chance. The celebration, complete with an exotic carnival midway featuring "The Half Italian Girl," "Ramona the Mind Reader," "Bozo the Fire Eater," and "Zippo the Monkey Man," provided a much needed diversion from the hard times. Congressman Byron Harlan stood up to speak amid a pie-eating contest, and a rocking chair marathon that lasted for three days even received brief notice from the Associated Press. Willing contestants competed in the "fattest woman" and "shortest man" contests. The only sour note came when rocking chair marathon contestant Bill Ross was disqualified by the judges for stealthily chewing on raw coffee beans in an effort to stay awake. Ray Simpson put out a daily newspaper throughout the week and at the carnival's end euphorically proclaimed the centennial celebration a great success.[24]

Celebrations aside, the Progressive Club could not ignore the consequences of the depression. It launched a Saturday night bingo operation to fund hot school lunches for needy children, putting the bite on local merchants for small prizes so that the club could keep the entire take. At Christmas time in 1933 it held a community-wide party in the refurbished Town Hall for all the children in the area. Nearly four hundred children received a small sack of candy from Santa Claus and watched a Western and a few cartoons. The annual Christmas party was continued until the late 1940s. The club's fund-raising efforts also included regular Saturday night dances in the Town Hall featuring Dean Pottenger's "Rhythm Makers." A descendant of Camden's original settlers, Pottenger made his living from his band's performances and by giving piano lessons to local youth; the big band sound made by his seven-piece group helped attract large crowds. The dances were immensely popular and continued throughout the 1930s, only to end with the war. Some fifty years later, many individuals identified the Saturday night dances, where admission was a mere dime, as a high point of their teenage years.[25] "In retrospect, the dances were pretty mild affairs," James Barnet recalls, marveling at the small number of fights that took place.[26]

The Progressive Club spread its revenues throughout the community. A fledgling Boy Scout troop got start-up money, 4-H clubs received donations to support their projects, and residents in need of eyeglasses were sent to an optometrist in Eaton. To the dismay of some residents, the Progressive Club seized upon the success of its centennial celebration and for the next quarter century sponsored an annual week-long "Homecoming" celebration in July, the main attraction of which was a sleazy street carnival, complete with a striptease dancer. It was the club's major fund-raiser, bringing in several thousand dollars in good years.[27] After the club fell on hard times in the 1960s, the carnival was continued by the Camden Lions Club, formed in 1948.

A few members of the Progressive Club also served on the board of a quasi-secret community organization that provided relief to needy individuals and families. Back in November of 1918 a huge white elephant sale held to raise money to assist the Red Cross during World War I had produced the sizable sum of $4,244, and when the war unexpectedly ended, it was decided to place the funds in a special Camden Relief Fund. A three-person committee was established to oversee the fund, which was used during the 1930s to alleviate acute cases of need. Using only monies generated by investment of the principal, the overseers anonymously paid for medical bills for local citizens, school lunches, clothing and shoes for disadvantaged children, and even burial expenses. Most Camden residents were unaware of the existence of the fund, and all awards were made confidentially. In 1986, with the health of the custodians deteriorating and the composition of the community substantially changed, the small account remaining was liquidated with a grant to the volunteer fire department and emergency squad.[28]

The importance of volunteerism in this small town was emphasized in the statement of appreciation issued by Presbyterian minister James E. Jones after the renovation of the Town Hall. "Among the chaos of depression, when every avenue of life is at the lowest ebb, when all things seem at a standstill, life still can be buoyant and egressive. The accomplishments in life, even in such times as these, are still possible though only when creative young manhood decides to accomplish its purpose. Such is the reason for the fine piece of work that the Progressive Men of Camden have done in remodelling the Town Hall."[29] Although Reverend Jones might have given way to rhetorical excess in his comments, he nonetheless captured both the dark mood of the depression and the emotional lift that the Town Hall effort symbolized to the people of Camden in 1933.

The pages of the *Preble County News* make it clear that Ray Simpson was reluctant to report major community problems. Like many small-town journalists, he knew that "good news" and the inclusion of everyone's name were what sold newspapers and advertising. A feisty editorial policy, as Will Hartpence had discovered fifty years earlier, was bad for business. Thus when we find Simpson commenting on such issues as the need to provide for the poor and to prevent malnutrition and even starvation, we can be reasonably certain that the situation was severe. In one of his infrequent editorials, Simpson wrote, "One principle must stand out clear and undisputed in these difficult times, and that is nobody in Camden shall be permitted to starve as long as there is food in the whole country. That is a joint obligation of society and of the government."[30]

The considerable voluntary community effort to help one another get through these difficult times stands out as a major theme of life in this small Ohio town during the 1930s. "I personally suffered little direct effect of the depression," a 1934 high school graduate recalls, "but I was very aware of the great suffering of many residents, both in my school contacts and in the community."[31] In the absence of adequate resources and the extensive coverage of today's government social programs, the actions of the Progressive Club, local churches, and private individuals gave strong testimony to the spirit of cooperation and volunteerism that has long been associated with America's small towns.

⁓

But in meeting that unwritten commitment to one's neighbors the earnest people of Camden encountered many frustrations. The two churches, the lodges, and the Progressive Club all lacked resources. Camden was merely one of thousands of communities caught up in a depression that was national, even international, in scope. A national unemployment rate of 26 percent and a devastated agriculture economy that had forced mortgage foreclosures on nearly 20 percent of the nation's farms produced human and social problems of unprecedented enormity. By the crucial presidential election year of 1932, demands for government action to assist the needy and to alter the nation's economic course filled the air. Even the prospect of revolution became a part of responsible political dialogue. "Unless something is done for the American farmer we will have revolution in the countryside within less than twelve months," the head of the Farm Bureau Federation told a congressional committee. The Chicago corporate lawyer and Democratic party leader Donald Richberg was equally pessimistic when he told a Senate committee, "There are many signs that if the lawfully constituted leadership does not soon substitute action for words, a new leadership, perhaps unlawfully constituted, will arise and act." [32]

Enter Franklin D. Roosevelt and the New Deal, pledging to "act and act quickly." And act the new president did, often in innovative and dramatic ways, sometimes stretching the limits of his constitutional powers. FDR's election in 1932 led to a new era in American life, one in which the federal government mounted an unprecedented intervention into local affairs. Camden residents had always instinctively subscribed to the traditional tenets of the Protestant Ethic. Self-reliance, individual responsibility, and the innate value of work were standards by which they judged themselves and others. A large, intrusive federal government assuming major social and economic responsibilities at the local level was not part of the value system to which the good people of Camden adhered.

Camden residents viewed the New Deal with a mixture of hope and trepidation. True to their Republican roots, they also viewed it with a healthy partisan skepticism. In the early stages of the New Deal, partisanship largely faded away as most residents watched the unfolding drama in Washington and hoped that it would result in solutions to the nation's problems. They, like many other Americans, agreed with Roosevelt that "this Nation asks for action and action now." Even Roosevelt's most ominous comment—that the "need for undelayed action may call for temporary departure from that normal balance of public procedures"—did not cause them to blanch. These abnormal times, they agreed, demanded an unusual response. [33]

The long arm of the federal government was felt almost immediately upon Roosevelt's inauguration with his declaration of a bank holiday. Until this point, the First National Bank in Camden had managed to weather the storm, but two Preble County banks, located in the smaller communities of Gratis and Verona, had been forced into receivership. Mortgage foreclosures and sheriff's sales had become routine events by this time. It was a bad sign that the assets of the First National Bank had fallen from $620,080 in 1930 to just $355,925 in July of 1933, a 43 percent decline. Thus everyone in town held their breath when the bank closed its doors on March 9, 1933, and Federal Reserve bank examiners from Cincinnati came calling. After four days of closure, bank president Howard Pattison announced that he had received authorization to reopen. The *Preble County News* reported that this announcement was "received to the general relief of business houses," and noted that the bank was one of the first in the region to reopen, "a sign of strength."[34]

The banking holiday came and went quickly, but announcement of the creation of the National Recovery Administration (NRA) raised important questions about the extent to which the federal government would become involved in the local economy. The NRA was a complex program that embodied the fuzzy concept of national economic planning, which infatuated many influential members of FDR's "Brain Trust." Roosevelt's intellectuals believed that the primary cause of the collapse of the national industrial economy was uncontrolled and often destructive competition. They contended that the establishment of national economic goals and guidelines, coupled with voluntary subscription to "codes of fair competition," would stimulate industrial recovery. The leaders of the NRA set out to create a new capitalist order, a rational, managed economy based on the concepts of national planning and cooperation among competitors. NRA leaders placed great hope in the "codes of fair competition" and started a national effort to get businesses to participate. Recognizing that such ideas were unprecedented and extremely innovative, NRA director Hugh Johnson decided to launch his program with a flurry of publicity designed to overcome anticipated resistance. He even had an art deco Blue Eagle designed as the symbol of the new agency and organized a national public relations campaign to get employers, workers, and consumers to join in his crusade.[35]

The Camden employer most affected by the NRA codes was Neff and Fry, which published a large advertisement in the *Preble County News* announcing that it had signed up for the program. The company agreed to follow the stipulations of the cement manufacturers code, which included adopting established wage guidelines and reducing the hours a laborer could work from fifty-one to thirty-six per week to create six more (albeit part-time) jobs. "We promise," Neff and Fry stated, "to support the code and cut the arguments." The company flew a Blue Eagle flag outside its office, and its advertisements carried replicas of the logo and the NRA slogan, "We Do Our Part."[36]

Through the Preble County Barbers' Association, Cliff and Harold Dearth, Camden's barbering brothers, announced that they had also signed on, agreeing with all barbers in the county that haircuts would cost thirty cents and shaves twenty cents, that weekday hours would be 8 A.M. until 7 P.M., and that they would remain open until 10 P.M. on Saturday nights to accommodate farmers.[37]

Forty-four other Camden businesses, although not signatory participants in the program, endorsed the Blue Eagle, pledging their support and cooperation. Their full-page ad in the *Preble Country News* ran: "We, the undersigned business firms of Camden, will cooperate whole-heartedly with the PRESIDENT'S wishes in supporting the NRA Code. It is our belief that the Code is a cure for the Depression and one that will do more than its share in relieving the strain that has been on the people of this community for the last three years, and on the Country at large."[38] That this group of independent small-town businessmen, overwhelmingly Republican in their politics, would endorse such a large federal intrusion into the daily affairs of private enterprise is indicative of the depth of the fears that were festering along Main Street.

But as the historian Arthur M. Schlesinger, Jr., writes, Hugh Johnson eventually paid a high price for "transforming a government agency into a religious experience" and by promising too much.[39] At the national level, the NRA soon ran into a political cross fire as liberals and conservatives alike took their best shots, denouncing it either for gouging consumers or for being an unnecessary bureaucratic interference in the affairs of private enterprise. By mid-1934 the Blue Eagle was a cooked goose, widely dismissed by its critics as the "National Run Around." Johnson had initially attracted a great deal of attention with all the hoopla, but within less than a year the NRA had served only to crystallize conservative opposition to the New Deal. Its impact on Camden was primarily psychological, helping to revive hope during the bleakest days of the depression.

❧

The bank holiday and the NRA set the stage for the acceptance of other federal programs. In the summer of 1935 some two hundred young men took up residence seven miles north of town in a Civilian Conservation Corps camp. Each day they worked on a series of soil erosion prevention programs. More than 150 farmers welcomed the corps onto their lands to plant trees and bushes, build small check dams, and assist in implementing new plowing and planting strategies designed to curb erosion.

After a few months their presence was taken for granted, and they remained until 1941. In 1935 ten local workers received wages from the Public Works Administration (PWA) for installing curbs and gutters throughout the town. Area road-construction projects funded by the Civilian Works Administration (CWA), the PWA, and the Works Progress Administration (WPA) became so numerous that after a time no one paid much attention.[40]

Before the 1930s, the only government agent to appear in town regularly (except for an occasional G-man pursuing bootleggers) was the agricultural extension agent. Now federal administrators and experts become an integral part of the local scene. Local politicians, businessmen, and professionals had to learn to share power with this new force. Initially they welcomed it, but doubts soon began to surface. The seductive lure of federal intervention was that it provided a new source of funds to pay for local needs.

Only a few months after Roosevelt took office, the Ohio office of the CWA announced that it would spend $500,000 dollars on emergency public works projects in the state during a six-month period beginning in December of 1933. Late in November, Camden mayor Oscar W. Taylor met with state CWA authorities. Taylor was encouraged by an announcement from Columbus that 165,000 unemployed workers statewide would be put on public works jobs by the first of December, and that $47,000 of the state's $500,000 budget had been allocated to Preble County. The mayor said that this meant that some Camden families would "have a merrier Christmas." Within a few days an astounding number of 800 men had applied for work. Only a small percentage of that number were fortunate enough to make it onto the CWA rolls, but by December 7 some 350 men in Preble County were busy on ten road repair and construction projects, with a weekly payroll of $2,143. Camden's CWA enlistees were assigned to pave the Old Trace Road east of town which closely followed the original path that General Wayne had followed 140 years earlier in his northward pursuit of Chief Little Turtle and his Miami tribesmen.[41]

By the time the CWA began its short-lived operations, Preble County farmers had already sampled the benefits of the New Deal. The same week that those 350 workers shouldered their picks and shovels to improve county roads, 108 of Preble County's largest wheat producers shared $46,000 in Agricultural Adjustment Administration (AAA) payments for participation in its controversial crop reduction program. In order to stabilize farm prices, which had fallen to historic lows owing to surplus production, the Roosevelt administration had embraced the "domestic allotment" theories of Montana State College agricultural economist M. L. Wilson. Thus in 1933 many Camden area farmers for the first time came face-to-face with the ironic reality of American farming: in order to receive government support to boost their badly sagging economic fortunes, they had to agree to reduce production. Over the pot-bellied stove at the train depot and at the grain elevator on South Main Street, area farmers weighed the economic merits and the moral implications of this drastic new program, the brainchild of Secretary of Agriculture Henry Agard Wallace.[42]

By late 1933 some eight hundred Preble County farmers had decided to forsake their independence for the new economics of artificially imposed scarcity. They agreed to reduce wheat, tobacco, and corn production by 20 percent and even to cut back on what had for so long been their major activity: pork production. When squealing litters of baby pigs were sent to an early grave by the AAA's effort to reduce the nation's hog population from sixty-five to fifty million, a national controversy exploded. Even Secretary Wallace could find little solace in an economic program that led to the early demise of six million baby pigs, or to the plowing up of ten million acres of southern cotton: these were, he confessed, "not acts of idealism in any sane society," but the only viable option for stabilizing the agricultural economy.[43]

At the annual Preble County Pig Roast in Eaton in December, John Wilson of distant Wood County, one of the architects of the Ohio crop reduction plans, informed the 600 farmers in attendance about the details of the program. Wilson described a scenario that would enable Preble County farmers to share in more than $1 million in crop and livestock subsidies in 1934. Some 1,450 county hog farmers would share $545,762 for reducing pork production. The welfare state arrived in Preble County during the early days of the New Deal, but those who received the vast majority of the federal largesse were among the county's largest property owners.

The pages of the *Preble County News* thereafter reported, without editorial comment, news of the latest Department of Agriculture pronouncements on its price stabilization programs. The federal government had become a major player in the economic life of Preble County. Writing about similar reactions by farmers in the Dakotas, the historian Catherine Stock concludes that the AAA and subsequent federal farm programs "gave real control over their fates as farmers and townspeople not to the familiar foes of weather, illness, or railroad rates, but to a new kind of middleman—the experts, advertisers, agents and advisors of the new middle class."[44] Camden-area farmers would forever after grumble about federal controls and bureaucratic red tape, but the farm support checks were not turned away. The new era of farming with a pen and a stack of government forms had begun.

~

Area farmers were swept into the fold of the AAA without major opposition or controversy. They had little option, and they learned to play the game in Washington through such powerful lobby organizations as the Farm Bureau Federation. The same did not hold true for the unemployed. Deeply ingrained attitudes regarding the work ethic underpinned this debate; it was widely believed that government handouts destroyed character and self-reliance. From the time the first timid public works programs were put forward by the Hoover administration, critics were quick to denounce them as "make-work" and "the dole." Allegations were made about "chiselers," individuals who accepted government "handouts" under false pretenses. In 1934 Republican gubernatorial candidate Clarence Brown, from nearby Highland County, told an Eaton audience, "The depression is a social problem, not a government problem" and promised to cut welfare to the bone. His successful opponent, Democrat Martin L. Davey of Kent, promised to jail all welfare cheats and cut the budget to the same bone.[45]

In Camden, the emotional issue of public works and accepting government handouts erupted in 1934 when the village council decided to seek funds from the PWA to install a city water and sewer system. For the first time since 1874, when a near riot had broken out when a few women temperance activists demonstrated vigorously in front of Frank Ramsey's tavern, the community was riven by controversy. The consensus that had for so long characterized public policy in Camden evaporated in a hailstorm of arguments and angry threats of lawsuits.

Should Camden accept federal public works dollars? Should the village council engage in deficit financing by issuing twenty-year revenue bonds to put up matching funds for Federal Emergency Relief Administration (FERA) dollars? Could the council force residents to commit to the proposed system? Would city officials condemn the private wells of those residents who refused as a means of forcing citizens to sign up? How could the community afford a new financial obligation during a depression? What would happen to property tax rates? Would a city water system actually reduce fire insurance premiums by 60 percent as promised? Did the town really want to use federal dollars to hire the unemployed? And, finally, the biggest question of all: Would the council force holdouts into the new system by making outdoor privies illegal?

The issue divided the town for more than two years. It began in September of 1933 when the council approved a motion to seek available FERA funds to put in a water and sewer system, an upgrade of the town's infrastructure that self-styled "progressive" members of the community had desired for some time. The use of private wells, septic tanks, and privies raised serious health questions, they said, and the high rates of fire insurance resulting from the lack of high pressure water rankled. But opposition immediately developed, citing fears of potentially exorbitant utility rates, unwanted federal intrusion, the cost of financing twenty-year bonds at 3.5 percent, and the loss of private wells. Many opponents simply seemed to fear change. Two local businessmen and would-be political activists, variety store owner Earl Shank and theater operator and oil dealer Orville Wood, led the opposition. In the nature of Camden politics, much of the debate was conducted one-on-one or in small groups over coffee at Doc Bryson's drugstore, around the depot stove, and at the morning church aid society meeting. The Progressive Club, as the organized voice of the town's business and professional elite, came out strongly in favor of the project. Its members dominated the council and the town's newly created Board of Public Affairs, which would oversee construction: "The Club feels that the project is an asset to our community and we will back it to the last stand," President Harry Neff said in a formal communication to the council. He proudly informed the council that he did so on authority of a unanimous vote of the membership. "Anything that the club can do to promote the idea to the people or anything else that you may desire in this matter you can feel free to ask for." [46]

In 1934 the council and the Board of Public Affairs finalized the project plans, which entailed the erection of a water tower on "Mt. Auburn," the hill guarding the west side of town; the drilling of several deep wells north and east of town to tap into massive underground water pools; the installation of a water filtration and pumping station; the laying of water and sewage lines throughout the community; and the construction of a sewage treatment plant on the far southern edge of town with the treated effluent to be dumped into the Seven Mile Creek. By late 1934 the board had firmed up its plans and received detailed specifications from an consulting engineering firm from Portsmouth, Ohio. Estimates of the cost approached the daunting figure of $40,000 at a time when the village government was operating on a total budget on less than $1,500 per year. [47]

In order to obtain $18,000 in federal funds, Camden's voters had to approve a revenue bond issue of $22,000. The bonds would be sold at 3.5 percent interest. State law required a vote of the electorate and mandated that 65 percent of those voting approve the bond issue. The informal politicking that preceded the elections in the fall of 1936 was intense. Although everyone took an interest in the Roosevelt–Alf Landon presidential campaign and the bitter battle between the flamboyant incumbent governor, Martin L. Davey, and his Republican opponent, John W. Bricker, most political discussion in Camden revolved around the water project. In a most uncharacteristic move, editor Ray Simpson published a strong front-page editorial urging voters to "take a progressive step forward" and support the bond issue. He warned that failure to pass the measure would entail "a step back into a rut which has for a number of years retarded public progress and convenience here."[48]

Simpson took the pragmatic position that the federal funds (which would now come through the recently established WPA) constituted "a gift of $18,000 from the government." The future of the town was at stake, he concluded: "It may be the last opportunity for Camden to accept an outright gift for municipal improvements." He noted that rival Eaton already had a comparable water and sewage system and concluded that "if it is voted down we will have to do it later at twice the cost to taxpayers." So the conservative, ever cautious Ray Simpson, Republican through and through, opted to take the New Dealers' money. After all, he was a member of the Progressive Club.[49]

Voter turnout on election day was extraordinarily high, and election night proved to be as dramatic as anyone could have imagined. As the hand-marked ballots were counted under the close supervision of local election officers, it was evident that the division would be very close to the required 65 percent margin. Eventually, it was announced that the proposal had passed by a vote of 332–178—a margin of one vote. Had just one additional voter cast a negative instead of a positive vote, the bond issue would have been rejected. (To be mathematically precise, the measure had passed by precisely one-half of a vote.) Simpson was a master of understatement in the following edition when he noted, "The result was a matter of doubt until the last vote was counted late Tuesday night."[50]

The opposition—Shank and Wood, joined by the venerable physician Jerrard "Doc" Combs—immediately demanded a recount and retained two attorneys from Dayton to assist in reversing the outcome.

They threatened to go to court to prevent the sale of the revenue bonds. Two weeks later, a recount was held at the Town Hall, and Simpson reported that a large crowd stood out front late into the evening to await the outcome. As Shank and Wood had anticipated, the original vote count was in error, but the new count of 328 to 173 meant that the measure had still passed, by 9/10 of a vote. Once again, just one more vote cast in opposition would have proved decisive.[51]

In January the village council unanimously approved the final legal documents and solicited bids; soon afterward a construction firm from Indianapolis began digging up the streets to put in the system. Except for supervisory and engineering personnel, local men were employed at basic WPA wage rates to do the labor.[52]

The Board of Public Affairs announced that hook-up charges for residences would be free for an initial period and set the monthly rate for water and sewer at $1.50 for residences and $2 for businesses.[53] The opposition quieted and talk about lawsuits faded. Orville Wood and Earl Shank were among the first to sign up for service.

By 1938 the new system was fully operational and the controversy forgotten. When in 1941 the National Youth Administration announced a grant of $4,000 to the school district to construct a modern shop for holding mechanical and woodworking classes, no one protested.[54]

~

Basketball made its first appearance in Camden in 1904 on a makeshift floor in the Opera House with the spectators perched on the stage. The game "made a popular hit," according to the *Preble County News,* which concluded, "The sport is here to stay. Camden has taken to basketball like the small boy has to Christmas." In reporting on a game between two local teams, the newspaper noted, "The initial game in the Opera House last Wednesday evening started out more auspiciously than any other sport ever introduced in Camden. The stage and entrance ways were packed with an appreciative audience and much enthusiasm was manifested, for the game proved most strenuous and interesting. John White was exceptionally good at placing the ball." For the historical record, a team patriotically named Stars and Stripes won 19–5.[55]

The game caught on. As interest grew and excitement intensified, so too did concern over the objectivity of the referees. In 1905 a local team got clobbered by an team from Middletown, and Camden fans believed the fault lay with the man with the whistle. The game was, the *News* reported, "a rank farce" because "the treacherousness of the referee was so boldly apparent and so disgusting to all lovers of fair play and the loud cries of 'put him out,' 'robber,' and the like rent the air from the start of play." On a much more positive note, and in the interests of gender equity, a high school girls team made its initial appearance in a game on the Opera House floor against a team from Liberty, Indiana, just a few weeks after the bullies from Middletown had stolen the game from the locals. Camden's "Fair Maidens" lost the game, the reporter concluded, because their "feminine sweetness" was taken advantage of by the "rough and tumble" visitors, who "used other than lady-like tactics."[56]

Thus did basketball come to Camden. The concept of sports as part of a public school educational program took time to gain a foothold. In 1910 a high school–sponsored team played a two-game season, but it wasn't until 1915 that the Camden Cubs made their first appearance in newly adopted school colors of red and black while their supporters urged them on with a fight song with wording adapted to the popular "Washington and Lee Swing." No one can recall the origin of the less-than-ferocious nickname, although an affection for alliteration and the popularity of the Chicago baseball team are likely reasons. In 1921 the county high schools held their first tournament, and large crowds came to cheer the boys and girls teams in the Eaton Armory. Camden High School lacked a gymnasium, but in a pinch the study hall could be used for practice, although its low ceiling made shooting difficult. Like the Stars and Stripes in 1904, the Cubs played on the main seating area of the Opera Hall with the chairs removed; spectators sat on the stage or in the small balcony. In 1930, ostensibly as a cost-cutting move but probably motivated by commonly held fears regarding the dangers of exercise to the reproductive organs of young females, the all-male board of education eliminated girls basketball. For the next half century, like most of their peers around the nation, Camden's girls had no competitive sports program. They could be cheerleaders for the boys' teams, however, and competition for spots on the cheer squad were intense.[57]

During the 1920s boys basketball gained strong community support as quality of play improved with better coaching. In small towns like Camden, where the numbers required for football made it nearly impossible to play and where at times it was even difficult to put a decent baseball nine on the field, the requirement of just five players and a few substitutes made basketball a better choice.[58] It was also a game that a young boy could practice by himself, shooting baskets at a hoop nailed over a barn door. The rules encouraged speed and skill rather than brute

Basketball loomed large in the life of most midwestern towns. Camden's town five posed for this picture in 1906. Courtesy Camden Archives.

strength, and the game made for an exciting diversion from the bleak grey skies that so often dominated the Midwest's cold winter months. Thus all across the Midwest, in towns large and small, basketball became the most popular high school sport.

In 1936 interest in the game grew even greater with the hiring of a new coach who came highly recommended for having produced several strong teams in Verona and Farmersville. Although the first team coached by Robert Davies registered a losing season, the next year he had his disciplined team routinely beating other county schools, and even giving teams from much larger urban schools stiff competition. Because the new coach had earned a master's degree from Ohio State University, unusual for the local teaching staff, he was given the title "professor" by the *Preble County News*. With a winning team, attendance soared. On Friday nights several hundred fans willingly paid the five cents admission charge and crowded onto the two rows of seats surrounding the floor, often overflowing the balcony and moving into standing room in the large entrance area. The seating was so close to the sidelines that occasionally players would trip over an extended leg; in one memorable game, an elderly fan reached out with his crooked cane and snared a visiting player, giving new meaning to the term "home court advantage." Community rivalries intensified emotions. During a hotly contested game with bitter rival West Elkton in 1945, a scuffle between players on the floor escalated into a brawl that quickly engulfed the overflow crowd. At least one cool head prevailed, however, and official timer and scorekeeper E. A. Bousman calmly brought the melee to an end by turning off all the lights.[59]

For its day, the new basketball facility upstairs in the Town Hall was one of the best in the county. There were no shower facilities, however, and home-team players had to dress at the high school two blocks away, while the visiting team dressed in the council chambers on the first floor. But the floor was sixty-four feet in length, much longer than most, and the ceiling was sufficiently high. Such spacious playing conditions did not always exist on the road: the ceiling in the New Paris gymnasium was just four feet above the rim of the basket, and local rules permitted ricocheting shots off the ceiling. The Lanier Township Tigers had learned to run special plays by utilizing the four wooden posts that stood in strategic spots on the floor holding up the ceiling, giving new meaning to the basketball term "post play." In 1938, after Coach Davies's team absorbed a 24–23 loss at West Alexandria, the *Preble County News* explained the loss to disappointed fans: "Although the Cubs played a much better game than that of the West Alexandria quintet, the low ceiling and rafters stopped a number of the locals' shots that might have gone for two points—hitting these rafters gave the opponents the ball out of bounds." On the plus side, the *News* commented favorably on the "nifty" new red-and-black team warm-up jackets the players wore for the first time.[60] That loss was a rarity in a year the team compiled a 15–3 record, winning the twelve-team county conference and the all-important postseason tournament.

～

High school basketball in winter, town team baseball in the summer. Baseball had been played on local lots—in Camden as in other small towns—ever since veterans brought the game back with them from Civil War camps. On September 10, 1894, the local team, the Camden Lathams, challenged the professional Cincinnati Red Stockings of the National League. The Camden team was named after the Reds' star third baseman, Arlie Latham, whose skills were much admired in town. Having won the county championship, the Lathams felt pretty cocky, and they raised enough money to get the "Reds" to come north for a challenge game. A crowd of fifteen hundred people streamed down Main Street, which was decked out in red, white, and blue bunting, and congregated around a new field built especially for the occasion. The final score, alas, stood at an overwhelming 16–1 against the Lathams, in large part because "Fournier's curves were too much for our boys"; but everyone had a grand time, and even the cocksure and tempestuous Arlie himself was moved to comment favorably on the determination and spirit of the team of farm boys that had appropriated his name. In congratulating the locals for their "good showing," the editor of the *Camden Gazette* sought to put the proper spin on defeat by noting, "The 'Reds' proved to the Lathams that we were out of our class in fast company, but we are swift enough for our neighbors."[61]

Since the nineteenth century, local men had played baseball on Sunday afternoons. In some years the team was little more than a disorganized group of men, but in others they sported uniforms and played in more-or-less organized leagues. So it was in the world of town ball all across the United States. In the 1930s baseball took on a greater degree of importance because residents were looking for inexpensive entertainment and diversion. Like motion pictures, town baseball provided a means of forgetting the sorry economic predicament for a few hours. In 1933 the Progressive Club donated $100 to purchase new uniforms and equipment for what was called the town's "semipro" team. Actually, it was anything but semiprofessional in quality, and the players did not get paid, but local fans nonetheless took its games with the utmost seriousness. When the locals took the field, located behind the high school, on Sunday afternoons, several hundred spectators showed up to watch, chat, and assist the volunteer umpire with close calls. The team was managed by Pennsylvania Railroad station agent E. A. Bousman. The manager was a feisty individual, headstrong and hell-bent on winning. Only his wife and a few close friends knew what the "E." stood for, because everyone knew him as "Bat." Ervil Bousman had gotten the nickname as a young man in his native Kokomo, Indiana, where he would pick up a few dollars in local boxing matches; over the years, his pugilistic nickname of "Battling Bousman" had gotten shortened to "Bat." Bousman led the local nine to many a victory, often accompanied by animated arguments with the umpires, and even an occasional threat of physical mayhem directed at visiting teams.

Baseball provided small towns everywhere with a sense of community identity. Natural rivalries developed with nearby towns, and the outcome of games became matters of civic pride. Baseball became a way

The Camden town baseball nine, about 1910. Courtesy Camden Archives.

of continuing old rivalries—over competition for canals, highways, and railroads; for regional economic supremacy; or for the location of the county seat or other government agencies. Thus Camden's games with county seat Eaton attracted considerable interest, sort of a mini David and Goliath drama, as did forays into nearby cities like Richmond, Dayton, Hamilton, and Middletown. Typically, the *Preble County News* was moved to denounce the tactics of the Eaton club, as in 1935 when the paper accused the opponent of employing "fast maneuvers" by hiring several "ringers" from Dayton for the fall Central Ohio League playoffs; such tactics, Ray Simpson noted with a sense of propriety, did not succeed, and Bousman's team battled to a crucial victory.[62]

Although Bat Bousman's team enjoyed considerable local interest, the team always struggled financially. Without a fenced field it was impossible to charge an admission fee, and a baseball cap was passed through the crowd during the seventh inning stretch to collect donations. The state of the economy meant that the cap was often returned with only a few coins in it, and more than once manager Bousman, who often advanced the team money from his own pocket to purchase balls and bats, threatened to cancel a season. At crucial times the Progressive Club contributed modest sums to keep the team afloat for another season.[63]

Town baseball and high school basketball provided a focus for the community during these harsh depression years, giving a sense of rhythm to the passing of the seasons. The two sports also provided a diversion from the cares of the day and a popular focus for local conversations at the barber shop or Deem's Half-Way Tavern. Although baseball fans had taken to listening to radio broadcasts of Cincinnati Reds games during the 1930s, the cost of travel and tickets precluded all but the most affluent from attending games at Crosley Field. Whenever locals made a trip to Cincinnati for a game, it was an unusual enough event to make the personals column. The popularity of basketball was attested to in 1938 when attendance at the county tournament forced school officials to move the games across the state line to Richmond, Indiana, where the Earlham College gymnasium held four thousand.[64]

Sports historians have observed that although major league baseball attendance declined precipitously during the depression years, public interest remained quite high. Fans continued to root for their teams, listening to radio broadcasts and reading the sports pages. The feats performed by such stars as Dizzy Dean, Frankie Frisch, and Lou Gehrig helped the American people to cope with the bleak days of the Great Depression. Local sports performed a similar function along the depression-riddled Main Streets of small-town America; the great popularity enjoyed by local teams is an important, if often overlooked, facet of the life of the small towns of America during this difficult time.

∼

Camden's economy essentially paralleled the slow and difficult national recovery that took place during the 1930s. By 1935 agricultural subsidies and WPA employment had introduced much needed cash into the local economy, and employment and farm prices slowly improved. Times remained tough and optimism was guarded at best, but the combination of federal programs and local efforts sustained the community. Major changes occurred in small towns like Camden during the 1930s, but some things definitely did not change. Although the New Deal brought money to workers and farmers, local voters were not inclined to switch their allegiance to the Democratic Party. By a slender margin, they had

Ray Simpson owned and edited the town newspaper from 1914 until his death in 1950. Here Simpson scans a 1942 issue of his newspaper delivering the news that town physicians Von Barnheiser and Charles McKinley have departed for military duty. Courtesy Camden Archives.

from census reports was not a revitalization of the rural town but the early stages of a trend that would contribute substantially to the decline of Camden and thousands of similar farm towns: the growth of the suburb. "The small town of the future is going to have the support of both the farm and the city, instead of depending almost wholly on the farm as in the past. It will not vanish from the picture as some big-town editors predict. Its future is brighter than it has been at any time in the history of the nation."[3] Simpson was not describing the future of Camden, as he hoped, but rather the advance guard of the suburban boom that would transform American society after World War II.

Throughout the dismal depression years Camden's newspaper editor never lost the faith. He remained confident in the ability of his town to survive and regularly told his readers that better times would soon return. Sprinkled among the many reports about sheriff's sales and the scramble of the unemployed for public works jobs were the items of "good news" that reassured readers there was a continuity and meaning to life in Camden. Front-page stories emphasized the ritual and routine that had been the stuff of small-town life for generations—births, marriages, high school graduations, funerals, meetings of the ladies bridge club, changes in ministers, high school basketball scores, the severity of hail storms and blizzards, destructive fires, summertime polio scares, installations of Worthy Matrons into the Eastern Star, and the ups and downs of the town baseball team. The 1940 census showed a continuation of the process of slow growth that had characterized the town since its founding: on the eve of World War II its population stood at 991, an increase of 103 residents since 1930.[4]

~

Political news revolved around the resurgence of the Republican Party in Ohio after the unforeseen Democratic tidal wave of 1936, when Ohio voters had supported Roosevelt over Landon by an astounding three hundred thousand votes and had also reelected the controversial and much-maligned incumbent governor, Martin L. Davey. With his administration beset with charges of corruption and malfeasance, Davey was able to ride the coattails of the Roosevelt landslide to narrowly defeat the popular Republican attorney general, John W. Bricker. But in 1938 Camden and Preble County contributed to the strong Republican majorities that Ohio gave to senatorial candidate Robert A. Taft and to Bricker, who this time easily won the governorship over Charles Sawyer of Cincinnati.[5]

As the years rolled by, Camden's economy slowly perked up. Farmers benefited from rising commodity prices that by 1938 had reached pre-1930 levels; subsidy checks received from the Department of Agriculture added substantially to farm income. The rebounding agricultural economy tended to have a salutary effect on business activity in Camden, since many of these dollars were spent in local stores and used to repay loans. Laboring jobs on public works projects tended to be temporary, but they contributed a modest infusion of cash into the local economy. After the nadir of 1933, Neff and Fry added workers to help meet a growing number of silo and storage bin contracts, and the company more than doubled its number of workers to sixty by the end of the decade. Bill Matt sold a few more new Fords each year, and the recently established Chevrolet dealer on the other end of Main Street also moved his small inventory. The two movie theaters enjoyed steady attendance, and several new stores appeared along Main Street. Bob Benson launched a popular meat market, and Jessie Roberts expanded her dry goods store to meet the needs of local women. In 1936 the new Blue Bird Restaurant featured "complete 25 cent dinners," offering "live music" on Saturday nights at no extra charge.[6]

The repeal of Prohibition in 1933 was followed by the opening of several taverns. The local branch of the once powerful Women's Christian Temperance Union attempted to fight this development, but it was no match for the resurgence of the town's tavern culture, which appealed primarily to working-class residents. Following repeal, Deem's Tavern enhanced its reputation as a popular place for "plate lunches" with its well-stocked bar. Whitey's Bar was ready to serve its customers at the first legal opportunity, and later in the decade Walt's Cafe developed a reputation for inexpensive sandwiches and soups. The H & H Cafe became a well-liked place to quench one's thirst and relax after a day's work, perhaps in part because of the alleged presence of a slot machine in the back room, which prompted an occasional visit by the county sheriff. The clientele of these establishments was overwhelmingly male and working class; few women were seen within their confines, even with a male escort. For women concerned about their social standing, the taverns were strictly off limits.

The economy thus continued its slow rebound. The net assets of the First National Bank in Camden steadily increased, reaching $430,00 in April of 1940, still well below what they were in 1929 but much better than the bottom level hit on the bank holiday of March 1933. Perhaps most encouraging was the fact that by 1938 mortgage foreclosures had fallen by 80 percent from the terrible year of 1933.[7] The school board had managed to keep things together during the depression years by cutting its budgets. As national defense spending began to trickle into the local economy in 1941, the school board even found a little extra in its budget to purchase new basketball uniforms. Reporting on a lopsided 33–16 win over Dixon Township, the newspaper commented: "The over capacity crowd, which jammed every available inch of space in the Town Hall, was very favorably impressed by the new suits sported by the Camden squad. They're white and look as good as the boys did Friday night."[8]

∿

Despite hardships, life in Camden and its environs maintained a continuity and rhythm that provided a feeling of security, of permanence. When a family encountered tragedy, the entire community seemed to come to its aid. In 1939 a farm family's home burned to the ground, and within hours the family had been provided temporary shelter, clothing, food, and enough household goods to get by. "We were so thankful," says Elois Johnson, remembering that devastating day in her young life. "There was no United Fund, Red Cross, or other service organization in Camden. Just people helping out their neighbors."[9]

The community provided a guarded environment in which young people could grow up and prepare for adulthood. Young boys earned money by mowing lawns and raking autumn leaves, or by running a newspaper route for one of the eight city daily newspapers that competed for local readers. When town boys reached high school they often took summer jobs as "hands" on area farms, working on threshing or hay baling gangs, where they experienced the realities of demanding physical labor. Young girls learned at a early age the expectations of their parents and the community. They helped their mothers with the housework and, once they reached the seventh grade or so, earned spending money from baby-sitting; later, the lucky ones secured jobs in local stores after school, if their parents were willing. In high school the great majority opted for home economics courses in preparation for marriage and mastered the essential secretarial skills of typing and shorthand. Although a few young women sought a college degree—nearby Miami University being the most popular institution—it was not unusual for academically talented young women to be denied the opportunity to attend college, much to the frustration of their teachers, because their parents did not believe a college education was proper or necessary for their daughters.

Camden's adults took their child-rearing responsibilities seriously. The overwhelming majority of teenagers regularly attended Sunday school and church. Discipline in the schools was strict, with a much feared paddle kept in the principal's desk drawer. The code of discipline was strongly supported by parents and the community; if a student was disciplined at school, many parents would impose additional sanctions at home. Outside school, teenagers were continually under community scrutiny. "As a youth I was encouraged, respected, helped, guided, and critically observed by my elders," 1948 high school graduate Donald Shields recalls.[10] Teenagers were permitted to test their wings, but the larger community was there to keep a watchful eye on behavior and to take action by placing pressure on parents if necessary. If a teenage boy was seen driving a little too fast in the family sedan, his parents were invariably informed.

Strong social sanctions encouraged young people to stay within well-established boundaries. Parents kept a close eye on their offspring, carefully guiding them through the perils of adolescence. One graduate of the class of 1940, Jacqueline Overholser Sylvia, remembers that in her senior year she was dating Bill Patton, a handsome young man who was both a star athlete and outstanding student. He happened to live a few houses away on North Main Street. On those rare weekend evenings when his parents permitted him to visit her home, at 11 P.M. his mother "would summon him home with a loud blast on a whistle from her front porch." Sylvia, now a retired public school teacher, wistfully recalls those innocent years on the eve of World War II: "Small town indeed! I was far too innocent to compromise him. Damn!" [11]

High school dances and post–basketball game parties went on without a hint of alcohol, and drugs were not even part of the consciousness of high school students. It was clearly understood that sex was to be postponed until marriage; boys considered a good night kiss a major triumph. Although dating was usually permitted after age sixteen, many girls were forbidden to date until their senior year in high school, and some had to wait until after graduation. Most social interactions with the opposite sex took place at church-sponsored youth meetings or school functions, less often at the movies or at the popular and heavily chaperoned dances in the Town Hall which featured Dean Pottenger's popular imitations of the big band sounds of Glenn Miller and Tommy Dorsey. [12]

In this protective, if not restrictive, social environment, it was uncommon for an unmarried teenage girl to get "in a family way." When such a situation occurred, it led to extreme embarrassment for the girl and her parents. A hastily planned wedding usually resolved the situation. Community standards, enforced by an unquestioning school board, required the expectant young lady to leave school. Informal school board policy mandated that if either a girl or boy married before graduation, they forfeited their opportunity to complete their high school studies. Local values decreed that it was time for the young husband to go to work to support his new family. During the war, however, circumstances forced a reevaluation of these values. On one occasion, when a high school senior married her sweetheart, who was on furlough from the army, the school board, after much discussion behind closed doors, permitted her to complete school.

These informal polices undoubtedly contributed to the high dropout rate once students reached the age of sixteen; enrollments fell by about 50 percent between the freshman and senior years. For girls not planning to go to college, marriage at an early age was a goal they knew their parents expected them to achieve. In keeping with the agricultural environment that pervaded the town, girls tended to marry a young man a few years older.[13]

~

In the 1930s Camden residents were firmly situated in the political mainstream of midwestern Republican isolationism. In an editorial celebrating the Fourth of July, Ray Simpson wrote, "We're happy because we are at peace with the world, and we want the world to know it. There's no chip on our shoulder; no hatred in our hearts; no ill will toward other nations."[14] The view of the world seen from Camden was precisely the same staunchly isolationist view that popular Senator Taft of Cincinnati embraced. The common perception was that the United States had been deceived into entering the Great War in 1917 and that a similar mistake should not be permitted to happen again. As war erupted in Southeast Asia and Europe in the late 1930s, Camden residents went about their daily lives with a gnawing apprehension that the United States would somehow be drawn into another war. Even after Germany overwhelmed France in June of 1940 and had knocked a groggy England onto the ropes, there was no upsurge of interventionist sentiment in Bob Taft country. Camden's view of the world was aptly summarized in a cartoon published in the *Preble County News* on the eve of the launching of the Blitzkrieg in 1940. This cartoon, distributed by a nationally syndicated service for small newspapers, was in the spirit of North Dakota senator Gerald P. Nye's neutrality hearings and subsequent legislation; it protested against greedy business interests that would attempt to lure America into another war for the sake of big profits. But foreign policy did not impinge much on the rituals of daily life; folks remained focused on the economic malaise that had yet to pass and quietly hoped to avoid involvement in the war.[15]

The meaning of the gathering storm became more personal to Camden residents when one of their three physicians, Dr. Von Barnheiser, was trapped in eastern Europe for several months after Germany invaded Poland on September 1, 1939. The popular physician and his wife were in Budapest attending a six-month seminar on new surgical techniques when war broke out. For several weeks the *Preble County News* carried reports about the efforts of the Barnheisers to return to the United States. Within eighteen months after returning to his Camden practice, Dr. Barnheiser would be drafted into the Air Corps medical service, and he would eventually return to Europe as part of the liberation forces.[16]

Residents followed news of the war in the daily newspapers and on the radio. Dramatic reports, such as pioneering electronic journalist Edward R. Murrow's on the bombing of London, helped prepare Camdenites for the inevitability of war. There were no public remonstrations when Congress, after impassioned debate, approved President Roosevelt's request for the establishment of the first peacetime draft in the nation's history. In the autumn of 1940 Camden-area male residents between the ages of twenty-one and thirty-five registered under the Selective Service Act. In December of 1940 the first contingent of thirty Preble County men, including Elwood Zech from a farm near Camden, departed for training at Fort Shelby, Mississippi, as part of the mobilization of the Ohio National Guard's Thirty-Seventh Division.[17]

As the likelihood increased in 1941 that the United States would be drawn into the war, President Roosevelt was able to overcome intense opposition in order to implement his Lend Lease program of making military supplies available as a means of helping England withstand an anticipated German invasion. In the summer of the fateful year of 1941 he placed an embargo on shipments of oil and steel to Japan, which created an increasingly tense relationship between the United States and the Rising Sun. In mid-summer no one was surprised when the popular coach and mathematics teacher, Robert Hallsted, resigned to accept a commission in the Army Air Force as a flight instructor. Sales of Defense Bonds were promoted at the bank and the post office, a sign not only of a renewed sense of patriotism but also of the resurgence of the economy, now rapidly accelerating under the enormous stimulation of defense programs.[18]

Nonetheless, the news of Pearl Harbor hit Camden—and the rest of the country—like a sledgehammer. The political dialogue about neutrality and a "phony war" ended shortly after noon on December 7, 1941, when the first radio reports about the attack were broadcast. No one could have anticipated the enormity of the changes that the war would have upon the community.

World War II constituted a major historical watershed for Camden. By V-J Day, the town's structure and its relationship to its immediate regional, political, and economic environment had changed substantially. The war ended the depression, introducing a level of employment and personal income unprecedented in the town's history. The impetus of the war-induced economic boom continued into the immediate post-war years, until the string ran out in the 1950s. The war intensified the integration of the town into the regional and national economies by stimulating commuting to attractive jobs in defense industries located in the ring of cities in which Camden was nestled. Not only did workers commute to these factories, but many families made the decision to move there as well. Thus began the departure of many of Camden's best and brightest, a process that would intensify after the war.

~

The immediate impact of the declaration of war was the departure of local men to serve their country. Some 275 men from Camden and Somers Township eventually entered the military, many of whom did not wait for the draft but enlisted upon graduation from high school. They were not happy about their lot, but they went without questioning the necessity of either the war or their role in it. Unlike the men who left Camden to fight in the Civil War, the Spanish American War, or World War I, they did not depart amid a blaring of trumpets and a public outpouring of patriotic rhetoric. They went quietly, keeping their emotions to themselves. Steadfastly patriotic, they were like the fifteen million other servicemen and -women who simply assumed that it was their duty to defend their country. Their parents, proud but fearful, sent them on their way to basic training. Eight would never return. Three times that number would return with their bodies malmed by enemy fire.

The historian Stephen Ambrose could just have easily been describing the men from Camden who went to the battlefronts across the world when he wrote of those who made the Normandy landing on June 6, 1944: They were "young men born into the false prosperity of the 1920s and brought up in the bitter realities of the Depression of the 1930s. . . . The literature they read as youngsters was antiwar, cynical, portraying patriots as suckers, slackers as heroes. None of them wanted to be part of another war. They wanted to be throwing baseballs, not hand grenades, shooting .22s at rabbits, not M-1s at other young men. But when the test came, when freedom had to be fought for or abandoned, they fought. They were the soldiers of democracy." [19]

The reality of the war was quickly brought home in early March of 1942 when the parents of Edward Leibolt were notified that the aircraft he was piloting had disappeared in the jungle over Burma. A 1934 graduate of Camden High School, Leibolt had trained at Kelly Field in

Texas in the late 1930s, had become an officer in the Army Air Force, and had volunteered to serve in the fabled Flying Tigers flying supply missions over the Burma Hump to the beleaguered Chinese army of Chiang Kai-shek. Apparently, Captain Leibolt was not shot down but was forced to parachute from his plane when it encountered engine failure. His body was never found. His family reported that he had become so taken with China that he had intended to return there to live after the war.[20]

As the young male population in Camden went off to war, the town moved to get behind the war effort. The *Preble County News* added a front-page feature "Camden Behind the Men Behind the Guns," which reported news about the activities and whereabouts of local servicemen and -women. The column reprinted portions of their letters and, through a local committee, solicited donations to purchase Christmas presents that would be sent to every Camden soldier; the gift packages included home-baked cookies, small personal items, cigarettes, and candy. The committee also arranged for the *Preble County News* to be sent to each person in the service. The American Legion Post erected a large signboard near the Town Hall that listed all area men and women serving in the military; if anyone was killed, a gold star was placed beside his or her name and a picture was displayed in the window of Bob Duskey's hardware store across the street.[21]

Given this atmosphere, the efforts of one local man to avoid military service caused a major stir. At age thirty-six, village councilman Orville Wood was at the high end of those eligible for the draft. One of the town's more affluent residents, this aggressive businessman and libertarian political activist operated a distributorship for oil, gasoline, and propane products and had major holdings in other local enterprises, including the two movie theaters and three area farms totaling some six hundred acres. When he was reclassified 1-A by the Preble County draft board, Wood sought a deferment based on his role as a "farmer," noting that the farms he owned produced far in excess of the number of "agriculture units" required for an exemption. Turned down in November of 1943 by the county board, whose members knew that he was anything but a day-to-day tiller of the soil, Wood brought suit in federal court in Dayton, seeking a reversal on the grounds that the 1-A classification was "arbitrary and illegal." He also requested a permanent injunction issued against the draft board preventing it from reclassifying him 1-A.

On December 2, the day that he and sixty-five other Preble County men were to report for final physical examinations, Wood did not show.

That night, unknown persons spattered his front porch, front yard tree trunks, and sidewalk with several gallons of yellow paint. The next day reports of the deed spread across town, and a parade of sightseers drove and walked by his South Lafayette Street home. The local constable was unable—perhaps unwilling, given community sentiment—to ferret out the vandals. The following week the court rejected his last legal gambit, and on January 20, 1944, citizen Orville Wood became Private Wood and entered the army at Fort Benjamin Harrison, Indiana. Wood served without further protest until the war's end.[22]

～

The resurgent wartime economy was good for Neff and Fry, and this small company moved rapidly to meet the unprecedented demand for its cement products. Not only did it soon have a huge backlog of orders for large storage bins as area industries expanded production, but the firm also became a major producer of 100-pound cement bombs used for training Army Air Force bombing crews. The war also was good for the specialized steel assembly shop operated by Joseph H. Gwynne; begun in 1935, this small concern secured several contracts during the war for customized steel structures used at the Wright-Patterson Air Force Base located on the northeast edge of Dayton. Gwynne had to scramble to find qualified laborers to fulfill his contracts.[23]

As more men left for the war, the problem of finding workers intensified. Throughout much of 1943 Neff and Fry ran a series of advertisements appealing for laborers: "Men wanted for Construction Crews and at Plant. Defense Work." By mid-1943 nearly two hundred Camden-area men had departed for the military, and there was an acute labor shortage. For an entire decade able-bodied men had searched for any type of work, and now jobs went begging. Some farmers were unable to harvest all their crops owing to the shortage of "hired hands." In April of 1943 unharvested corn from the previous growing season stood rotting in the fields. In a startling reversal of accepted employment practices, Neff and Fry hired approximately 125 women to do heavy industrial work in their Camden cement stave factory.[24]

The shortage of workers was not merely the result of military service. Good jobs, and plenty of them, were available in the cities that ringed Camden. Thus many men and women took jobs in Richmond, Dayton, Middletown, Hamilton, even relatively distant Cincinnati. Many kept their residencies in Camden and carpooled, carefully husbanding their precious gasoline rationing stamps. Some simply moved to the cities to be close to their new jobs. This was part of a national phenomenon: one out of every seven Americans moved during the war in response to attractive new jobs, and seven million Americans left the rural areas for the cities or the military, creating a major labor shortage in towns and on America's farms.[25]

Unfilled professional positions also lacked qualified applicants. A shortage of certified teachers created a serious problem for public schools throughout the United States as male teachers either left for the military or abandoned their teaching careers for better paying jobs in the expanding economy. Camden lost several male teachers in 1942 and 1943, and those who remained were forced to assume additional extracurricular responsibilities. Each August the newspaper carried reports of vacancies still unfilled for the upcoming school term beginning in September. For two years there was no science teacher on the high school faculty, and the longtime superintendent, E. W. Schwing, filled in on a temporary basis.[26]

All across the United States, communities suffered from a lack of adequate medical personnel. Camden was no exception. Its two most active physicians, Drs. Barnheiser and Charles McKinley, were among the first to be drafted, leaving the 1,800 residents of the area dependent for a time on the services of Dr. Combs, who was now in his mid-seventies. In late 1942 Dr. James Glier came to Camden from Greenfield, Ohio, to establish a general practice for the duration of the war; he even served on the village council for a time.[27]

≈

Within a few months after Pearl Harbor, signs of the war effort were evident. Scrap drives became a part of community life, spearheaded by the American Legion and the Progressive Club. Acting under orders from Governor John Bricker, Mayor Lloyd Townsley created a Camden Defense Council; more than seventy-five Camden men and women assumed duties on several committees, although as fears of enemy attack waned, so did the committees' efforts.[28]

Civil defense became a major focus of local activity, and for the first time the heartland of America contemplated its vulnerability. State officials warned direly about the possibility of enemy bombing. Although such an eventuality was not even remotely likely, participation in air-raid drills made everyone feel connected to the war effort. Camden's close proximity to major defense installations and arms factories intensified concern. "Did you know that 20% of all war material made in the

United States is produced within a radius of 45 miles of Camden and that this section would be one of the first attacked by the enemy?" Ray Simpson warned his readers in the summer of 1942. A few months later, perhaps responding to depressing news of the American war effort, Simpson became much more alarmist, suggesting that Camden could be a major enemy target. "It takes only a few bombers to annihilate a small community," he threatened, "whereas a whole fleet of airships is needed to cause noticeable damage in the metropolitan area."[29] When insufficient numbers of air-raid wardens and fire watchers volunteered to patrol Camden's streets and alleys, Simpson prodded them by noting, "A great many people in Camden will say this is foolish and 'it can't happen here'—well a dozen nations in Europe said the same thing two years ago, but it did happen there and it can happen here."[30]

As a consequence, a sufficient number of volunteers, many of them veterans of World War I, signed up for the local civil defense board and coordinated a series of air raids. The drills were scheduled during convenient weekday evening hours, and volunteer air-raid wardens and fire watchers went through a training program. It took a while to get the drills organized, and it was not until early in January of 1943 that Camden had its first full "blackout." An obviously pleased Ray Simpson reported that within less than two minutes after the fire siren on top of Town Hall had given its coded signal, the town had been doused in darkness.[31]

≈

Although residents strived to maintain a normal life, the war's impact was felt in many ways. A few months after Pearl Harbor, Simpson reported that "Camden is already beginning to feel the pinch of the war." The impact of gasoline and rubber tire rationing required serious modification of driving habits. Drivers struggled to keep their speeds below the new 35 mph national limit imposed by a fuel-conscious Congress. Because "the Japs" (as they were routinely called in the newspaper) now controlled Southeast Asia, the traditional sources of rubber were shut off, and Simpson implored his readers to comply with the new speed limit. Camden participated in another fuel reduction program—the "dimout" of lights in homes and streets after 9 P.M. Residents were urged to turn off most lights each evening and even to retire earlier than usual. "After nine o'clock in the evening, Camden looks like a ghost town," Simpson reported with satisfaction.[32]

Red Cross drives for blood and funds became routine, and residents labored in their backyard Victory Gardens. Viewers flocked to the movies to watch the Pathe News summaries of the military action of the previous week and such compelling feature films as *Hitler's Children*. The use of rationing stamps for meats and sugars was a constant reminder of the war effort.[33]

Only a few sour notes surfaced. Bob Benson, operator of a popular butcher shop, became so frustrated with the paperwork and inconsistent regulations of the Office of Price Administration that for a time he closed up shop. "OPA restrictions have made it necessary for me to close my business," he said in a paid advertisement in January of 1943. "I am unable to determine what I can do and what I cannot do under the present restrictions."[34] Benson quietly reopened his shop in March, but over coffee at Doc Bryson's drugstore, Ray Simpson heard many other locals complain about rationing and price and rent controls. He attempted to see the big picture, and he urged his fellow citizens to persevere: "The flower of our young manhood has been called to arms," he wrote in 1943. "Our job on the home front is to preserve the freedom of this, their America, and to keep the necessary war materials flowing to them. The hearts of the American people are with their soldiers. While they may be somewhat confused at times by the veritable patchwork of government regulations and counter-regulations they establish, they are honestly, fervently and conscientiously doing their best."[35]

⁓

By the summer of 1942 the full impact of the war had been driven home to Camden residents. A few local men had already been involved in naval duty in the Atlantic and Pacific, where they were exposed to enemy fire. William Brilhart from nearby Dixon Township was taken prisoner in the Philippines, an event that was announced in the *Preble County News* under the headline "Former Fair Haven Boy Held Prisoner by Japs." An Eaton youth was reported killed in a naval battle in the North Atlantic.[36] The gossipy "Camden Behind the Men Behind the Guns" column informed readers in July of 1943 that William Grimstead had sent a letter from North Africa, which had somehow got through the military censors, reporting that he was now "out of danger" after seeing plenty of frontline action against Rommel's forces, but that a former Camden Cub basketball player, William Laney, had died of wounds sustained at Anzio.[37] As the island hopping progressed in the South Pacific, and as the North Africa and Sicily campaigns unfolded in 1943, the residents of Camden closely followed the war news, always with an eye on events where they thought members of their family or the boy next door might be stationed.

The invasion of France was a long awaited event, one heralded by an unusually large headline in the *Preble County News*. In Camden, as in the rest of the United States, people followed the news from Normandy closely, huddling over radios in stores and homes to get the latest news bulletin.[38] Many stores closed their doors at noon, taping a handwritten notice on the door: "Gone home to listen to the news." In the evening of that fateful Tuesday, June 6, 1944, hundreds of apprehensive Camdenites participated in prayer services at local churches. The *Preble County News* reported that initial reports of the invasion were "met with moderate calmness." A week later the newspaper noted that everyone was asking the same question: "How are our boys doing on the coast of France?" It reported that the invasion, although expected, nonetheless produced a great deal of "surprise" throughout the community—and a great deal of apprehension.[39]

Approximately one hundred Camden-area youth participated in the invasion, and at least two were seriously wounded during the early days of the assault on the beaches of Normandy. Another young man, Marvin Alcorn, was killed shortly after the breakout from the hedgerows in July. Nearly everyone in Camden felt personally involved, even if they did not have a family member in General Dwight Eisenhower's enormous task force. As farmers they had greatly increased their production to meet wartime quotas, and many others had worked overtime in area factories—in the steel mills in Middletown; the airplane propeller factory in Moraine, an industrial suburb of Dayton; the machine shops in Hamilton; even in the modest practice bomb shop on South Main Street—to crank out the material of modern warfare. For many Camden workers, the results of their labor were now on the line. Many had dutifully filled out Internal Revenue Service forms for the first time to pay taxes to help bear the cost of the nation's Herculean military effort. Like all American communities, Camden, with its men, its taxes, and its labor, had made a significant contribution to the assaults on French beaches that now carried such American names as Utah and Omaha.

As the months following D-Day rolled by, the news from the two fronts continued to occupy everyone's attention. The status of local servicemen filtered back to town: much of the news was good, some of it very bad. Bombardier Clarence Doan was reported missing in action over Hungary and was later identified as a prisoner of war. Earl Pitsinger received a Purple Heart, having been wounded "somewhere in the South Pacific." Dale Doty, just two years earlier a popular high school athlete, was now being held in a German prison camp after seeing action at the Battle of the Bulge. Sandy-haired Dale Thomas, a reserve guard on the 1941 basketball team, lost a leg at the Battle of the Bulge, receiving four Purple Hearts and four bronze stars; Paul Felton received serious burns when the Navy cruiser he served on was hit by Japanese fire. Charles Keller managed to survive a kamikaze attack that sunk his minesweeper, but he earned a Purple Heart and carried severe burn scars by which to remember that frantic day off the coast of Okinawa. Others were not as fortunate. Dale Patterson died on August 18, 1944, in France; and Ned Sebert, previously decorated for bravery on D-Day, died in eastern France, ironically on Armistice Day, November 11, 1944. Adolph Willeford had been killed three weeks earlier in the same region. And just a few days before the fighting ended on May 6, 1945, Clayton Andrews died near the German town of Aachen.[40] Virtually everyone in Camden knew all of its young men who had made the ultimate sacrifice.

~

Rifleman Donnie Ferris landed on the treeless volcanic beach of Iwo Jima in the ninth wave of Marines to go ashore on the first morning of the invasion, February 19, 1945. Just turned twenty years of age, Ferris was one of seven children raised on a small farm a few miles west of Camden, a member of the Camden High School class of 1942. Like many of his classmates, he did not wait for the draft but enlisted in the military shortly after graduation. He completed special training as a radio operator in Logan, Utah, but the Marines discovered they had more radio operators than they needed, so Ferris became a Marine grunt, officially a "rifleman-stevedore," shipping out of Treasure Island and San Francisco Bay shortly before Christmas in 1944.

"When we hit the beach I could hear the Japanese machine guns. We took cover along a shoulder of the beach," he later recalled. There he lay, within a few hundred yards of the base of Mount Suribachi on what the military planners called "Green Beach," flat on his stomach, spread-eagled, just as he had learned in training. Listening to the furious Japanese fire whizzing over his head, Ferris remained pinned down at the water's edge of the small island for about twenty minutes. Then a landing ship, an LST, came onto the beach nearby, drawing a flurry of Japanese mortar fire. One of the mortar shells landed squarely between

Ferris's legs and buried itself in the loose, black volcanic soil before detonating. That fortuitous fact saved Ferris's life by muffling the impact of the exploding shell. "I didn't feel any pain. I just knew that I had been hit." Forty-five minutes later, medics removed him to a hospital ship. But they left both of his legs on shore.

Nine days after Ferris had been hit, some of his buddies from his Twenty-Eighth Regiment of the Fifth Marine Division raised the American flag atop Mount Suribachi, their effort captured by photographer Joe Rosenthal in what would become the most famous photograph of the war. Military experts agree that the battle in which Ferris participated for less than an hour was one of the fiercest battles in all of American history. Much of the fighting involved hand-to-hand combat between the Marines and determined Japanese defenders. Ferris was one of 25,851 casualties that the Americans sustained during the thirty-six days of fighting to take this small pork-chop-shaped island. Only five miles long, it would be some of the most precious real estate ever taken by U.S. Marines. In the end, 6,821 Americans were killed while more than 20,000 Japanese soldiers died defending this strategic island, one of the last major hurdles facing the Americans before they could launch a much anticipated invasion of the Japanese mainland. Located just 640 miles from Tokyo Bay, Iwo Jima was coveted by the military as the site for an air strip from which long-range B-29 bombers could be deployed against Japanese mainland targets.[41] But Green Beach and Mount Suribachi were a very long way from Camden, Ohio.

The wounded farm boy was shipped back to the United States on a hospital ship filled with other wounded young men. He spent seven months in the U.S. Navy Hospital in Philadelphia, receiving treatment and being fitted with prostheses. One leg had been severed above the knee, the other just below the knee. Ferris returned home in October of 1945. After sufficiently mastering the use of his artificial limbs, he enrolled as a freshman at Miami University on the GI bill. After graduation he learned the harsh reality of being a handicapped veteran once the euphoria of victory had melted away; he was turned down for several jobs after prospective employers learned of his disability. Long before American law protected those with such handicaps, employers frankly told him that he was "not physically capable."[42]

Disappointed but undaunted, Ferris enrolled in the School of Law at Ohio State University in Columbus, married a Camden school teacher, passed the bar examination, and entered private law practice in Hamilton in 1952. In addition to developing a substantial general law practice,

Ferris served four terms on the Hamilton Board of Education, became active in local Democratic politics, practiced for a time as an assistant county prosecuting attorney, and even made an unsuccessful run for Congress in 1966 in a heavily Republican district. He and his wife raised four children, including a son who eventually joined him in his law office. In 1985, as the fortieth anniversary of the invasion of Iwo Jima neared, Ferris talked with a young reporter about the day that changed his life forever: "It was a part of my life I would not have missed for anything. We had a known enemy, a known objective. We had a strong feeling that it was them or us and we had a preference for us." And, with a wave toward a calendar on his office desk, he ruefully observed, "I have no trouble remembering this time of the year."[43]

～

The double headline that spread across the top of the *Preble County News* on August 16, 1945, told it all: "Crushed Japs Surrender! World War II is Ended!" President Harry S. Truman's declaration of the cessation of hostilities set off a noisy celebration in Camden. Happy locals drove through the streets honking their automobile horns, church bells pealed out the joyous sounds of victory, and the fire siren atop Town Hall, which had blown often during the conflict to announce an air-raid drill, joined the action. Even "the weather man chimed in," Ray Simpson noted, "with several loud claps of thunder as a rain storm was approaching."[44]

The celebration did not last long, however, and it was not especially exuberant. V-J Day was, at best, a bittersweet event. Nor was it unexpected, because everyone had anticipated an end to the fighting in the wake of the atomic bomb blasts over Hiroshima and Nagasaki. The war had taken a heavy psychological and personal toll on the American people. Like most Americans, Camden residents had approached the war with a workmanlike attitude, hoping to get it over as quickly as possible, but public support was largely devoid of the emotion and enthusiasm that had swept Camden in 1917–18. Eight local men had died, and more than a score, like chubby-cheeked Donnie Ferris, had suffered horrible wounds that would affect the rest of their lives. Recognition that an incredibly powerful new weapon had been unveiled was cause for further reflection on the meaning of the war.

The surprise announcement on August 6 by President Truman that the United States had dropped a new kind of bomb on the industrial city of Hiroshima was initially greeted with great cheer, for everyone believed the president when he said that use of the atomic bomb would prevent hundreds of thousands of American casualties anticipated in the invasion of the Japanese mainland. Many Camden soldiers, recently arrived home from Europe, were enjoying a brief furlough before shipping out for the Pacific and the dreaded invasion that was scheduled for late 1945. If the Japanese soldiers fought as tenaciously as they did at Okinawa and Iwo Jima, how would they fight when Americans attempted to land on their home soil? Truman's use of the new weapon met with these soldiers' approval because they knew that the likelihood of becoming an invasion casualty was high. Among those on furlough was Clyde Puckett, one of five sons his parents had sent off to war. His brother Labon had received a Purple Heart for wounds received in France. Clyde had escaped injury during the invasion but had been captured by the Germans at the Battle of the Bulge and spent nearly six months in prisoner-of-war camps; when he was liberated in late April his weight had fallen from 170 to 100 pounds.[45]

Thus did the pall of death, of lost limbs, even the awesome image of a strange mushroom-shaped cloud dampen Camden's victory celebration. Nuclear weapons and the dawning Atomic Age produced a new set of ethical issues and prompted Ray Simpson to tell his readers that he didn't know "whether to rejoice or worry" about the unexpected way in which the war had ended. He feared that "civilization will destroy itself." "Those with loved ones in the South Pacific will rejoice because the invasion will not be required," he conceded. Simpson even injected a little local pride into the news about the atomic bomb, noting that Neff and Fry had produced "some specialized concrete materials" for the "mystery plant" in Oak Ridge, Tennessee.[46]

The *Preble County News* also carried ominous news from occupied German territory. A letter from Germany written by Edward Keith White described his role in helping liberate the Nazi S.S. concentration camp in Oachan. He related his shock and horror upon seeing "gas chambers and crematoriums," and some hundred dog pens into which victims had been tossed to be eaten alive by packs of vicious animals. "I have been out looking the place over today and I would not have believed a lot of the things that have been going on here, if I hadn't seen them. Some of these things I am going to tell may not be so nice to read, but it really is what has been going on here and I think you should know it." He reported seeing the corpses of victims whose heads had been severed by "long knives," and he told of the hundreds of survivors who "are starving, insane, many having been beaten horribly. . . . There are some ropes still hanging from trees where some people were hung." White concluded his letter by noting that American officers estimated that at least three hundred persons a day had been executed by the Nazis over a period of several years.[47]

Edward White's grim tale was not the only one reported by locals in the column "Camden Behind the Men Behind the Guns." In early May of 1945 Lt. Margaret House of the Army Nurse Corps unburdened herself of the atrocities she had witnessed in eastern Germany, including one where an estimated nine hundred civilians, including many children, had been jammed by Nazi S.S. troops into a large hay barn, which was then sealed and set on fire. "It's something unbelievable, and hard to imagine how any people can be so cruel," she wrote. "I just returned from the scene and I'll never forget it so long as I live. . . . I know it's true because I saw it."[48]

~

News of the Holocaust and such atrocities as Margaret House had witnessed quickly faded in a midwestern community anxious to put aside the sacrifices and tragedies of war and return to a normal life. Although many leading economists and political leaders had expressed fears that the end of the war would lead to a resumption of the depression, Camden residents saw encouraging indicators everywhere they looked. By March of 1945 assets at the bank for the first time exceeded one million dollars, more than a doubling since Pearl Harbor. The spectacular increase in the bank's fortunes, even considering inflation, provided a fairly accurate measure of the turnabout in the town's economic condition produced by the war effort.

Camden people were anxious to spend the money they had made in the war, when rationing and shortages had meant that there were no appliances or automobiles to be purchased. Much to the consternation of many who now had plenty of money in their savings accounts, Bill Matt could not promise a new Ford until at least 1947. Americans everywhere were anxious to buy a new house or remodel their existing one. Returning veterans—many who had married during the war—looked forward to settling into family life and needed housing. It was a time to rejoice in the hard-earned victory to which everyone had contributed. It was also a time to plan for the good life that everyone hoped lay just around the corner.

6

The Last Picture Show

The years immediately following V-J Day were euphoric ones in Camden. Across the United States the economy expanded, in part owing to the stimulus derived from the enormous expenditure of federal defense dollars, but also owing to pent-up consumer demand resulting from fifteen years of depression and war. The country was about to enter a period of sustained growth that would carry American society to a level of affluence and economic strength unprecedented in history. Five years after the war ended, the economic expansion showed no signs of abating; the postwar economic boom made even the heady days of the 1920s pale in comparison.

For several years, like many similar towns scattered across the United States, Camden participated in the postwar boom. However, by the mid-1950s, although metropolitan areas continued to expand, the boom in Camden began to ebb. By the 1960s an ominous pattern of economic stagnation had set in. The contrast to nearby cities was obvious. While the urban areas of southwestern Ohio grew in size and economic diversity, Camden found itself struggling and was eventually unable even to maintain its position. Although the spectacular growth occurring across the Sun Belt received the preponderance of media attention, major urban growth also affected older sections of the country, including southwestern Ohio. Within two decades following V-J Day, Camden had been whipsawed by a series of events that undercut its economy and altered the very character of the town.

～

The powerful postwar economic expansion stimulated a massive urban housing construction boom. Much of the growth took place on the edge of the larger cities, and new rings of suburban developments transformed the structure of American urban life. Seldom did a month go by in Dayton or Cincinnati that yet another subdivision did not announce its "grand opening."[1] Central cities were undercut not only by residential suburbs but also by shopping centers and industrial parks as both commerce and manufacturing relocated to the urban fringes. The central city of Cincinnati, for example, grew by only 50,000 between 1940 and 1960, reaching a total of 502,000; in sharp contrast, its metropolitan area expanded by 225,000 to reach a total population of 864,000. Dayton's metropolitan area also expanded, the population of Montgomery County increasing from 295,000 before the war to 527,000 in 1960. Most of Cincinnati's new manufacturing and service enterprises were built on inexpensive land in its northern suburbs and across the Ohio River in northern Kentucky, rather than in the traditional industrial core located near the central business district. Such long established Queen City companies as Kroger Foods, Crosley Manufacturing, Procter and Gamble, Lever Brothers, and several local breweries also expanded their operations.

Dayton's traditionally large employers also participated in the national economic expansion: National Cash Register, DELCO, and General Motors, including one of its major subsidiaries, Frigidaire. Adding to Dayton's healthy economy was the enormous expansion of Wright-Patterson Air Force Base, which became home to a major wing of the Strategic Air Command, complete with B-52 jet bombers, sophisticated electronics, and nuclear weaponry. In Hamilton, such established firms as Mosler Safe, Ohio Casualty Insurance, Champion Paper, and Niles Machinery expanded operations, but the largest employer now was Fisher Body, which opened a modern factory that employed five thousand workers to manufacturer automobile bodies for General Motors. This new plant was located just south of Hamilton in the rapidly growing suburban community of Fairfield. A few miles farther south, on the northern edge of Cincinnati, General Electric opened an industrial complex to manufacture jet aircraft engines, another major economic stimulus to the Ohio economy provided by the cold war. The huge blast furnaces and rolling mills at the Armco plant in Middletown, having been awakened from a decade-long stupor by the war, now produced the steel demanded by a booming American industrial economy. And, shrouded in secrecy, some ten miles southwest of Hamilton near the small community of Harrisonville, a mysterious new factory opened. Its employment statistics were kept secret, but passersby noted several hundred cars in its parking lots. Located behind high chain fences and surrounded by an inordinate level of security, this subsidiary of the Renauld Corporation manufactured radioactive components for America's growing arsenal of nuclear weapons.

These and many smaller employers offered jobs that proved irresistible to the men and women of Camden. Those who had established homes in the town became part of the growing national army of long-distance commuters. With gasoline prices under twenty-five cents a gallon, they willingly drove a hundred miles round trip each workday, sometimes even farther. Those whose roots were not as well established in Camden moved to Hamilton or Middletown, or to such new suburban communities as Fairborn, Beavercreek, or Kettering near Dayton, or to Fairfield or one of the many new suburban developments clustered around Cincinnati. The younger the individuals, the more powerful the lure of the city seemed to be.

This outward migration was intensified by the growing importance of a college education. Increasing numbers of Camden High School graduates, sometimes approaching 20 percent of a senior class, now opted for college; the most popular institution was Miami University, just fifteen miles away in nearby Oxford. The majority of graduates, however, never considered college. Young women sought urban positions as typists, clerks, and receptionists, and their male counterparts frequently looked to the military as a way of making the transition between adolescence and adulthood. After spending a few years on active duty, they returned to live and work in one of the area's industrial cities.[2]

~

A destructive cycle thus took hold. Camden provided a secure haven in which young people were reared and educated, but on reaching adulthood they left for greater opportunities than those available in their hometown. This pattern emerged incrementally. It was masked for many years by the postwar economic expansion and the optimism it generated. During the immediate postwar years, a large number of veterans returned home, often marrying their high school sweethearts and establishing themselves locally. As veterans made the transition to civilian life, "Camden Behind the Men Behind the Guns" was replaced with a "Back From the Service" column.[3]

Some of the returning veterans, like former star high school athlete

Stanley Humphrey, took advantage of the educational benefits of the GI bill. He enrolled at Ohio University and earned a degree in education. After teaching in Camden for two years, he departed for a better paying position in northeastern Ohio.[4] Most Camden veterans, however, decided to forgo their GI education benefits in order to enter the growing labor market. The pattern they confronted could be found elsewhere in America. Morrison Colladay, writing about his hometown in upstate New York, lamented what he saw as the beginnings of the "passing of the American village." He reported that there were a hundred World War II veterans unable to find work in this agricultural community. "Most of those who left Eastcamp during the war are home and they want to stay home. But how can they? What can they do to make a living?"[5] In Camden, some veterans secured jobs in service stations or stores or at Neff and Fry, but there was a dearth of good-paying jobs, especially those with the possibility of long-term advancement. The most fortunate were the young men who took over operation of their parents' farms. To many Camden-area youth, the prospect of entering farming was very attractive. Having been born and raised on a farm, they understood and enjoyed the lifestyle. The most perceptive of these young men recognized the major trends toward increased sophistication in American farming and enrolled in the College of Agriculture at Ohio State University to equip themselves with the scientific and managerial skills necessary to operate a complex farming operation.

Most veterans, however, were not going to inherit a farm and had to look elsewhere for a livelihood. Consequently, a pattern emerged which saw many of the best and the brightest depart. A common route went like this: first, a job at Champion Paper Company in Hamilton required the young husband to commute down narrow Route 127 five days a week. After his wife took a secretarial position at the home offices of the Ohio Casualty Insurance Company in the same city, the couple decided to rent an apartment in Hamilton to save time and money. A few years and two children later, using the GI bill housing benefits, the "Camden couple" purchased a tract home in a new Hamilton subdivision. They were gone.

Encouraged by an expanding economy that masked the departure of Camden's future, the town's leadership focused attention on civic improvements and community activities. That very few new houses were being constructed in town during an unprecedented national housing construction boom did not register on them. Nobody suggested a program to stimulate economic diversification and community development. The same lack of foresight could be found elsewhere. In Montana, a Rockefeller Foundation planning grant for developing a statewide strategy to encourage the economic development of small towns was allowed to expire by an unconcerned legislature. In a prescient comment, Colladay, whose essay on rural New York described a similar pattern, lamented that "now the little towns in Montana are back where they were when the experiment started. Unfortunately, their plight is shared by thousands of other little towns all over the country. Towns die slowly, but they do die, and today the blight has attacked too many of them."[6]

The housing shortage in Camden did not encourage young couples to remain. One of the most pressing of all postwar problems throughout the United States was a national housing shortage, estimated by Truman administration housing officials as exceeding twelve million units. The housing shortage produced a national political crisis of the first magnitude.[7] Veterans returned home, often to begin married life, and found few available houses or apartments, despite the financial assistance provided by Federal Housing Administration or Veterans Administration mortgage insurance. In Camden, few veterans used their benefits to build a house in town—undoubtedly a telling sign of their long-term plans—and instead moved in with their parents for a short time or rented an apartment.

Although the postwar Camden housing market supported the construction of only a few new homes, it did stimulate a substantial remodeling movement. With the cessation of wartime rationing, many residents threw themselves into the process of remodeling, often seeking to modernize houses that had been constructed in the nineteenth century. Local painters, carpenters, plumbers, electricians, and handymen found themselves with more work than they could handle, a sharp contrast from the prewar years. Those few merchants who dealt in furniture and appliances were unable to keep pace with demand as families sought to replace outmoded stoves, refrigerators, and washing machines.

∾

For several years following V-J Day the local job market provided continuing employment opportunities for day laborers. Neff and Fry reduced its workday from twenty-four to eight hours, but its payroll stabilized at about a hundred, well above prewar levels, and Joe Gwynne's steel fabrication company and the revitalized Camden Cement and Tile Company, a small manufacturer of cement blocks and bricks, each employed about twenty men.

Little attention was paid to the most significant change in the local job market: the immediate return of the 125 working women at Neff and Fry to their traditional roles as homemakers. As soon as the defense contract for concrete bombs expired, the company immediately terminated all women laborers. Just as Rosie the Riveter left Henry Kaiser's ship-building factories in Oakland, California, for the hearth and stove, so too did Camden's version of feminism, Cindy the Cement worker.[8] Ironically, for the first three years after the war Camden's major employers struggled to find sufficient male labor. Prevailing social attitudes did not permit the retention of women in jobs considered to be for men only (at least in peacetime).

Employers were even forced to advertise for workers. Gwynne promised steady work, emphasizing that his company had had "No layoffs in Thirteen Years." Neff and Fry believed that "The FUTURE LOOKS BRIGHT!" An advertisement that appeared for several months proclaimed, "We have a large backlog of essential and priority business! We have plans for plant improvement! We have much to be done and we need men to help do it. Working conditions good, work steady, pay periods weekly with overtime pay. The Neff and Fry Company is a well established, fast growing company with a good postwar future. Come into our office and talk it over—you'll like this work."[9] Given the accepted social assumptions under which it operated, the company did not need to mention that "women need not apply."

Since during the war many analysts had feared—quite wrongly, as it turned out—that the economy would tumble into recession, or worse, once the war had ended, it was with a mixture of relief and reserved optimism that Ray Simpson wrote shortly after V-J Day: "No unemployment situation exists here. Despite the fact that the public hears much these days from certain parts of the Nation regarding a pending unemployment situation, this problem does not exist in Camden . . . as there are many positions open here. Rodney Neff, president of Neff and Fry Company, stated this week that instead of an unemployment situation there is a serious labor shortage."[10] What Simpson did not mention, however, was that the shortage was due in part to the jobs created when the women laborers were sent home after the war.

In fact, Joe Gwynne and Rodney Neff could not compete with Fortune 500 companies like General Motors, Champion Paper, and Procter and Gamble—or with the federal government, which was paying top dollar as it rapidly expanded Wright-Patterson AFB to protect America from the Soviet menace. General Electric entered the employment fray in 1946 when it opened its huge jet aircraft factory in a northern suburb of Cincinnati. Its personnel department took out large advertisements in the *Preble County News* urging local workers to consider its total package of "Top Wages, Scholarships, Vacation With Pay, Training for Advancement, Accident and Sickness Insurance, Savings Plans, Retirement Pensions, Profit Sharing, and Free Life Insurance!"[11] What ambitious small-town fellow could resist seriously considering such an opportunity?

$\sim$

While attractive employment opportunities were opening up on a regular basis elsewhere, in Camden a traditional form of employment was drying up. Few persons paid much attention because the process had established itself years earlier and had been steadily, if unspectacularly, taking its toll. Farm labor had long provided employment for many Camden males. In some instances these positions required considerable managerial and agricultural expertise, such as operating a farm for an absentee owner. Most farm labor jobs placed a high demand on a strong back and an admirable tolerance for repetitive work. The work was seasonal and low paying, but for decades it had provided many Camden-area men with the rudiments of their livelihood. Farm labor, however, was steadily being eliminated by advances in agriculture technology and science. New hybrid seeds, better crop rotation systems, improved pesticides and fertilizers, advances in animal science and veterinary medicine—the result of the combined efforts of the Experiment Station and the Extension Service of Ohio State University's College of Agriculture—not only markedly improved production levels but also reduced the demand for unskilled labor. The universal adoption of tractors and sophisticated power equipment accelerated the declining need for unskilled labor. Combines replaced the traditional threshing gangs. Hay balers, power-driven corn pickers, and milking machines all reduced demand for manpower. In a distinct parallel to the changes occurring in manufacturing, on Ohio farms machines were quietly but surely replacing humans.

A revolution was affecting American agriculture, and Camden was not immune. "Underlying the current mechanization trend," the anthropologist Art Gallaher wrote of postwar "Plainville," "is the acceptance of a new style of farming. The farmer now defines his role mainly as manipulator of machines designed to do what formerly were irksome, time-consuming agricultural tasks." Whereas not too many years earlier a farmer took great pride in the amount of physical labor he could put forth, now he looked upon extensive physical exertion as demeaning. "This new role involves a redefinition of farm labor and the acceptance of new criteria for assessing industriousness. Thus, men who a few years ago gained prestige by working long hours at physical labor are remembered today as 'slaves' to hard work and long hours, and if one of them still manifests these qualities he is ridiculed as 'behind the times.'"[12]

~

Few people paid much notice to this fundamental change in the nature of Ohio agriculture because it happened unobtrusively over several decades, but everyone recognized the pressures created by the postwar baby boom. It had begun during the early years of the war and now affected the public schools, driving enrollments in Camden up from 400 in 1940 to over 550 by 1950. Because of the hiatus created by the depression and the war, there were few certified new teachers available in the United States until the GI bill drove college graduation rates upward in 1949. Thus Camden's school administrators found themselves continually scrambling to hire even minimally qualified teachers. The high turnover rate was exacerbated by noncompetitive salaries, and many of the most qualified teachers left for better-paying positions in the urban school systems of southwestern Ohio.

New classroom facilities were essential to cope with increased enrollments. In 1945, after much deliberation, the Camden school board put a bond issue to a vote and supporters mounted a low-key campaign to secure the necessary 65 percent of the vote. Because the needs were so great, there was no formal opposition, and in November a $179,000 bond issue, authorizing construction of much needed new facilities, including a modern multipurpose gymnasium, was approved by a 520–153 majority.[13] Camden's voters, traditionally suspicious of increased taxes, this time responded overwhelmingly to the needs of their youth.

The vote brought to an end the long tradition of Friday night basketball in the cramped upper floor of the Town Hall. The new gymnasium was designed to provide for a myriad of activities. With a seating capacity of 1,500, 50 percent larger than the town's population, it testified to the importance of high school basketball in Camden. This community jewel included state-of-the-art glass backboards, locker rooms with hot showers, a music room, a spacious stage for plays and concerts, and bleachers that folded against the walls to provide space for physical education classes. Included in the package was the construction of five new classrooms, including the school's first real chemistry laboratory, and a large kitchen to serve community dinners as well as provide for the school's hot lunch program. The new facility stood as a monument to the community's confident view of the future.

Opened in 1950—its completion suffered delays due to problems with the architectural design and initial cost overruns—the gymnasium became the focal point for community activities, rendering the top floor of the Town Hall obsolete; this once proud community icon soon fell into disrepair. The new gymnasium proved to be a functional multi-purpose facility, serving the community as theater, concert hall, dance floor, convention center, banquet hall, and sports arena. During the winter months on Friday evenings it rocked with the noise, enthusiasm, and tension that only a high school basketball game with a hated rival could generate. It also stimulated a modest expansion of performing arts programs and physical education classes.

∼

The new gymnasium provided tangible evidence that Camden was a progressive town, ready for the challenges of the postwar era. This major construction project mirrored the activities of the Progressive Club, which had modified its orientation from helping individuals cope with economic depression to boosting major civic projects. In 1946 the Progressive Club made its largest contribution to the town by modernizing the high school baseball field. At a cost of $4,000, the club erected lights and constructed a grandstand and refreshment booth. More than a thousand fans were on hand on September 1, 1946, despite unseasonably cold weather, to see Camden's first night baseball game. Very few towns of its size had outdoor lighting for baseball, and a sense of pride surged through town. Even those who cared little for baseball showed up that night to watch a doubleheader, a softball game against Oxford and a baseball game between Bat Bousman's team and a collection of "all-stars" from the Central Ohio League.[14] Unfortunately, the Oxford softball team got its signals confused and failed to appear, and the "all-stars" soundly whipped the local nine.

The lighted ball park was a first for Preble County (although several other communities soon followed suit), and, as many a citizen commented, a sign of a town with good prospects. During the next four years, from May until September, a six-team fast pitch softball league used the facility five nights a week. Central Ohio Baseball League games were played on Sunday afternoons before large crowds. For a time, the

Two proud officers of the Progressive Club, Harry Neff and Herschel Brown, pose beside a 1947 Chevrolet that was raffled off at the annual Homecoming carnival. Courtesy Camden Archives.

spectators overflowed the eight rows of bleachers behind home plate. Some fans watched from the comfort of their cars ringing the outfield, where occupants could unobtrusively sip on a can of beer.

∽

The year 1947 was a very good one for Camden, both for the local economy and for the town baseball team. Viewed from the perspective of half a century later, it stands out as perhaps the most upbeat and productive year in the community's history. Good economic times provided an aura of optimism and confidence not seen since the 1920s. Jobs were plentiful, agricultural commodity prices remained high, and community activity and involvement reached an all-time level.

Perhaps symbolic of this good year was the success of the town baseball team. The Merchants, as they were called, were now managed by one of the town's best longtime players, railroad maintenance foreman Bob Elston. The oft-contentious Bat Bousman now devoted his energies to the business side of this marginal operation, including maintenance of the field and the new lights. Elston's 1947 team included two future professional baseball players, both pitchers, one of whom was Elston's eighteen-year-old son, Donald, who would systematically work his way through the minor leagues and spend seven years with the Chicago Cubs.[15]

The most compelling member of the 1947 team, however, was substitute second baseman Dale Thomas. A 1942 graduate of the high school, this sandy-haired, bespectacled young man had lost a leg in the Battle of the Bulge. Nonetheless, he gamely hobbled around the infield on his artificial limb, fielding ground balls and even helping to turn an occasional double play. To some fans, Thomas's entrance into the lineup in the late innings was always a good sign that the game was well in hand; to the more reflective, however, it was a poignant reminder of the community's sacrifices in the war just ended.

The team spent the entire 1947 season in first place in the Central Ohio League, then swept undefeated through the postseason playoffs, winning the championship over a team representing the much larger community of Miamisburg. Camden's 5–4 victory was witnessed by an estimated 1,500 cheering fans.[16] This banner season came on the heels of the high school baseball's team stunning spring season, which saw them win the district tournament in Dayton and come within four games of winning the state championship.

The good fortunes of its baseball teams set the tone for the town. Every man who wanted a job could get one. Neff and Fry continued to advertise for workers, announcing that it was paying new employees the federal minimum wage of ninety-five cents an hour. Ford dealer Bill Matt struggled with the problem of not being able to get enough new automobiles to meet demand. By early 1946 he had a waiting list that was so long it took nearly eighteen months to deliver a new vehicle to impatient customers. Brownlee Borradaile, an energetic farmer turned car dealer, was now selling as many Chevrolets as Matt was Fords. Business was so good that Borradaile abandoned his small, rented Main Street location next to the Dover Theater and built a large showroom and maintenance shop on the north edge of town. At the time it was the largest commercial building in the county.[17]

Three new restaurants opened along Main Street, and Clarke Ledwell, who had repaired watches in his home for several years, felt sufficiently emboldened to open the town's second jewelry store. A new bakery, an ice cream parlor, and an additional grocery added to the action on Main Street. A large furniture store replaced the one that had closed during the depression. In October, a popular local automobile mechanic, Dave Campbell, entered the automobile competition when he opened a Kaiser-Fraser dealership on South Main Street. His opening day celebration attracted over six hundred curious visitors eager to see the new, innovatively styled automobiles produced by the now famous West Coast shipbuilder and industrial tycoon Henry Kaiser.[18]

Christmas season brought unprecedented crowds into local stores. Two years after the war, American manufacturers had overcome the shortages of most consumer items. Harry Simpson, now in the process of taking over the editorial responsibilities from his semiretired father, reported in the *Preble County News* that local stores were doing "a capacity business." More people seemed to have more money than ever before. Having endured the depression and the war, they were happy to enjoy the benefits of good times. "Most families are having a bigger Christmas this year than last," Simpson wrote. "Merchants have a bigger supply of merchandise and a wider variety to select from. More toys have been on the counters and some of the hard-to-get items have been more available this year." [19]

"Main Street is a 'little Broadway' these days." Simpson cheerfully noted. "Shoppers are jamming the streets and stores. Retailers report the volume of Christmas business has been 'exceedingly large.' Most people are still gainfully employed and making reasonably good money. This Christmas has offered them the opportunity of obtaining many things they have wanted for some time." [20]

In 1948 a Lions Club was chartered with thirty members. As one of its service projects, the club sponsored a drive to raise $1,200 to buy uniforms for the thirty-five-member high school band. The sparkling new red-and-black uniforms of the band became a source of community pride, and the high school musicians were invited to perform at many local functions. The popularity of the high school band was another sign of the changing times, as public schools assumed roles in the community previously filled by other organizations. Lou Sterzenbach's Camden Band had disbanded after its leader's death in 1948. For nearly three decades this popular group of local musicians of all ages had held its summertime Thursday evening concerts at the corner of Main and Central. [21]

And so it went. Jobs were plentiful, farm income was increasing, modern diesel engines replaced the coal-fired engines on the Pennsylvania main line, businesses were prospering, the new high school gymnasium was under construction, and the town baseball team had brought home a championship. Evidence of "progress" and success abounded. The future seemed bright along Main Street. And the newly outfitted band played on.

≈

The ten-year-old boy walked down South Main Street as dusk turned to dark one warm May evening in 1948, a bag of groceries tucked under his arm. He was on his way home after running an errand for his mother to Ernie Jefferies's grocery store. As he approached a recently opened appliance store, he noticed a cluster of people standing on the sidewalk peering into the display window. His eyes were drawn to an unusual flickering, silvery luminescence emanating from the window. At that moment he saw, for the first time in his life, a television screen. He immediately became transfixed—almost hypnotized—by what he saw. The small ten-inch image was somewhat blurred, and more than once store owner Fred Schmidt had to crawl into the display window to fiddle with several dials to keep the picture from flipping over and over. But the small screen more than adequately portrayed the images of men engaged in a wrestling match. The young boy had never seen a wrestling match before, and the wild antics of the performers were captivating. The announcer said that the program was being "telecast" live from a studio in Cincinnati. Several times the boy told himself that it was time to return home. His parents gave him permission to explore the streets and alleys of town by foot or bicycle during the day, but like most parents in town, they also kept him on a short leash: "We want to know where you're going to be, whom you'll be with, and when you'll be home." That was the cardinal rule for him and his friends, but as the minutes, and then an hour, and even more, went by, he remained frozen in front of the flickering Philco. He knew the rule and he knew he was in serious violation, but he stood as if paralyzed. That fuzzy picture in the window was the most incredible thing he had ever seen.

By the time the boy—who would later become the author of this book—finally arrived home a little past ten o'clock, he was confronted by two very upset (and worried) parents, and even his story about the flickering black-and-white wrestling match he had watched in "Smitty's" window did not prevent a serious, one-sided conversation about obeying the rules. Given the extenuating circumstances, the young boy escaped serious punishment. Neither he nor his parents could have begun to anticipate just how much their lives would be affected by the advent of the age of television, which he had encountered for the first time that warm spring evening.[22]

By the summer of 1948 three stores sold television sets in Camden. In addition to Fred Schmidt, the Camden Hardware Store and Vernon Caskey plunged headlong into the television sales and repair business. The ever aggressive Caskey, his business stimulated by increased cash flow in his grocery store, purchased an adjoining building and opened a small furniture store, complete with a line of home electronic entertainment equipment. As a portent of things to come, his large advertisement in the

Preble County News on September 1, 1949, proclaimed: "Be Sure and See The WORLD SERIES ON GENERAL ELECTRIC TELEVISION. Big 10" Tube only $189. 12" Tube only $289. Ohio State and Notre Dame Football Games!"[23]

Television transformed the community. Large television antennae, the ultimate status symbols, began to appear on the rooftops of the more affluent families. Firmly clamped to chimneys, antennae were aimed at Cincinnati to pick up WCPO and WLW, or at Dayton to receive the signals of WHIO. Local conversations now contained such new vocabulary as "snow," "vertical control," "contrast," and "coaxial cable." The relative merits of the wrestling prowess of Gorgeous George and Don Mohawk stimulated many an argument at Bob Barber's restaurant, and activity in town slowed during autumn afternoons when a World Series game was being telecast. Friday nights meant boxing from Madison Square Garden with Don Dunphy describing the bouts for Gillette Blue Blades, and Tuesday nights featured Milton Berle's *Texaco Star Theater*. In 1952 most sets were tuned to *I Love Lucy* on Monday evenings. The spectacle of wrestling seemed to be on some channel every evening, but overexposure led to its virtual disappearance until it was rescued by cable television in the 1980s.

During the first years of commercial television broadcasting, many Camden families could not afford their own sets. In order to tap into this market, the management of the H & H Cafe placed a television set above the bar and enjoyed the benefits of a rapidly expanding clientele. Competitors in the beer-and-sandwich trade, Ted Girton's Girt-Inn and Deem's Half-Way Tavern, soon followed suit.[24]

Families that purchased the town's initial television sets had delicate social problems coping with friends and relatives who devised ingenious ways to visit during prime evening hours. Television parties replaced evening bridge or canasta games, and the ubiquitous "TV tray" became a popular wedding gift. The traditional living room underwent substantial design change, and the television set became the focal point of the room, replacing a piano or reading area. Evening meals were often eaten in front of the black-and-white screen in a semidarkened room. Teachers observed that homework was not being completed, and town librarian Hattie Ward reported a sharp decline in patronage.

These changes in the patterns of daily life were not unique to Camden, of course. They were taking place across America, in large cities as well as isolated farming communities. Television accelerated the domination of small-town life by urban America, reflecting initially the values of New York City and later those of Los Angeles. Similarities of clothing and hairstyles, slang phrases, and music preferences were among the superficial manifestations of a much more important phenomenon—the standardization of thought and values and an accelerated diminution of unique regional and local cultures. Television intensified the erosion of local autonomy begun earlier by the railroad, automobile, radio, and motion pictures. By 1955 about 65 percent of American homes had a television set.[25]

Although Vernon Caskey made a lot of money selling Dumont and Crosley television sets, another business in Camden—the movie theater business—suffered grievously from the arrival of television. In October of 1950 the Dover Theater, which had already limited its operations to showing detective/Western double features on weekends, closed its doors forever. Later that year the Majestic Theater also ceased operations. On some weeknights owner Orville Wood could count the number of tickets sold on his fingers. Wood could recognize a bad business trend when he saw it, and he judiciously bailed out. In April of 1951 the Majestic reopened "under new management," but the competition of the "cool medium" of television was too much. Just thirteen months later it closed for good, a victim of the changing American entertainment scene. William Bendix and Kirk Douglas, starring in the forgettable film *Detective Story,* were the last Hollywood heroes to appear on the silver screen in Camden.[26]

Born in the depths of the Great Depression, the once proud Majestic Theater had been a boon to a severely wounded town, but now it was gone, a victim of the new age of television. Editor Harry Simpson lamented the passing of an era: "Closing of the theater will be quite a blow to the community, leaving Camden with no amusement center." He identified "low attendance" and, curiously, "high federal taxes" as the culprits. For some reason, perhaps not wishing to belabor the obvious, he made no mention of television. All across the country the impact was similar. In 1951, the journalist-historian David Halberstam reports, 134 motion picture theaters closed in southern California alone, the victims of television. That same year, in novelist Larry McMurtry's fictional windswept plains town of Thalia, Texas, Sonny and his Korean War–bound pal Duane watched Audie Murphy in *The Kid from Texas,* that town's last picture show. By 1952 movie attendance nationwide had fallen nearly 40 percent since 1947.[27]

The inherent power of television was manifest in the waves of fear and anxiety that rushed through Camden each summer. Polio! The seasonal outbreaks of paralytic poliomyelitis produced panic throughout American society. Although its most famous victim, President Franklin D. Roosevelt, was thirty-nine years old when he was stricken, most of its victims were children. Adding to parents' fears was the fact that each year the number of victims in the United States increased. Television news, although in its infancy, recognized the value of an emotional story. Local and national television news departments exploited the drama of the disease, showing pitiful small children encapsulated in huge iron lungs or struggling heroically in a rehabilitation clinic to get their withered legs, supported by ugly metal braces, to move again. The threat of contracting the virus was undoubtedly real—it was, after all, afflicting over thirty thousand Americans a year—but television coverage intensified apprehension.

In 1937 Camden experienced its only known polio victim, seven-year-old Ruthayn Dearth. As a high school student in the late 1940s she bravely went about her life on crutches, her paralyzed, severely atrophied legs supported by fifteen pounds of metal braces. The sobering image of Ruthayn pulling herself slowly down the corridors of the high school, or on a visit to a local teen hangout with her friends, made the threat of the disease seem very real. Like towns everywhere, Camden held many benefits for the March of Dimes—donkey softball games under the new lights, church bake sales, school candy campaigns. Canisters to receive donations were on store counters near the cash register.

What worried parents did not know was that the disease often struck infants, who showed few symptoms but who, unbeknownst to parents or family physician, had thereby acquired immunity. It was those who contracted the disease later in life who endured major debilitating effects.[28]

Since they did not know the etiology of the disease, parents sometimes went to extreme lengths to protect their offspring. A few purchased "polio insurance" from William Eikenberry's general insurance agency, whose advertisement suggested that such protection "Might Come In Handy."[29] Some parents essentially restricted younger children to their homes and backyards for the duration of the summer epidemic months, permitting them to venture out only when accompanied. During the peak months of July and August, many boys were forbidden to swim in the murky waters of the Seven Mile Creek. Some were even forbidden to exert themselves in active play. Parents who could afford to do so opted to spend the time away from the hot and humid Camden summer climate, somehow convincing themselves that the cooler temperatures of a Michigan lakefront were safer.

The town council, eager to do something to help, conducted weekly sprayings to kill the unknown cause of the disease, a popular effort that continued until the Salk vaccine became available in 1954. The spraying, it was reported in the newspaper, was "a precautionary measure against any possible outbreak of polio cases in Camden."[30] Every Wednesday evening during the months of July and August, members of the volunteer fire department rode through the alleys of the town in the bed of a pickup truck, dousing everything in sight: weeds, rocks, buildings, and especially garbage and refuse cans. Unfortunately, the chemical spray of choice was the then popular pesticide DDT, now known to be a carcinogen. As the pickup maneuvered slowly down the dirt alley ways, children, for whose protection this effort was designed, often stood along the side to watch the action, sometimes getting themselves thoroughly exposed to the misty spray. Since no new cases of polio occurred, the reasoning went, the spraying might be doing some good. So the DDT campaign continued each summer until the miracle wrought by Dr. Jonas Salk eased the minds of concerned parents and city fathers. No subsequent study was ever made on the effect this carcinogen had upon the health of Camden's residents.

~

The closing of the Dover and Majestic theaters stands as the beginning of the end of an era. By 1952 the outburst of community activity and civic improvement that had developed after the war had run its course. The out-migration of families was evident by this time; the good jobs were in the cities, and there Camden's younger generation moved en masse. Despite earnest efforts by the Progressive Club, now attempting to act in the capacity of an economic development agency, no employers of any significance could be lured to town. Other than relatively unattractive teaching positions, there were few professional opportunities to entice college graduates to return to their hometown.

By the early 1950s most high school students perceived that their parents expected them to leave town after they completed their education.[31] Parents viewed such departures as evidence of their success in raising their children. Enrollments in the public schools leveled off at about six hundred students. The 1950 census reported 1,084 residents of the community—a 10 percent gain since 1940   but owing to the increased mechanization of farming, the population of the rural Somers Township showed no gain. Although Paul Stowe opened a small Willys Jeep dealership in 1952, Dave Campbell's Kaiser-Fraser agency had closed with the demise of that ill-fated automobile company.

Interest in civic affairs began to sag. Each summer the Homecoming carnivals drew smaller crowds, and the midway attractions seemed to grow ever more sleazy. Attendance was no longer high enough to support a lottery with a new automobile as the main prize. For a few years after the war the *Preble County News* had expanded to six pages to accommodate a spurt in advertising, but by 1952 it was back to its basic four-page format. Interest in the town baseball team declined as fans now watched their favorite team, the Cincinnati Reds, on television. In 1952 CBS introduced its Saturday "Game of the Week," featuring such baseball stars as Jackie Robinson, Mickey Mantle, and Ted Williams. The town team, the Merchants, its drab gray uniforms now showing the results of several years of wear and tear, could not compete with the antics of announcer Dizzy Dean and major league games televised live from Yankee Stadium. The Merchants played their last season in 1953.

Symbolically, the demise of town baseball was very important. For decades the team had carried the hopes and pride of the community on its shoulders. Now, without a whimper, it had died. Town ball was vanishing all across the United States, and a tradition that stretched back to the nineteenth century was coming to an end. Only occasionally did the bright lights stand out in Camden on a summer evening, usually to illuminate a youth team playing in front of parents and relatives.[32]

≈

The sagging fortunes of the town were vividly underscored in the local elections in November of 1951. There were only two candidates for the council listed on the printed ballot, and no one filed for mayor. Informal nominating committees, including the Progressive Club, could not secure commitments from even minimally qualified persons to run for local office. Older leaders contended that they had met their responsibilities and believed that it was time for a younger generation to take its turn. (In a society dominated by men, no one apparently thought to consider women candidates.) Perhaps the apathy stemmed from the lack of compelling issues to attract candidates.[33]

The immediate crisis of securing candidates was resolved when four individuals, under heavy pressure from a hurriedly created "Committee for Camden," agreed to assume office if their names were written in on election day. The community was thus spared the embarrassment of not having a functioning local government. Three write-in candidates for the council and the two on the printed ballot were elected without opposition. High school principal William E. Browning received 173 write-in votes and became the town's forty-eighth mayor. He also was an ordained minister of the Church of the Brethren and occasionally appeared in local pulpits. A man of considerable ego, he soon became a controversial figure by ordering a crackdown on speeders, many of them out-of-towners passing through town on Route 127. A high school driver's education teacher who had become obsessed with driving safety, Browning felt little sympathy for the offenders who ended up in his mayor's court. There he presided in magisterial fashion, routinely handing down fines and sometimes a condescending sermon about automobile safety to transgressors. Browning and the new council suffered a serious political rebuff in the fall elections of 1952, however, when their revenue-generating plan of installing parking meters in the business area lost by a resounding 2–1 margin after angry residents forced a referendum election on the issue.[34]

~

What went unrecognized at the time was that the social fabric, which had long provided a sense of community responsibility and unity, had begun to unravel. What was happening in Camden was being replicated in many towns of similar size across the country, such as Art Gallaher's "Plainville." Television tended to isolate families inside their homes during evening hours, reducing the amount of visiting between neighbors. Instead of sitting on the front porch greeting evening strollers, residents now closeted themselves to watch Jackie Gleason. Over time, neighbors became more distant; newcomers sometimes remained strangers. Attendance at the three traditional churches became a subject of concern, while the recently established evangelical Church of God and the First Baptist Church enjoyed an influx of new members, primarily from the middle and lower classes. Saturday nights provided prime television programming, and merchants suffered a steady decline in their trade on that most important of evenings. Store owners also knew that when farmers and townsfolk went shopping now, especially for major purchases, they got into their automobiles and headed out of town. Their clientele increasingly looked to them only for the low-cost necessities of everyday life. Even local grocery stores lost market share to distant supermarkets.[35]

The growing number of residents who commuted to work extracted a heavy toll on the community; commuting loosened local ties in many ways. It was more convenient for commuters to stop after work for groceries or other routine purchases in one of the sparkling new automobile-friendly strip malls along the highway from Hamilton or Dayton. And the daily grind of traveling up to a hundred miles a day reduced the time and energy that individuals had available to participate in community activities. When they arrived home after a long day they found themselves less inclined to attend a meeting and much more interested in simply plopping in front of the television set to watch *Leave It to Beaver.* Thus did Camden enter into the early stages of becoming another American commuter bedroom community, but one that lacked most of the modern services and conveniences of the new suburbs.

The convergence of these trends in the mid-1950s led to the melancholy sight of a near empty Main Street on Saturday nights. For decades, families had flocked to the business district, not just to shop, but also to socialize. After completing their errands, a husband and wife would often sit in their parked car on Main Street for extended periods of time, happily conversing out the window with passersby. Within a year after the arrival of commercial television, the Saturday night crowds became markedly smaller. Main Street merchants felt themselves under siege but had no way to counterattack. The enemy was too pervasive: the high volume, low-pricing policies of chain stores, new shopping malls, ever more sophisticated Sears catalogs, the automobile, television . . . the enemy was, in fact, modern America itself. Television and the automobile had combined to kill an American tradition—Saturday night along Main Street.

∼

Life at mid-century in this small southwestern Ohio town reflected other social and economic changes occurring across the United States. The changing attitudes and behavior of local teenagers created concern in Camden even before Indiana native James Dean rebelled. Relaxed parental rules enabled some teenagers to cruise Main Street until late in the evening. Ducktail hairstyles, black leather jackets, cigarette packs arrogantly carried in rolled up T-shirt sleeves—feeble mimicry of the movies' portrayal of restless, rebellious youth—soon made their appearance in Bob Barber's restaurant, a popular teenage hangout. School officials pondered whether to permit such clothing and hairstyles in school, and the school board listened patiently to more than one parental complaint about the playing of rock 'n' roll music at postgame sock hops. An occasional late-night drag race awakened residents. In response, the council passed the community's first curfew; all persons seventeen years of age and younger had to be off the streets by 10 P.M. on weeknights, midnight on Saturdays. Enforcement by the town's only part-time law enforcement officer, however, proved to be a sham, since lack of widespread parental support for the curfew doomed its effectiveness.

Reports of increased crime also began to filter onto the pages of the local newspaper. A series of break-ins of businesses and residences stunned local citizens, who began to lock their doors even during daytime hours. Few residents considered the relationship of juvenile behavior and rising crime rates to national trends because they naturally tended to view life from the perspective of their daily lives and their local community. Also, they tended to know their neighbors less, thus increasing the level of suspicion and lowering their sense of security.[36]

~

This parochial view was especially true in relation to the complex issues raised by the cold war. It was a topic that seldom entered daily discussion because it was beyond the scope of most persons' understanding or interest. Camdenites' traditional view of the world—Republican, isolationist, conservative, Protestant, patriotic—provided a prism through which world affairs filtered into town. Many residents despaired at the defeats of Bob Taft at the hands of the eastern elite at the 1948 and 1952 conventions and accepted the conventional wisdom that the Soviet Union constituted a dire threat to American security. Although no one had ever known a Communist, everyone was naturally opposed to them. Social studies teachers in the high school dutifully emphasized the evils of Marxism and the Soviet threat to American security. When President Truman, who received only 35 percent of the Camden vote in 1948, fired military hero General Douglas MacArthur in the spring of 1951, the conventional wisdom at Deem's Half-Way Tavern was that Harry was leading the country down the road to oblivion.

The confusing nature of American policy as the cold war unfolded was revealed in the town's reaction to the Korean War. Although several local young men served in what Truman termed a "police action," interest in the conflict remained strangely muted.[37] There was considerable interest in the safety of Marine Lt. Bill Patton, a popular former high school athlete and student, who was among those trapped at Hagamari when massive numbers of Chinese troops flooded across the Yalu River in November of 1950. The community was cheered when news arrived that the local graduate of the U.S. Naval Academy had survived, although he suffered serious frostbite.[38] A feeble effort to revive the committee to provide moral support for Camden's servicemen that had been active during World War II died aborning; the "Camden Behind the Men Behind the Guns" column ran twice in 1951, contained little information, and disappeared. No Christmas packages were mailed from the community. The concept of a limited war seemed somehow foreign, perhaps "un-American," to the regulars sipping their morning coffee at the drugstore.

The cold war made an official appearance for a brief time in Camden in the form of the U.S. Air Force Ground Observer Corps. This program was designed to supplement the nation's radar defense system by visually observing and reporting, over a special telephone network, all flying aircraft that appeared above the United States. Only during these, the most frigid days of the cold war, could such a program have been taken seriously. Supposedly, somewhere in a supersecret command center, every airplane aloft over the continental United States would be tracked. For several weeks during the summer of 1952, a group of volunteers, primarily patriotic retirees and curious teenagers with nothing better to do, manned around the clock a tent pitched on top of Mt. Auburn, using a secret telephone number to report all Piper Cubs and other equally suspicious aircraft that penetrated Camden's air space. Presumably, all across the United States, other vigilant patriots were simultaneously reporting air traffic to the same secret command center, and somehow all of this information was being assimilated and evaluated in time to prevent a Russian sneak attack. By the time school resumed in September, however, and with no Soviet bombers yet in sight, interest in the project waned. As the first frosts of autumn tinged the maple trees in brilliant hues of red and orange, the Camden Observer Corps quietly folded its tent.[39]

~

Considerably more interest was expressed in stopping the speeding on local streets than in reporting enemy bombers. A concerted effort by the town council and its aggressive new mayor led to the writing of numerous traffic tickets, to the point that Camden, under the mayoralty of the good Reverend Browning, developed a modest reputation as a "speed trap." However, it was the loud roar from "glass pack" exhaust pipes that local young men installed on their '46 Fords and '49 Mercs, coupled with the squeal of tires as their cars blasted away from intersections, that produced a crisis of law and order. The Methodist minister, James Misheff, recently graduated from the seminary and a popular community figure—albeit somewhat of a clerical maverick—became so angry at the flouting of local traffic laws that he got himself sworn in as a police officer and for several months in 1951 spent the evening hours in his family sedan, a red light taped to the roof, patrolling the streets and earnestly writing traffic tickets.[40]

Such shenanigans as these, of course, distracted attention from the things that really counted. The inexorable movement of young families to nearby cities and the departure of high school graduates steadily gained momentum. Another downward trend was the migration of substantial numbers of retirees to Florida, a change that over the next several decades stripped the town of affluent senior citizens while leaving those with limited retirement income behind. Well-to-do farmers were now as likely to retire to the Sun Belt as to "move to town," as had long been the custom. The Census of 1950 brought the good news that the town's population had exceeded a thousand for the first time; but it also revealed that Camden's growth had not kept pace with other Preble County communities located closer to rapidly growing Dayton. Camden now ranked as the county's fifth largest community, down from second in 1940.[41] The transformation of Camden from a relatively self-sufficient community into a bedroom community for commuters and a haven for the poor and for retired citizens living on Social Security had begun in earnest.

Not that the community did not try to fight back. In 1947 the Progressive Club worked hard to attract a garment factory that would have employed fifty persons. This deal fell through at the last minute, but in 1951 hopes rose when the Atlas Plywood Company opened operations near a railroad siding north of town to construct heavy-duty shipping boxes and components for mobile homes. For a brief time this seemed to be a major coup, but the company proved incapable of competing successfully in its markets and hired no local managers. Most of its jobs were of the minimum wage variety, and the company periodically laid off workers because of minor fluctuations in demand. The "box factory," as it was called, did not last until the end of the decade.[42]

More serious was the sharp decline in the fortunes of the Neff and Fry Company. In 1942–45 the company had operated three shifts and employed up to 175 men and women. Business remained good for a time after the war, and its construction crews roamed much of the

United States and parts of Canada erecting concrete silos and storage facilities. Although its silo construction business started to decline, demand for its large industrial storage bins soared. For several years Neff and Fry employed over two hundred men, who assembled bins as far away as Maine, Florida, and California, bins designed to hold such diverse commodities as cotton seed, fertilizer, coal, cinders, clay, lime, and chemicals. Some fifty employees were kept busy at the Camden plant producing cement staves. Not adverse to horizontal diversification, the company also developed its profitable line of sealed burial vaults. Company leaders attributed their success, as quoted in a national business newsletter, to "a small town location where they are near sand and gravel, where labor is steady and taxes low." By the early 1950s company revenues exceeded $2 million, a not insubstantial sum for a small-town-based firm, but it proved impossible to maintain this rate of growth.[43]

The swift decline of the company began with two deaths. In 1947 cofounder Charles Neff died at age seventy-four. Not only had he remained active in an advisory capacity as the company expanded during the 1940s, but as a member of the board of directors of the First National Bank he was a major player in the Camden business establishment. His cautious leadership and business acumen had guided the company's steady expansion since he and Merle Fry had founded it in 1916. Neff's son Rodney had already assumed the company's presidency and had demonstrated an enthusiasm and understanding of the industry that boded well for the company's future. However, in February of 1950 the fifty-five-year-old executive was killed on a business trip in Louisiana when his car smacked into a parked lumber truck in a heavy fog.[44]

The company's leadership then fell to a competent senior administrator, D. H. Herbster. But he encountered serious health problems and was unable to travel or to provide the daily stewardship the increasingly vulnerable company required. For a sustained period of time following his tragic death, Rodney Neff's large holding of company stock was tied up in a trust fund administered by a Cincinnati bank, which inserted itself into the company's internal management, thereby complicating decision making at a crucial time in the company's development.[45]

It was especially unfortunate that as Camden moved into the pivotal 1950s its primary nonagricultural employer encountered serious internal management problems that were not adequately resolved. At the same time, the company faced strong competition from two major corporations seeking to establish themselves in the storage facility business, Martin Marietta and International Harvester. Neff and Fry's weekly payrolls grew ever smaller.

The company's decline had an adverse impact on other local economic interests. It led to a loss of contracts for three small local welding and steel fabricating operators, and especially to a drop in demand for aggregate from the White Gravel Company. In the end it was impossible to reverse the downward spiral. Over the next few years, the cumulative effect of these many problems contributed to the closing of local businesses.[46]

~

Just five years after that euphoric Christmas buying spree along Main Street, when the jingle of cash registers provided sweet music for local businessmen, the holiday season brought few reasons for cheer. Now those same cash registers remained all too quiet. By Christmas of 1952 changes in shopping patterns had become so pronounced that near panic had set in among merchants. They could not compete with the large chain stores and sophisticated department stores like Rike-Kumler's in Dayton or Shillito's in Cincinnati. The frequent appearance in the "Around Camden" personals column of brief notices like the following told the tale that Camden's shoppers were taking their business elsewhere: "Mrs. Harry Woodard and Mrs. E. L. Travis were Dayton visitors Tuesday."[47] Advertisements in the *Preble County News* by the popular Dayton department store carried a disturbing message for small-town merchants all across the Miami Valley: "Rikes is Ready for Christmas! Dazzling Toyland! Main Floor Fairy Land!" or "Plan a trip to Rike's in Dayton as a Christmas treat for your whole family."[48] Up and down Main Street store owners simply could not compete.

As they witnessed their customer base continue to erode, hard-pressed merchants launched a counterattack. Like Hitler's last ditch gambit in late 1944, it would prove to be Main Street's own Battle of the Bulge, producing a momentary gain after which they would be overrun by superior forces. In the spring of 1951, under the aegis of the Progressive Club, local merchants announced the "Camden Retail Merchants' Profit Sharing Plan." Throughout the week, tickets were given out by participating local merchants for sales of $1 or more. Then, every Saturday night at 9 P.M. a drawing was held in front of the Town Hall. Cash prizes totaling $100—two $25 prizes and the grand prize of $50— were given to winning ticket holders in attendance. For several months hundreds of people appeared at the appointed hour to check their handful of tickets when the winning numbers were announced.

Just as Art Gallaher reported about "Plainville," whose beleaguered merchants conducted a similar lottery, things did not go as planned.

Parents, preferring to remain at home in front of their television sets, sent a teenager to check out the numbers, or they pooled tickets with neighbors. The ticket holders who did come appeared shortly before 9 P.M. and then quickly retreated to their homes; only a few bothered to drop by a store to make a purchase—the primary reason for holding the drawing on Saturday evening. Initial curiosity produced large crowds and a temporary bump in sales, but interest and attendance soon fell. There was no evidence that the program slowed the surging amount of out-of-town shopping. Before a year had passed, the "Camden Retail Merchants' Profit Sharing Plan" was shelved. Even cash drawings could not revive the traditional Saturday nights of an earlier era.[49]

The fate that befell many of America's small towns in the years following World War II was cruel and ironic. Cruel because the towns suffered irreparable economic damage that would lead to stagnation and severe decline. Ironic because it happened during a time when the national economy was enjoying its greatest period of growth and expansion in history. By 1955 the fate of Camden had essentially been determined. It faced a future that offered little hope and considerable despair. By 1955 the town that erected prominent highway signs in 1949 proclaiming itself the "Birthplace of Sherwood Anderson, Famous Author" had entered into a new phase, one that constituted a significant break from its 150-year history.

7

Main Street in Repose

The bright red tower reached arrogantly toward the skies. To many Camden residents, "Woody's tower" symbolized the soaring potential of their town. To others, the tower was merely another publicity stunt by the local maverick. Erected in 1949, the tower rose a majestic 232 feet out of Orville Wood's backyard on South Lafayette Street; rumor had it that it was probably the tallest amateur radio tower in the world. Another curious first for the struggling town.

In truth, most residents did not know what to make of the enormous skeleton of steel. Because the town had no zoning regulations and no land use plan, would-be opponents lacked the legal power to prevent its construction. Although no formal opposition developed, many in this conservative town questioned Wood's priorities. The cost of the tower, rumored to be $12,000, became a local scandal. How could anyone spend that much money on a hobby?

The real criticism developed after Wood began to broadcast from his towering antenna; sometimes his powerful ham radio signal washed beyond its assigned amateur radio band and thrust itself onto standard television and radio broadcast frequencies. His signal often overrode the speakers of the first generation of delicate television sets, producing many an angry outburst in Camden living rooms. Just as the murder mystery was reaching its dramatic conclusion, or so it seemed, the actors' voices would be overridden by Woody babbling in ham radio jargon to a farmer in North Dakota. A few local residents became so riled that they telephoned him and complained. But most just groused behind his back, some linking their frustrations over his interference with

Erected in 1949 amid a flurry of gossip and second-guessing, Orville Wood's 232-foot tall ham radio tower—now rusting and in need of a new paint job—still towers over the community half a century later. Courtesy Camden Archives.

their evening's entertainment to his unpopular legal gyrations to avoid the draft in 1943. As the years passed, Wood's interest in ham radio waned, but the tower remained. In the decades to come, as Camden's economy continued its downward slide, Woody's tower, its red and white paint now faded and peeling, increasingly symbolized no longer a town's great aspirations but its irrelevance.

~

It is impossible to pinpoint the moment when the forces of economic and social decay took hold in Camden, but the years 1956–61 are pivotal. During this brief period, a series of isolated events, over which the town's leadership had little control, undercut the fragile economy and set the stage for the emergence of a new form of community, one that had little relationship to the proud and vibrant one it replaced. In the same period, similar patterns of decline were emerging in thousands of small towns across the United States.

One major setback involved changes in the public school system, always a focus of community life and pride. The people of Camden had placed a priority on providing the community's youth with a fundamentally sound, no-frills education. Despite a primordial resistance to property taxes, voters regularly supported bond issue elections to build new facilities and to operate the educational program at a level that met all State of Ohio mandates. In 1955 voters strongly supported a $270,000 bond levy to construct a new elementary school building.[1] In keeping with the voters's wishes, school board members were careful to operate the system in a prudently fiscal manner. In addition, administrators strove to keep the school in touch with community values, and teachers were reluctant to discuss local controversies in their classes. Cautious instincts prevailed throughout the system. Thanks in part to the lack of divisive issues in matters regarding public education, residents held their school system in high regard. In 1952 the Camden public schools, after years of preparation and planning, received full accreditation from the North Central Association of Schools and Colleges. This was a substantial achievement for such a small school system, and the accomplishment was proudly proclaimed on the front page of the *Preble County News.*[2]

As with small-town school systems throughout the United States, Camden's not only provided local students with a basic educational program but also played a central role in the social life of the community — offering plays, concerts, lectures, Christmas musicals, potluck dinners, dances, Halloween carnivals, and boys' sports events. At times, town and school became virtually indistinguishable, especially when it came to the fortunes of the boys' basketball team. Few persons doubted that these sixteen- and seventeen-year-old boys carried the good name and honor of Camden upon their shoulders, especially when it came to intense battles with the neighboring towns of Gratis and West Elkton. These games, which occasionally led to postgame fights in the parking lot — not to mention the often recalled free-for-all during a game against West Elkton in 1945 — added a modicum of anticipation and excitement to bleak winter days.

This special relationship between school and town disappeared with the "consolidation" movement that swept across Ohio like a prairie fire in the 1950s. School consolidation enjoyed strong support among state legislators and educational planners in the state capital of Columbus; larger school districts offered the benefits not only of economies of scale but also of enriched academic and extracurricular programming. Modern buses made the transportation of students over relatively long distances logistically and financially feasible. Advocates of consolidation noted that Camden's school system did not offer guidance and counseling services, that it had no special education program, and that its music and art offerings were minimal. With only a small percentage of graduates going to college, educational consultants were correct to criticize the lack of adequate vocational programs. The high school did not offer automotive, welding, or electrical programs and did not even have a vocational agricultural program, a deplorable gap for a public school located in the midst of a rich farming area. Enrollment was so small it could not even field a football team. Nonetheless, arguments on behalf of consolidation failed to persuade many townspeople, especially those who cherished their identification with good old "CHS." The strength of the town's feeling for its boys' basketball team proved to be one of the most powerful deterrents to consolidation.[3]

However, the inadequacies of the small school district were too obvious and the strength of the political forces supporting consolidation too powerful. The Preble County Board of Education recognized the political realities and began exploring the possibilities of consolidation. The pressure on small, marginal districts was mounting, but the swiftness with which action was taken in Camden was shocking. On the eve of the opening day of classes in September of 1956, the West Elkton school board, facing the dual problems of an inadequate budget and a severely constricted educational program, voted to send its fifty high school students to Camden. The Camden Board of Education agreed to accept these students in exchange for tuition. The ramparts had been breached, and within a few months the West Elkton elementary grades were also "consolidated" with Camden's.

After a new board of education was selected, one of its first items of business was choosing a name for the new school. The board appointed a committee of thirty persons—parents, alumni, and students—to pick among some two hundred names suggested in a contest. After quickly passing over the one with the most individual entries, Elvis Presley High School, and seriously considering such historical names as Anthony Wayne High School, St. Clair High School, and Wayne Trace High School, the committee eventually selected the Indian name of Shawnee. The new name proved to be a popular choice, although a few historical purists pointed out that the Shawnee tribe had never resided in the area (its closest known permanent encampment was some forty-five miles to the east near the modern day city of Xenia). In 1963 the Shawnee school district expanded to include the Gratis schools. By this time the consolidation movement had taken hold throughout Preble County. Where there had once been thirteen separate school systems, there now were just five.[4]

For the next seventeen years Shawnee High School remained in

Camden, occupying the venerable yellow brick facility constructed in 1916. The immediate success of the new basketball team, dubbed the Shawnee Arrows, helped heal some of the wounds inflicted on local pride. Coach Lee McDaniel's basketball team, combining the best athletic talent of former rivals, powered their way to the district Class B tournament finals in their first two seasons, and the regional finals in 1959 before losing a close game; three more wins would have made them the champion of some seven hundred Class B Ohio schools.

But the success of the basketball team and the introduction of football in 1965 were not enough to satisfy those who mourned the passing of good old Camden Hi. Nor did the fact that students now had an enriched educational program. Many Camden residents, especially dedicated alumni of the high school, felt that they had lost part of their heritage. Although those sensibilities slowly ebbed with the passage of time, many Camden alumni felt an acute sense of personal loss.

In 1980 a new high school building, with an unconventional modern design, was constructed in a rural area roughly equidistant from Gratis, West Elkton, and Camden. Although the new school system enjoyed general community support, the six miles of travel eastward to the new high school, standing amid corn and alfalfa fields, was a substantial psychological barrier for many Camden residents who had previously regularly attended sports and cultural events. Students undoubtedly had improved educational opportunities, but the vulnerable town of Camden had lost its most prized of community icons.

∼

Each year traffic on Main Street seemed to become worse. The increase in cars and trucks resulted not from the growth of Camden but from the steady growth of highway traffic. Even the advent of the two-car family had little impact on the growing number of vehicles on Main Street. Not that gridlock had arrived, but each year the flow of through traffic increased, as did concerns about safety and the increased level of vehicular noise along Main Street. Ever since the early settlers arrived, the trail/road/highway that came north out of Hamilton and paralleled the Seven Mile Creek had provided the main corridor between Cincinnati and points north. U.S. Route 127 was an important link in the midwestern urban network. In 1956 the Eisenhower administration secured congressional approval for the new interstate highway system. This modern network of multilane, limited-access highways eventually connected Cincinnati with Dayton-Toledo-Detroit and Columbus-Cleveland, but that development lay nearly a decade in the future.

Meanwhile, a sizable amount of the north-south traffic that I-71 and I-75 would eventually absorb plowed through the heart of Camden.

Although the increasing number of automobiles created some concern, most irritating was the noise made by the large transport trucks, which shook windowpanes and drowned out Arthur Godfrey's ukulele in living rooms along Main Street. The loud roar of powerful diesel engines as their drivers ran through the gears irritated many citizens. The noise of heavy traffic, however, sounded like sweet music to the owners and operators of several service stations and the restaurants along Main Street. At a time when franchised motels were beginning to make their presence known along America's major highways, several Main Street families still took in overnight guests attracted by modest "Tourist Rooms" signs. Just north of town, a cluster of small cottages, relics of the 1920s, still attracted families seeking the privacy of "tourist cabins." All things considered, Camden business leaders were happy to put up with the irritants and inconveniences of heavy traffic in return for the dollars that flowed into local cash registers.

But highway planners across the country were taking dead aim at small towns that slowed traffic. Lobbyists representing highway construction, petroleum, automobile, rubber tire, and trucking interests, together with spokesmen for the American Automobile Association, now prowled the halls of state legislatures and Congress in a relentless quest for appropriations to fund highway construction projects to end mounting urban traffic congestion and the nagging bottlenecks produced by small towns. State and federal highway planners had Camden and many towns like it in the middle of their crosshairs well before creation of the interstate system. No one was surprised in 1958 when state highway officials announced that they planned to reroute Route 127 from just north of Hamilton to the south edge of Camden, bypassing the small towns of New Miami, Seven Mile, and Somerville. Nervous Camden merchants were pleased that the traffic would still have to traverse Main Street, past the town's several tourist-oriented businesses.[5]

The following year, however, state highway planners decided to extend the project to two miles north of Camden at an additional cost of $1.7 million. Scheduled for completion in 1961, this new stretch of highway would be moved four blocks to the west, where it would slice through the west edge of town at the foot of Mt. Auburn. The proposal stirred a modest opposition from local merchants, who feared it would "make Camden a ghost town."[6] Several merchants protested at a public meeting in Eaton, but to no avail. Public opinion in town actually seemed about evenly divided; those without direct business interests seemed relieved to get the noisy "six wheelers" off Main Street, while those in the tourist trade feared the economic consequences. It is important to recall that at this time the impact of what was officially called the Interstate and Defense Highway System—the multi-billion-dollar extravaganza of the Eisenhower administration that would reshape the nation's urban network—was just in the planning stages. Ten years later, a large body of literature would lament the extreme economic disloca tions that the interstate system created when it bypassed towns and cities, but that perspective was not available in 1958.

When the new highway opened in 1961 the impact along Main Street was immediate and severe. Within a year several service stations and restaurants had closed. In order to survive, Ray O'Dell moved his popular South Side Service station from its prime location at the southern edge of town to the new intersection, appropriately renaming his business West Side Service. The "tourist rooms" signs soon disappeared from the front yards of Main Street homes, and the neat white tourist cabins with green roofs stood abandoned, relics of an earlier era.

~

Although Camden's business leaders mounted little concerted opposition to rerouting the highway, they resisted strenuously when the Pennsylvania Railroad, citing declining demand and growing deficits arising from its modest Camden operation, announced its intention to halt all regular freight service in 1961. Passenger service had been terminated in 1951, an inevitable result of the decline of America's once-proud passenger train service before the onslaughts of air, bus, and automobile travel. By 1960 most local businesses received the great percentage of their shipments via truck, and farmers had been relying on trucks to haul their livestock to market ever since the 1920s. But the loss of freight service would mean that the depot, an important part of the community since it was built in 1896, would be closed—a symbolic setback that town leaders very much wanted to avoid.

At the time of the announcement, local stationmaster Bat Bousman had just recently retired, after presiding over his domain at the depot for thirty-nine years. He remained as feisty as ever, though, and his anti-management views, stemming from his career as a dedicated member of the railway union, quickly surfaced. Bousman considered the announcement a personal affront and started to rally the community behind him, charging the railroad with insensitivity and a preoccupation with "making a paper profit."[7]

Given the conservative attitude of the town, the organization of a spirited protest was no inconsequential event. Bousman, ever the battler, pushed a fiery resolution through the town council before a packed hall. The council even authorized the extraordinary measure of hiring an attorney to press their cause with the Public Utilities Commission of Ohio (PUCO), which had the authority to grant or deny the railroad's request. The Progressive Club, its membership having dwindled to thirty, bestirred itself to pass its own resolution of protest. In September of 1961 PUCO took a quick look at revenue figures, listened sympathetically to Eaton attorney (and state senator) Bill Tyrrell and a statement from the Progressive Club, and then unanimously approved cessation of freight service. "The action will be very harmful to the welfare of Camden and seven other nearby communities," Harry Simpson glumly informed his readers. In the summer of 1962, 110 years after the first fiery cinder- and smoke-snorting engine pulled in from Hamilton, regular local train service to Camden ended.[8]

These two major changes in its transportation system greatly altered Camden's relationship with the urban network of southwestern Ohio. Within a few years, grass was growing out of cracks in the pavement and sidewalks of Main Street. The abandoned depot soon began to show the effects of neglect; vandals tossed a few rocks through its windows. In 1972 the depot was razed to make way for a small, non-descript hamburger joint that took the ironic name of Depot Dairy Bar and Restaurant.

~

In the fall elections of 1955 Mayor William E. Browning was soundly defeated in his bid for a third two-year term. To some Camdenites his loss was just deserts for his imperious attitude. Others viewed Browning's record as mayor as a frustrated effort to save Camden from the forces of stagnation and decay, forces whose harmful effects were now being recognized. Browning's lopsided defeat to, of all people, Orville Wood in the November elections was paralleled by the resounding rejection of a modest increase in the property tax levy to pay for improvements in police and fire protection and upgrades in the street and sewer systems. Browning's support for this much needed small tax increase had alienated many voters. His advocacy of parking meters shortly after his election and his stern enforcement of traffic laws had also contributed to his diminished popularity.

The outspoken Methodist minister, and one-time traffic cop, James

Misheff saw the election as a failure of civic responsibility on the part of voters. In an open letter to the community heavily laced with sarcasm, the reverend took aim at the voters while praising the outgoing mayor: "You [Browning] were wrong in trying to enforce traffic regulations. The best way to stop speeding and other violations is to wait until a child or elderly person is killed. Then we shall call a citizens' meeting and indignantly demand that 'something be done.'" The irritated minister boldly continued, knowing that many of his parishioners had voted against Browning: "You were for the town tax levy. That was a mistake, too. All intelligent people know that it doesn't require money to operate a town. Since you were for the bond issue, Camden defeated the tax levy, thus getting even with you. That is good sense; it is better logic. Mr. Browning, I suggest that you shake Camden's dust from your feet. We are not worthy of you."[9] Perhaps Misheff felt secure enough to publicly admonish voters because he knew that he was about to be reassigned to another church. The following June the Ohio Methodist Conference promoted him to a large suburban Cincinnati church, and it was he who shook the dust of Camden from his boots.

~

The election of amateur radio operator and political libertarian Orville Wood did not produce a major political upheaval in Camden. Quite the contrary, for Hizzoner had a distinctly constricted view of town politics, later saying that he ran for public office primarily to prevent the passage of laws regulating business and to keep property taxes as low as possible: "Camden don't have any [housing] codes and don't have zoning [sic]. We haven't lost a damn thing by not having them. I'm proud of that. That's the main reason I stayed on the council all those years. So I could help keep them out."[10] Wood served only one term as mayor—he did not run for reelection—and later reclaimed a seat on the council that he had held off and on since the late 1940s.

Did Wood's election in 1955, coupled with the decisive defeat of the modest operations levy, deteriorating streets notwithstanding, indicate that the town had essentially surrendered? Certainly the new mayor's limited outlook did not bode well for a town fighting for its life. When asked in 1958 by a Dayton newspaper reporter about the town's increasingly evident state of economic atrophy, Wood curiously blamed geography for the growing blight along Main Street, suggesting that the Seven Mile Creek prevented expansion. Journalist Carl Beyer, however, easily recognized the culprit: "The lack of growth can be explained in two words—no industry." The closing of Atlas Plywood had cost eighty-five jobs, Beyer noted, and Neff and Fry was now down to about twenty-five full-time employees. "The bulk of the laboring population must find jobs in Middletown, Hamilton, Dayton, and Richmond, Indiana. Local businesses feel a 'pinch' due to Atlas' shut down." [11]

Beyer also found a considerable amount of frustration in the town, quoting one anonymous citizen, "We could have a lot more businesses in Camden if the businessmen would band together to bring it in, instead of just complaining about how bad things are." Easier said than done, of course. Economic development requires expertise, capital, and a willingness to develop new infrastructures. Camden lacked all three. But Beyer got to the core of the matter when he concluded, "A conservative attitude is most common throughout the village. It reflects the rural atmosphere which has prevailed here for so long, and carries over into all walks of life." Taking note of the impressive statistic that the town operated on a total budget of just $4,481 for fiscal year 1957, including water and sewer operations, Beyer had discovered the essence of the community's outlook. Quite obviously, improved roads and water systems, which any major employer would require, would not be provided by Camden's parsimonious residents. [12]

Beyer's depressing but accurate assessment contrasted vividly with an *Eaton Register-Herald* editorial that had appeared only eight years earlier. Editor Ace Elliott had noted with approval, "Camden continues to be a progressive village, as evidenced by the growth of several manufacturing plants in the past few years, not to mention the advance of several and varied business establishments which continue to serve a wide area of southern Preble County. . . . New homes, apartments and buildings are a constant assurance that population is on an increase." [13]

By the early 1960s that cheery assessment no longer held true. Within less than a decade, Camden's economy had slid into a state of sustained atrophy. "Out of business" signs appeared on storefronts, and up and down the major and side streets commercial buildings and residences began to show the effects of neglect: peeling paint, grass growing in streets, deteriorating sidewalks, unkempt yards, trash and litter strewn about, and broken windows in abandoned buildings. Under a headline that read, "Majestic? Deserted Theater Belies its Name," a 1961 article in the *Dayton Daily News* reported, "There hasn't been a movie shown here in more than nine years. A few ghosts of the past may still lurk in the long deserted auditorium, but there's little else. The plush seats have long been removed as has the projection equipment. Windows of the ticket booth have been knocked out and the litter of many seasons have blown in." [14]

When difficult economic times struck, Camden lacked the resources, both human and financial, to respond. It had lost its economic base. It had also lost its will to fight. There was no chamber of commerce to stimulate much-needed critical evaluations; there was no economic development plan in place. Government was no more than a caretaker body. The organization that had tacitly accepted many of these responsibilities, the Progressive Club, had suffered a steady decline in membership. As older members dropped out, many to retire in Florida, they were not replaced because younger men displayed less and less interest in the organization or the community. These men were mostly commuters who lived in Camden but worked and shopped elsewhere. Most of these individuals had less motivation to dedicate large amounts of time and energy to community affairs; their involvement tended to be restricted to their church activities. By 1965 the Progressive Club had fewer than twenty-five members and had become a paper organization.

Camden also lacked an essential ingredient for community action: an aggressive town newspaper. The venerable *Preble County News* had long followed a policy of reporting all of the good news and overlooking, or at least treading very lightly upon, the bad. Catering to the sensitivities of readers and advertisers had been a central editorial principle since Will Hartpence got run out of town in 1880. Ray Simpson was a kind and genial individual, dedicated to his town and its people. But from the day he assumed ownership in 1914 it was apparent that he was not equipped with the temperament or steely resolve to challenge his readers. Simpson simply did not consider his role to be that of town conscience or ombudsman. If major problems needed to be brought to public attention, they most likely would not appear first on the pages of the *Preble County News*. Investigative or advocacy journalism were foreign concepts to Simpson.

Week after week, year after year, the *Preble County News* appeared on Thursday afternoon, devoid of editorial comment on local issues and conditions. When Ray's son Harry took over the newspaper in the late 1940s, no change in policy occurred; if anything, the newspaper became even less interested in printing hard news. Harry was himself a modest local politician, serving as an elected member of the Somers Township Board and the board of education; that this might constitute a conflict of interest for an independent journalist probably never crossed his mind, or that of his contented readers. When a recently hired male teacher and coach was summarily fired during the middle of a school term (and indeed, during the all-important basketball season), the event was not mentioned in the newspaper; local rumors, however unsubstantiated, were left to fill the news vacuum. The man in question—whether rightly or wrongly—had been accused of homosexuality. The week after the abrupt termination, the name of the new coach was casually mentioned in a sports story without so much as a comment on either the suddenly departed individual or on the new coach, who came from Indiana to assume command of the team in mid-season.

The *Preble County News* lulled the sensibilities of a town long given to complacency and indifference about community economic development and planning. Whether or not an aggressive editorial policy, urging the importance of mounting a vigorous community development plan, would have made a difference is impossible to discern. What is certain is that the community did not have the benefit of a newspaper that was willing to take an occasional risk, one that was capable of goading the community to ask hard questions about itself and its future. Ultimately Camden paid the price for not having a newspaper serve as the catalyst and champion for the essential process of ongoing self-evaluation and strategic planning.

~

Even the collapse of Neff and Fry, which dealt the community a powerful body blow from which it never recovered, was treated only in the most general of terms in the pages of the *Preble County News*. The company had provided employment for local residents for nearly half a century. During the 1950s, a combination of internal problems coupled with competition from Fortune 500 corporations led to its collapse. In 1961 it was acquired by Peter and Ronald Rutten of Plainfield, Illinois, who operated a family-owned company engaged in agricultural storage and equipment leasing. The new management continued to manufacture storage bins with about twenty local employees until 1977, when it shut down the Camden operation. In 1980 the once proud company suffered one last indignity when its outmoded equipment and office furniture were sold at a sheriff's sale.[15]

Hard times fell not just on Camden's primary employer. Merchants who had been in business for decades were reaching retirement age. Their customer base had declined to the point where many were unable to find buyers to take over their businesses. They held "going out of business sales," ran thank you notes in the newspaper, and shuttered their doors. Clarke Ledwell abandoned his jewelry store, and Lee Danser's jewelry store went through a succession of owners after he retired in 1948. By 1960 there was no jewelry store left in town. Bill Matt sold his last Ford in 1960 and, unable to find a buyer, closed his shop and retired; for a time his building was occupied by a Chevrolet dealership, but by 1970 Camden had lost its last automobile dealer.[16]

One of the last hold outs was Burdette Collett. A 1915 graduate of Camden High School, he had taken over his family's men's clothing business in the early 1920s, operating it out of the same brick building in which his grandfather had first opened for business in 1855. Collett had served faithfully as a charter member of the Progressive Club, and had been a regular worshipper at the Presbyterian Church. He continued operating his store long after losing most of his clientele, apparently because he had nothing else to do. He died in 1969 without heirs, and the following year the imposing Collett brick Victorian home, constructed in 1880 and located around the corner on Central Avenue, was razed to make way for a bank parking lot. "This fine structure was home to Colletts for three generations," the *Preble County News* reported.[17] What the writer did not say was that one of the town's most precious architectural legacies had been leveled to make way for a seldom used parking lot.

Atlas Plywood shut down its operations north of town in 1950 and was replaced amid a flurry of optimistic publicity by a prefabricated home company, President Homes. This enterprise lasted barely two years before entering Chapter 11.[18] Shank's Variety Store, long the butt of jokes for its slapdash operation but nonetheless a symbol of continuity along Main Street, ceased operations in 1970. In that same year, Jessie Roberts, who had operated an eclectic notions shop—a combination of clothing, dry goods, and knitting and sewing supplies—shut her doors at 40 South Main after serving customers since 1913. Such closures left holes that were not filled by a new generation. By 1970 the business district had more vacant buildings than occupied ones, presenting a depressing atmosphere that discouraged both shoppers and would-be investors.[19]

The downward spiral continued throughout the 1970s. When longtime grocers John Porter and Ernie Jefferies retired, their stores closed even though they still enjoyed loyal patronage. New owners were simply not in the offing. By 1980 the number of full-service grocery stores had declined to just one modest-sized IGA chain store. The manager of the grocery told a reporter in 1985, "It is hard to keep people from going out of town to shop" and wistfully expressed his wish that more locals would make their food purchases in their own community.[20] A pool hall, a few secondhand stores, seldom open dusty "antique" stores, a few grimy bars, and small pizza emporiums filled some of the dilapidated storefronts on a haphazard basis, but increasingly they were converted to low-cost housing. Although George Deem opened a small restaurant along the relocated highway, only one marginal eatery remained on Main Street.[21]

~

Camden's economic decline accelerated rapidly. By the mid-1970s Camden was but a shell of its former self, its business district decimated and its population increasingly reflecting two major demographic groups, the aged and the poor. Once-noble Victorian houses that had been proudly occupied by the town's leading families now stood in silent humiliation, their sagging roofs, peeling paint, decrepit porches, and unkempt yards mute testimony to the tough times upon which Camden had fallen. Many large houses and several abandoned stores were purchased by speculators and converted into small apartments for recently arrived low-income families, many of them poorly educated refugees from the depressed regions of rural Appalachia. The central business district was thus converted into a shabby row of low-income housing. Many of these new residents were underemployed, forced to rely on public assistance programs. By the mid-1980s over 40 percent of Camden's children attending the Preble Shawnee schools participated in the federal school lunch program.[22] In 1995 the town council devoted an entire meeting to discussing possible ways to require property owners to clean up and maintain their neglected properties.[23]

Like many rural communities, Camden found it difficult to maintain adequate medical services. In 1966 the sixty-seven-year-old Charles McKinley died suddenly of a stroke, leaving the town temporarily without a physician. He had followed a seven-day-a-week regimen as a general practitioner ever since coming to town in 1930. The popular Von Barnheiser had already died of a heart attack in 1955, possibly the victim of stress from his relentless schedule. In 1975 a recently arrived physician dropped dead of a heart attack at age forty-five, and the town was once again without a physician.[24] For several years Camden endured the not untypical small-town problem of lacking a resident physician, as several individuals came, stayed for a time, and then departed for nearby cities and more lucrative practices. For some residents this meant seeking medical services in other towns, but for many others it meant essentially going without regular medical care.[25]

~

Three of the most important institutions in any small town are the local newspaper, the school, and the bank. Eventually, Camden lost all three. In 1972 Harry Simpson died, and Camden lost one of its most popular citizens. Not only had he worked on the family paper since the late 1920s, but Simpson had been a charter member of the Progressive Club and had faithfully served on the school board and the township board of supervisors, as well as being a deacon of the Presbyterian Church.[26] For the next twenty years the *Preble County News* was published by a printing firm located in Oxford; whatever the limitations of Harry Simpson's benign stewardship of the newspaper, he was a local resident with deep loyalties. Increasingly, the absentee owners published what looked more like a shopping news than a newspaper. In 1991 even that came to an end as the dearth of local businesses made the sale of sufficient advertising an impossibility. For the first time in 114 years, Camden did not have its own newspaper.

In 1980, with the construction of the new facility east of town, the high school building in Camden was closed. Two years later the First National Bank in Camden, with assets now approaching $15 million but unable to compete with the challenges of branch banking, was absorbed by a Cincinnati banking holding company. President Herschel Brown cited the inability of small independent banks to offer the range of services expected by modern-day customers.[27]

~

By the time the cluster of nearby industrial cities encountered severe setbacks in the 1970s, Camden had already lost its economic vitality. The economic hardships that hit the Rust Belt in the 1970s also affected Camden because it had become essentially a bedroom commuter community for industrial and service workers. Dayton's depressed economy reflected the loss of business to international competition endured by General Motors and National Cash Register. Armco Steel, the economic dynamo that propelled Middletown, suffered major setbacks because of its inability to compete with the modern steel manufacturers in the Far East. The staged closing of the Fisher Body plant during the late 1970s dealt Hamilton a blow from which it never fully recovered.

The economic malaise that overtook the heartland of industrial

America exacerbated Camden's economic problems. The options for many workers were not pleasant: they could enter into a forced early retirement, take much lower paying jobs, or move out of state in search of better employment prospects. If they were financially able, workers took retirement, many departing for the warmer climes of the Sun Belt.

As Camden's economy continued its downward slide, the community also suffered a proportionate decline in community spirit. Paradoxically, it was during this extended period of economic atrophy that its population grew at a much greater rate than at any time in its history. The population stood at 1,500 in 1970, and two decades later the federal census reported a population of 2,210. But increased population did not produce economic revival. Although Camden's population doubled between 1950 and 1990, this increase did not include an infusion of much needed entrepreneurial or professional talent. Rather, as noted above, Camden attracted mostly unskilled workers and nonaffluent retirees. In the mid-1970s Camden welcomed a modest housing development built on the town's north edge—a twenty-unit mobile home park. In 1980 a Lancaster, Ohio, firm constructed Camden Way, an attractive apartment development that included a twenty-unit complex designed specifically for the elderly. Not a nursing home—those services were available in Eaton and Oxford—Camden Way epitomized the fate of Camden as a home to the aging, a role increasingly being assumed by many small towns across the nation.

～

The fate of the Town Hall provided an apt metaphor for the town's collapse. Once the symbol of community pride, in the years following the construction of the high school gymnasium the building had been permitted to fall into a condition of serious disrepair. In 1971 Mayor John Matt, son of the former automobile dealer, forced the community to confront the issue when he urged placing on the ballot a referendum calling for a modest three-year increase in property taxes to pay for $30,000 of renovations. The overwhelmingly negative response he received to a mailed questionnaire forced the mayor to shelve the plan.[28] The building continued to deteriorate. In 1985 it was condemned by the state fire marshall, and the town government was forced to move its modest operation into the building that had once housed Bill Matt's Ford dealership. The volunteer fire department moved to new quarters around the corner on Lafayette Street.

Tragedy struck just a few months before the Town Hall would have reached its 100th anniversary. A fire of undetermined origins, but probably caused by faulty wiring, gutted the entire structure on the evening of December 22, 1988. The intense fire opened gaping holes in the roof and brought the upper floor—once home to the dignified Opera House and the site of exciting basketball games—crashing down on the council chamber and fire truck garage. Once the flames were stilled, only a blackened brick shell remained. A few long-time residents were eager to rebuild the hall, to make it as sparkling and exciting as it had been the day it opened on May 11, 1889 . . . or at least like it was when it was reopened in March of 1933 after the successful renovation effort led by the Progressive Club. Advocates of rebuilding emphasized the structure's historical significance, recalled the many dances and basketball games held there, and quietly reflected on the depressing symbolism that the gutted structure held for those who cared about the town. Eventually, Jack White, a 1947 high school graduate and the descendant of a pioneer Camden family, assumed leadership of a fund-raising drive. After consulting with historical preservation experts and architects, his Committee to Rebuild the Town Hall announced that the needed renovations would cost $260,000.[29]

The committee's first effort was to seek passage of a special bond levy that would have increased property taxes by a modest amount ($50 for the average homeowner) for a twenty-year period. In February of 1990 the voters defeated the levy 169–148, and White's committee was left with the daunting prospect of raising the funds privately. White recognized the enormity of his task: "It's not a place of beauty now, and I guess I wouldn't say it was a place of beauty before it burned, but if we did a first class job on restoration, it would be recognizable. It would be something to be proud of." White understood that the community of his birth, where his parents, grandparents, and great-grandparents had lived and worked, sorely needed a morale boost. The image—perhaps the future—of Camden seemed to be at stake. Agreeing with this assessment was octogenarian Herschel R. Brown, onetime grocery store manager and bank president, founding member of the Progressive Club, and now an enthusiastic member of White's committee: "I can remember when we had the best school system and the nicest town around this area, but our town doesn't look as good as it once did," he told a newspaper reporter. In 1993 White's group created the Camden Area Historical Preservation Foundation in hopes of attracting tax deductible donations.[30]

But five years after the fire, a burned-out brick shell still stood in the heart of Camden—a blight on the community. The restoration committee's efforts had generated little enthusiasm from either current or

A wreck of its former self, the Camden Town Hall, built in 1889, stands as a daily reminder of better days. Condemned by Ohio safety officials in 1985, its interior was destroyed by fire in December of 1988. Efforts to raise funds to restore the facility have fallen short, and the village council cannot afford the $50,000 to have it razed. Photograph taken 1997 by Archie Armstrong.

former residents, and it had raised less than 5 percent of the $750,000 which a Dayton architectural firm specializing in historical preservation now estimated would be needed to accomplish a complete renovation. In fact, the committee had failed to raise even the $25,000 necessary to put a new roof in place. The town council had to admit to the ultimate humiliation: it could not even find the money to raze the building. And so its hulking ruin provided a daily reminder to residents of better days. Jack White's discouraged committee still plugged away, holding dances and bake sales, selling bricks inscribed with the donor's name for $50, hoping that a wealthy benefactor might emerge.[31]

∽

In 1972 reporter Roz Young of the *Dayton Journal Herald,* possessed of a perceptive eye and a sharp pen, published a three-part story on the town in which she emphasized the presence of elderly citizens, took note of the grass in the sidewalks along what remained of the business district, and acidly observed that even the tombstones in the cemetery, like many of the houses and business structures, were in need of substantial repair. Her stories were laced with acerbic comments about the lack of business and professional activity, empty streets at midday, boarded-up businesses, middle-aged residents sitting on Main Street stoops during workdays smoking cigarettes while watching their scruffy children playing in the streets. She was also struck by the lackadaisical quality that the community exuded, and quoted with relish one senior citizen, Harvey Douglass: "Camden's a great town. It's got six churches and five bars so I guess you can go either way." To Young, "Harvey's philosophy pretty well sums up how it is to live in Camden. It's a quiet town. Nobody is in much of a hurry. Everybody knows everybody else. The main road has passed Camden by and hardly anybody goes there unless he lives there or knows somebody. Six churches and five bars. You can go either way, whichever you've a mind to."[32]

Thirteen years later, and with no improvement evident, another reporter, this time from the *Middletown Journal,* surveyed the town and concluded that it was a victim of "the apathy of the 1970s," when "buildings in the town began to show their age, and some of them were allowed to disintegrate beyond repair. Town Hall, once a show place for miles around and a center of action for the town, was condemned by the state because of the hazard it presented to the community."[33]

Shortly before the Town Hall fire, another conflagration had gutted the prominent Dearth Building in December of 1988. This stone and brick building had occupied the northwest corner of Main and Central since the 1850s. The anchor of the business district, it had housed the drugstore on the ground floor and business offices and apartments on the upper two levels. By 1988 it had been relegated to the ignominy of housing a pizza parlor, whose greasy ovens probably caused the fire. The charred remains were cleared, leaving the ugly scar of an unpaved makeshift parking lot as the centerpiece of what was left of a ravaged business district.[34]

⁓

With its Town Hall condemned and its premier business location now a dirt parking lot, Camden approached the twenty-first century severely wounded. Like so many small towns, it had fallen victim to the forces of modernism. In his insightful study of the decline of small towns

The Dearth Building had anchored the northwest corner of Main and Central since it was built in the mid-1890s. After it burned in December of 1988, it was razed to make room for an unpaved parking lot. Courtesy Camden Archives.

in southwestern Minnesota, Joseph Amato writes, "Natural decline has appeared in rural Minnesota. The young are gone and the old are hanging on. The prairie is no longer a magnet for distant capital. Tracks have been ripped up; downtowns are coming undone; amenities—like schools, recreation, and medicine—vanish; populations don't coalesce; leaders do not cohere. The initiative of civilization has been lost. The ideal of a new commercial order . . . fades."[35]

But life goes on in Camden. Although residents worry about losing essential services, they can still purchase daily essentials in the one remaining grocery store, a small drugstore, and a couple of service stations. Downtown Camden has never been able to attract a franchise fast food emporium, but people can get a modest meal at Loretta's Restaurant on Main Street, and they have three options for local pizza. The small library, now a branch of the county operation, serves a steady clientele, and six churches still minister to the needs of their communicants. An attorney offers legal services from a dingy storefront, and a branch of the Bank of Southwestern Ohio provides financial services. Residents must go elsewhere for clothing, specialized medical care and basic dental services, and all durable goods. A public recreation program offers youth summer baseball and softball, and the Shawnee Consolidated School District struggles to meet its students' needs under tight budgets.

In 1987 a few optimists established a chamber of commerce, announcing exciting plans for the future. Its early professions of the coming of a new and glorious age were the stuff of wishful thinking. The Homecoming carnival is still held over an autumn weekend, with sponsorship provided by the Lions Club. A Black Walnut Festival in October — the major project of the chamber of commerce — attracts visitors who browse through handicraft booths and sample walnut delicacies.[36]

Hope remains that a miracle will occur and a benefactor will contribute three quarters of a million dollars to refurbish the Town Hall. In a faint echo of the earnest conversations of the 1950s, some residents still talk about putting in the necessary infrastructure for an industrial park. The Philomathean Club still meets once a month to discuss books and cultural issues, and the chamber of commerce takes hope from the sizable crowds that attend the walnut celebration. A few new middle-class residences are built each year, located as far from the town's decayed core as possible, providing housing for the recently retired or another family anxious to escape the deteriorating social conditions of a nearby industrial city. As the visitor reflects on the past and ponders the future, the question comes to mind: How would Sherwood Anderson, the town's most famous son, react to the present-day reality of the town to which he so often fled in his dreams?

⚭

In the spring of 1987 a brief meeting of the Progressive Club took place in the home of eighty-four-year-old Herschel Brown. In this town that America has left behind, the three surviving members of the Progressive Club, all in their eighties, closed the books and formally voted to disband the organization.[37]

Camden: The Town We Left Behind

In a series of comments made in 1994 and 1995, current and former residents expressed their disappointment over the condition of Camden. The town had become "run down" and had "a large number of people on welfare." "It looks almost like a ghost town." "The town is dead compared to when I lived there." "It's a small town in need of a lot of repair of its streets, houses, and buildings." "Mostly older people live there." "There is an alarming rise in the number of transients who live in town for a short period to take advantage of low rents."[1]

Mayor Jerry Wood, now operating his father Orville's fuel business as well as following his footsteps into local politics, echoed these comments during a conversation in 1995: "We have a lot of people move in here, stay a while, and then leave. They don't contribute much of anything to the town. We often don't even get to know them before they are gone." The son of the long-time political activist, businessman, and general tree spirit identified the lack of "community spirit" and "apathy" as preventing Camden from mounting an economic comeback. He described himself as frustrated with his job, especially with the lack of funds to operate even a bare-bones governmental operation. Echoing earlier leaders, Wood expressed hope that someday he could convince residents to vote for a bond levy to pay for the extension of roads and utilities to an area on the north edge of town that has long been designated to become an industrial park. The same project has been on the drawing board since the 1950s.[2] Nothing has happened yet, and most likely never will.

The leader of the effort to renovate the Town Hall, Jack White, returned to Camden in 1976 to live in his family's large 1920s bunga-low-style home on the south edge of town after retiring from a mana-gerial position in Dayton. He remains hopeful but realistic about his hometown's future: "There is much to be said in favor of living in a small village such as Camden, but local job opportunities will never be adequate to retain talented youth. The educated leave and seldom re-turn." Even the most positive spin he can put on the future of Camden is sobering: "Our future at best will depend upon lower middle class families who feel it is important to support the community."[3]

Was the collapse of Camden inevitable? Would the presence of strong, imaginative leadership during the crucial postwar period have made a difference? Was it asking too much of town government and the informal male leadership network connected to the Progressive Club to have demonstrated greater vision by formulating an economic devel-opment program? If such leadership had emerged, would it have been able to convince others of the crisis that their community faced? And could they have then raised enough money to mount a sustained effort to build a viable economic base in the town?

The obvious answer to all these questions is no. It would have been asking too much of relatively unsophisticated small-town operators to whom economic planning and development were, at best, vague and unfamiliar concepts. There are thousands of towns whose leaders fol-lowed the same path of least resistance and permitted similar patterns of decline to take hold. State and federal governments also failed to anticipate future problems. Once the downward spiral of small towns became evident during the 1960s, policy makers demonstrated little in-terest in taking corrective action. Lacking a sufficient voter base, the small towns were easily ignored as politicians rushed to combat the media-hyped "crisis of the cities."

∼

One of the overlooked tragedies of modern American history has been the trashing of its small communities by federal policies. That, coupled with a persistent policy of benign neglect, all but assured the contem-porary malaise of the small town. These communities were certainly not singled out for special assistance, and whatever federal programs they were able to access were largely formula-driven programs targeted else-where. Sometimes well-intentioned federal programs—such as federal highway and agricultural policies—ended up wreaking extreme damage upon small towns.

The political realities of the postwar period were clear: the "crisis of the cities" was threatening the future of America. This explosive issue dominated postwar social and economic planning at the federal level, from the Housing and Urban Redevelopment Act of 1949 through the myriad of programs that were part of Lyndon Johnson's Great Society during the mid-1960s. The condition of the cities became one of the highest priorities of domestic policy, and the nation's villages were overlooked. Much has been written about the devastating impact of the interstate highway system on the towns that it bypassed, and much more needs to be written about this tragedy from the perspective of the communities thrust aside by insensitive highway engineers and their political allies. Although the highway lobby must be held accountable, so too must the farm lobby, which succeeded in greatly expanding price support programs for its powerful agribusiness constituencies. Since their inception in the 1930s, federal farm subsidies and related policies have favored large-scale individual or corporate agricultural interests, thereby accelerating the demise of the small family farm and contributing markedly to the depopulation of America's farmlands. The cumulative effect of federal agricultural polices was to encourage migration of rural residents to the cities on new interstate highways, a migration that reduced even further the economic base of the nation's farm towns while it exacerbated congestion and other social ills of the cities.

The confluence of several divergent federal urban policies also worked to the detriment of the small town. Federal mortgage insurance programs, such as the GI bill and FHA, although available to home buyers in small towns, tended to encourage large-scale housing subdivisions by well-financed developers in metropolitan areas. These spiffy new subdivisions encouraged residents of small towns to relocate nearer to their place of work. Very few smaller communities participated in the federal public housing program, since they lacked the capital necessary to fund community renewal or housing agencies as well as the political and financial wherewithal to mount a viable redevelopment program. They also did not have the administrative resources or an adequate tax base to assemble land and administer such programs; consequently, small-town America is riddled with substandard housing and has received little federal assistance for low-income housing.

Because small towns lacked political clout, they all too often fell through the cracks, overlooked or simply ignored by the policy makers in Congress and the Departments of Agriculture and Housing and Urban Development. Lack of interest on the part of the federal government was replicated in the state capitals. Except for an occasional dollar or two expended by state tourism bureaus, towns seldom received direct support from state legislatures other than through population-based, formula-driven programs. Instead, the towns were left to fend for themselves in the national and international marketplaces. Private industry contributed little to the towns. Even Wal-Mart—the megacorporation whose roots are firmly grounded in the small Arkansas town of Bentonville and whose executives profess special concern for the future of small-town America—has often been accused of driving Main Street merchants out of business by its high volume, low price strategies.[4]

Despite all these negative forces, America's small towns have somehow survived, but they have become much different and less attractive and viable communities. The architectural historian Richard Francaviglia seeks to put a good front on this development, concluding his study of land use planning and architecture with the observation that Main Street America has merely entered into an new era: "Rather than bemoan the loss of Main Street and condemn strip commercial areas, one would do well to see them as part of the rich visual variety of the American landscape today—a variety that reflects how much America has changed in the twentieth century."[5]

∼

Camden is thus a case in point for what the historian Catherine Stock has described as "Main Street in crisis."[6] That diagnosis, however, must be mitigated with the observation that some small towns have been able to beat the odds. In my forty-four state tour conducted in 1995 I had the opportunity to visit hundreds of communities, a few of which have avoided, to a greater or lesser extent, the pressures of decline. One such town is Elkton, Virginia, located in the Shenandoah Valley. This small town received an unexpected economic boost during the early 1980s when Colorado-based Coors Beer built a huge brewery on the edge of town. This economic break did not result from Elkton's efforts at economic development but happened simply because company geologists discovered an enormous pool of pristine underground water that made possible the production of enough "Coors Light" beer to quench the thirst of much of the eastern half of the United States. The anticipated economic boom in Elkton did not fully materialize, however, because the majority of the brewery's workforce opted to live in the city of Harrisonville, located twenty miles to the west. The only tangible changes in Elkton were the construction of a modest number of apartment buildings and new homes and the opening of a McDonald's. It even subsequently lost its high school to a rival town in the ongoing process of school consolidation. The downtown business district remained an unattractive patchwork of small stores interspersed with vacant buildings.

Another southern town's economic development program fared somewhat better. Faced with deteriorating economic conditions in the early 1980s, the business and political leaders of the small county seat of Tylerville, located in the south-central part of Mississippi, used a low tax base and proximity to the port of New Orleans to attract several small automotive, specialty linen, and machine milling firms. Its local economy enjoyed a substantial boost, but like Elkton, Tylerville's new jobs attracted many workers who commuted from several nearby towns and the cities of Macomb and Hattiesburg. The economic growth resulting from Tylerville's development program, although halting the town's population and economic decline, has been less than spectacular. But the town's condition has stabilized, its business district remains viable, and the future looks much less bleak than it did when local leaders launched their effort in the early 1980s.

Many towns have sought to capitalize on unique geographical or ethnic factors to reverse bad fortune. For example, the farm town of Oakland has promoted a cultural-economic renaissance by declaring itself the "Swedish Capital of Nebraska." The annual Swedish celebration in this eastern Nebraska town attracts thousands of visitors for a June weekend, and town residents have gotten into the spirit of things, sprucing up the community by placing colorful Swedish decorations on their homes, businesses, and street signs—and even the water tower. Construction of a new school building, renovation of the town park, the opening of a new outdoor community sports center, the refurbishing of a town auditorium, and the continued operation of a nineteen-bed hospital during the new bottom-line era of health maintenance organizations are directly attributable to this manifestation of civic pride, Swedish-style. Like Tylerville, Oakland also benefits from a lively local newspaper that is unafraid of stirring up controversy on local issues. The *Oakland Tribune* is in the image of its upbeat and aggressive editor, Dewaine Gahan, who was one of the primary proponents of the Swedish campaign.

However, the community spirit that local leaders attribute to the Swedish gambit has not led to any notable infusion of nonagricultural jobs. Several storefronts stand vacant, and the population remains static. The shrinking farm population can be attributed to the influence of the high tech, large-scale agribusiness that now dominates the region's fertile farmland. Oakland is certainly a more lively place to live in than it was before the celebration of its Swedish heritage was initiated, and the community has made a creative effort to remain vital, but the harsh realities of modern economics suggest that its future is at best problematic.

One of the more audacious efforts to revitalize an economically moribund small town occurred during the mid-1990s when Rising Sun, Indiana, home to 1,500 residents, succeeded in landing an $85 million capital investment in the form of a riverboat casino complex, complete with a large hotel, an upscale golf course, several restaurants, and a modern version of a nineteenth-century stern paddleboat capable of hosting three thousand gamblers at its slot machines, green felt tables, and roulette wheels. Located fifty miles to the southwest of Cincinnati along the Ohio River, this agricultural community has bet its future on the seductive promises of Hyatt Corporation executives.

Within six months after the modern replica of an antebellum river boat, the Victoria Queen, took its first load of gamblers for a ride on the Ohio River in August of 1996, the town had received an infusion of $250,000 in tax revenue, a bonanza that produced a flurry of local projects, including street pavings, refurbishing of the business district, and special remodeling grants to some owners of older houses with architectural or historic merit. New schools and other major projects are now within the realm of possibility. Awash in tax revenue, town leaders even contemplate the impossible: sharing their new wealth with nearby towns. This economic success, however, has failed to convince a vocal minority of skeptical residents of this conservative agricultural town, who wonder if the transformation of their sleepy town into a gambling mecca for Ohio River Valley residents will be worth the social, environmental, and psychic costs.[7]

A few towns have unique features that cannot easily be replicated. The well-heeled mountain town of Peterborough, New Hampshire, the community on which Thornton Wilder based his classic play *Our Town,* has long been a haven for writers and artists. The affluence of its permanent population, and especially its many summer residents, provides for stability without the need for economic development. The picturesque southern Oregon community of Ashland has grown from small farm town to sixteen thousand residents since the 1950s because of the success of its nationally acclaimed Shakespeare Festival. Ironically, Ashland's growth in the 1990s has been such that its citizens have found themselves embroiled in impassioned debate about how (or whether) to curtail further development in order to protect its small-town ambience, the very atmosphere that attracts upscale tourists by the thousands each week.

No tour of American small towns can skip a visit to Clyde, Ohio, and Sauk Centre, Minnesota. Clyde is the real Winesburg, once home to the young Sherwood Anderson. It now has a population of four thousand and is no longer the sauerkraut dynamo that Anderson knew. Today Clyde is home to a large kitchen appliance factory that provides the major source of employment, but as in Elkton and Tylerville, many workers commute from substantial distances and do not live or shop in Clyde. A small museum highlights the career of its famous author, and a local restaurant displays a humorous mural depicting the major figures in Anderson's novel, although locals seem oblivious to it while they sit sipping their coffee and eating homemade pie. The *Clyde Enterprise,* the weekly newspaper that once employed a youthful Anderson as a reporter, still publishes on Thursdays. Its enthusiastic editor, John Brewer, regularly prods his readership with editorials about the importance of the Main Street redevelopment project, which seeks to restore the business district with a late 1880s look in hopes of luring tourists. The visitor wonders what Sherwood Anderson would make of all of this bright paint, antique street lights, and antiquarian signs. To the contemporary visitor, however, they evoke an all-too-familiar image of Disneyland's take on small towns.

As in Clyde, the residents of Sauk Centre have long since gotten over their exasperation of having one of their own write negatively about the community. Located northwest of the Twin Cities, Sauk Centre continues to serve the farming population of the fertile western Minnesota prairie. The community has benefited from its location on Interstate Highway 94 in the form of a few restaurants and service stations clustered on the interchange. It also benefits from its role as county seat and from the fact that no larger towns exist nearby to steal local consumers (except for major shopping expeditions to the Twin Cities). A well-manicured golf course, tidy neighborhoods, and the lack of vacant storefronts on Main Street attest to the town's vitality. Most of all, the Sinclair Lewis Visitors Center attracts hundreds of visitors daily, and tours of the restored home of Dr. E. J. Lewis and his family keep a few docents busy. Carol Kennicott would still not find Sauk Centre an exciting place to live, but the rough edges that town's most famous son so vividly described have long since disappeared.

$\sim$

Such exceptions notwithstanding—ordinary or exceptional as they might be—the great preponderance of America's towns have been left far behind as modern America has moved into the postmodern era. They have become neglected appendages to America's dominant urban culture. Only a fragment of their once viable mercantile bases remain, usually in the form of a small grocery store, a coffee shop, a tavern or two, a feed store, perhaps a modest hardware store. Many have become bedroom commuter communities for regional cities, providing inexpensive housing for those willing to drive up to a hundred miles round trip to work. Those towns located beyond a commuter's reach of a city have suffered especially large population losses; they have not had the option available to Camden of becoming a commuter bedroom community and have nothing else to offer would-be residents.

As several scholars have observed, America's small towns have become the repository of aging men and women who are living out their lives along shaded side streets, getting by on modest pensions, carefully monitored savings accounts, Social Security, and Medicare. These individuals have spent most of their lives in or near the same communities. While some of their more affluent friends and neighbors have departed for Sun Belt retirement communities, they lack either the resources or the desire to relocate. Many have been attracted by the inexpensive cost of living, especially housing. In these declining communities, houses sell at deep discounts, and property owners have converted commercial buildings into inexpensive apartments. Many of the younger families attracted to this inexpensive housing are run by single parents, swelling the welfare roles of small towns, putting heavy burdens on underfunded local schools and social agencies. One-third of the children attending the elementary school in Camden, for example, participated in the free lunch program in 1995, and 1990 census data confirms that those 11,897 towns of less than ten thousand people contain larger concentrations of the poor and elderly, on a percentage basis, than America's cities.[8] Catherine Stock accurately observes that "rates of poverty and unemployment in small-town America have crept close to those in the nation's largest cities; domestic violence, substance abuse, and teenage pregnancy increase without even the minimal services provided in urban areas. Perhaps most frightening to residents themselves is the inadequacy of rural health care."[9]

~

Be it in South Dakota, Maine, South Carolina, east Texas, or my adopted state of Nevada, most American small towns present a familiar, even predictable, appearance. Many houses are badly in need of new paint, their yards uncared for, with rusting appliances, or even an occasional stripped automobile, sitting in the side yard. Playgrounds and parks are unkempt, and the streets are in advanced stages of disrepair. A visitor who enjoys a competitive game of tennis cannot help noticing the sagging nets and the grass growing in the town's cracked cement courts. Aging school buildings reflect the damage inflicted by deferred maintenance budgets. The former high school building has been redesignated an elementary or middle school, the new consolidated high school having been located miles away in a larger magnet city. The central business district is in a state of advanced deterioration; many of the aging brick or frame buildings are now empty, their windows often broken or boarded. A faded marquee provides a distant memory of Saturday night at the movies. Faded "For Sale" signs abound. From their front porches, elderly residents watch intently as a vehicle with unfamiliar license plates slowly moves down one of the town's residential streets. On one side of town, along the state highway, will be found a trailer park and nearby a small cluster of dingy bars, mom-and-pop restaurants, a convenience grocery store and service station, perhaps an automobile and farm implement repair shop, its front and side yards filled with discarded transmissions, axles, and rusting automobiles with four flat tires, the assembled clutter of many years of inattention to appearances.

Along another residential street, however, the curious visitor comes upon a throwback to an earlier and more promising day: scattered throughout these communities are still a substantial number of houses that have been kept in prime condition, their neatly manicured yards resplendent with flowers and mature trees, an American flag proudly flying from the front porch. So it is a mixed picture, to be certain, but one that does not indicate that a renaissance is around the corner.

Nonetheless, although they might be on the ropes, America's small towns have not yet given up. The concerned and hopeful observer quietly departs, convinced that they will somehow muddle through. But daunting negative forces are much in evidence. The lack of economic activity is unmistakable. Why is it that so many of the remaining businesses are secondhand stores or antique shops operated by widowed women? Conversations with a waitress, a local newspaper editor (if the town's weekly is still publishing), or a shopkeeper leave the visitor with the distinct impression that the future is anything but bright. Young adults are a distinct minority; most leave as soon as they can. The people who remain are conservative, quietly but intensely patriotic in an admirable old-fashioned way—the large number of American flags in evidence is striking—but the tenor of their conversations and their body language indicate that they are living in quiet resignation. They will not leave their town, but the spark they once knew has disappeared. Progressive Clubs are not to be found anymore, and Lions Clubs are largely venues for retired men to reminisce about the good old days. Churches provide a haven for many elderly women as they gather to sew, discuss the Bible, and socialize. Most folk are comfortable in these towns, perhaps complacent. They are quick to compare their town favorably with the crime and drug ravaged cities, but they seldom speak of their town with any sense of pride; the future is not promising, and longtime residents tend to talk about "what used to be" and shrug their shoulders when asked about the availability of medical services, the quality of public schools, or opportunities for meaningful employment.

Even when imaginative rural and community development programs have been able to provide attractive employment opportunities and to stabilize local economies, the potential for a downward spiral is always lurking nearby. The continuing decline of America's family farms before the onslaught of corporate farming threatens even further depletion of the farm population upon which these towns have long depended. Where employment opportunities still exist, local leaders select their words carefully to express their guarded optimism, because they know that they are only one corporate relocation, downsizing, or offshore deployment decision away from catastrophe. Each and every day the automobile does serious damage. The instrument that Henry Ford intended to make rural living more attractive has had the reverse impact. Automobiles not only transport locals to regional shopping centers but also, if a new employer can be lured into town, bring workers from other communities to take what were intended to be local jobs.

∼

All of these less than sanguine factors, however, do not lead to the conclusion that Main Street America will disappear. The small towns may have been left far behind, but they will remain a part of the American landscape. Thanks to fortuitous circumstances, a few exceptional towns will actually thrive, but most will have to be content with maintaining the status quo, and some with mere survival. Eclipsed by regional cities, overlooked by federal and state policy makers, and ignored by no-nonsense bottom-line corporate executives, they will fill those small niches that remain open to them, getting by on the margins of American life. Once the very marrow of a young and growing nation, now hollow shells of their former selves, they are condemned to live in the shadows of a new America. In his "My Hometown," pop singer Bruce Springsteen is not far off the mark: "Main Street's closing down. . . . No one wants to come down here anymore."

Notes

Prologue. Plainville, U.S.A.: The Towns We Left Behind

1. Quoted in Glaab and Brown, *A History of Urban America*, pp. 269–70.

2. A Village Trustee, "Are Small Towns Doomed?" *American Mercury*, May 1934, pp. 74–79.

3. Sinks, "The Old Home Town Fights to Live."

4. Colladay, "The Passing of the American Village."

5. Withers, *Plainville, U.S.A.*

6. Gallaher, *Plainville Fifteen Years Later*; Atherton, *Main Street on the Middle Border*, p. xv.

7. Vidich and Bensman, *Small Town in Mass Society*.

8. Martindale and Hanson, *Small Town and the Nation*.

9. Amato, *The Decline of Rural Minnesota*, p. 12.

10. Johnson, "It's Not Hep to Stay."

11. Heath, "Parts of Nebraska Are Just Plain Deserted."

12. Lewis, *Main Street*.

13. The literature on the postwar "urban crisis" is enormous; among the most significant of the major books on this subject are Salisbury, *The Shook-Up Generation*; Editors of *Fortune*, *The Exploding Metropolis*; Jacobs, *The Death and Life of Great Cities*; Keats, *The Crack in the Picture Window*; and Martin Anderson, *The Federal Bulldozer*.

14. See Keillor, *Lake Wobegon Days*; Kuralt, *On the Road with Charles Kuralt*; McMurtry, *The Last Picture Show*; Heat-Moon, *Blue Highways*; and Steinbeck, *Travels with Charlie*. See also the sentimental touch of Helen Hoover Santmyer, whose novels and remembrances of life in Xenia, Ohio, have earned her high praise. See especially "*. . . And Ladies of the Club*," and *Ohio Town*. For the influence of small-town nostalgia on Walt Disney and his empire, see Eliot, *Walt Disney*, pp. 231–33; Findlay, *Magic Lands*, pp. 84–95; and Watts, "Walt Disney: Art and Politics in the American Century," pp. 106–8.

15. Anderson, *Winesburg, Ohio*, pp. 244–48.

197

Chapter 1. Dover: The Building of a Community

1. There are several useful biographies of Sherwood Anderson and a large number of critical appraisals of his writing. See especially the biographies of Kim Townsend (1987) and Irving Howe (1951), which both carry the utilitarian title *Sherwood Anderson.*

2. Townsend, *Sherwood Anderson,* pp. 1–108; Howe, *Sherwood Anderson,* pp. 3–90.

3. Burbank, *Sherwood Anderson,* pp. 61–77; Townsend, *Sherwood Anderson,* p. 150; Howe, *Sherwood Anderson,* pp. 91–109.

4. In an undated document found in the Sherwood Anderson Museum, an unknown resident of Clyde provides an intriguing comparison of names of major and minor figures, as well as some businesses, that appear in *Winesburg, Ohio,* with real individuals and enterprises that existed at the time Anderson lived in Clyde. It is readily apparent that Anderson borrowed heavily from real names and places. Pawsey's Shoe Store appears in the novel and existed on Main Street. "Turk Smollett" drew upon the three Smollett families of Clyde. "Skinner Leason" of the novel was similar to Frank "Skinner" Letson; "Winny's Dry Goods" was adapted from the real Winnie's Dry Goods; and the "Spaniard Nursery" had to have been inspired by the French Nursery. See the one-page duplicated "Characters from Winesburg," n.d., Sherwood Anderson Museum, Clyde, Ohio.

5. This theme appears in many critical analyses of Anderson's writing. For example, see Irving Howe, "The Book of the Grotesque," pp. 90–103, and Rex Burbank, "The Populist Temper," pp. 32–43, in Ray Lewis White, *The Achievement of Sherwood Anderson.*

6. Anderson, *Poor White* (1920); Townsend, *Sherwood Anderson,* pp. 150–55; Howe, *Sherwood Anderson,* pp. 123–30.

7. Miller, *The Colossus of Maroussi,* p. 34.

8. See Townsend, *Sherwood Anderson,* pp. 1–2, 294, for a discussion of his fantasies about Camden; see also *Tar: A Midwest Childhood,* pp. 13–18.

9. Anderson, *Tar: A Midwest Childhood,* pp. 17–18.

10. Hurt, *The Ohio Frontier,* pp. 4–142; Knepper, *Ohio and Its People,* pp. 14–23; Roseboom and Weisenburger, *A History of Ohio,* pp. 63–70; Bond, *The Foundations of Ohio,* pp. 275–348.

11. Bond, *The Foundations of Ohio,* pp. 13–15; Knepper, *Ohio and Its People,* pp. 17–19.

12. Hurt, *The Ohio Frontier,* pp. 178, 211.

13. Ibid., pp. 143–78; Bond, *The Foundations of Ohio,* pp. 14–15; Knepper, *Ohio and Its People,* pp. 6–8; Faragher, *Sugar Creek,* p. 10.

14. Bond, *The Foundations of Ohio,* pp. 7–12; Knepper, *Ohio and Its People,* pp. 2–3; Dayton Power and Light Company publication, n.d. [ca. 1950], Camden Archives. Harper, *Ohio in the Making,* pp. 58–72, provides a concise summary of the periods of glaciation in Ohio; see also Whittlesey, *Geology of Ohio,* pp. 4–8.

15. Hurt, *The Ohio Frontier,* pp. 120–42; Bond, *The Foundations of Ohio,* pp. 312–48; Knepper, *Ohio and Its People,* pp. 24–81.

16. Bond, *The Foundations of Ohio,* pp. 349–95; Roseboom and Weisenburger,

A History of Ohio, pp. 109–17; Knepper, *Ohio and Its People,* pp. 81–102, 120–24; Utter, *The Frontier State, 1803–1825,* pp. 130–31.

17. Lowery, *A History of Preble County, Ohio,* pp. 292–93; *History of Preble County, Ohio,* pp. 141–42; *Camden Gazette,* May 31, 1900; Morgan, *Directory of Preble County, O.,* pp. 49, 107; *Preble County News,* September 10, 1925, and August 16, 1933.

18. *Camden Gazette,* April 22, 1897; Morgan, *Directory of Preble County, O.,* p. 191; *History of Preble County, Ohio,* p. 299; *Preble County News,* August 18, 1933; *Camden Herald,* June 2, 1877.

19. Faragher, *Sugar Creek,* pp. 10–15; Slotkin, *Fatal Environment,* p. 126.

20. See Faragher, *Sugar Creek,* pp. 62–63, for a concise summary of the attitudes and practices of settlers on the frontier regarding the decimation of the native forests. For a detailed description of the early stages of settlement in Ohio, see Hurt, *The Ohio Frontier,* pp. 240–43; and Utter, *The Frontier State,* pp. 137–45. See also Knepper, *Ohio and Its People,* pp. 121–22; and Harper, *Ohio in the Making,* pp. 76–77.

21. Heistand, *Preble County, Ohio,* p. 253; *Preble County News,* November 25, 1915, providing a historical review based on interviews and other data; *History of Preble County, Ohio,* p. 310; Utter, *The Frontier State,* p. 240; Jones, "The Introduction of Farm Machinery into Ohio Prior to 1865."

22. *History of Preble County, Ohio,* p. 307; Neff, "A History of Camden, Ohio," pp. 44–47.

23. Neff, "A History of Camden, Ohio," pp. 51–52; *History of Preble County, Ohio,* p. 313.

24. Aaron, *Cincinnati,* pp. 13–18; Hurt, *The Ohio Frontier,* pp. 187–89, 353–56; Wade, *The Urban Frontier,* pp. 22–27, 53–59; Utter, *The Frontier State,* pp. 156–57; Knepper, *Ohio and Its People,* pp. 127, 133.

25. Aaron, *Cincinnati,* p. 35.

26. Cronon, *Nature's Metropolis,* p. 228; Knepper, *Ohio and Its People,* p. 133; Aaron, *Cincinnati,* pp. 31–37; Wade, *The Urban Frontier,* pp. 195–97; Hurt, *The Ohio Frontier,* p. 356; Trollope, *Domestic Manners of the Americans,* pp. 88, 90.

27. Utter, *The Frontier State,* pp. 152–56; Knepper, *Ohio and Its People,* pp. 125–27.

28. Utter, *The Frontier State,* p. 156; Weisenburger, *The Passing of the Frontier,* pp. 70–71.

29. Jones, "The Introduction of Farm Machinery into Ohio," pp. 1–8; Utter, *The Frontier State,* pp. 146–72.

30. Utter, *The Frontier State,* pp. 146–72; Weisenburger, *The Passing of the Frontier,* pp. 56–88; Knepper, *Ohio and Its People,* pp. 125–29.

31. *History of Preble County, Ohio,* pp. 309–10; Lowery, *A History of Preble County, Ohio,* p. 294; *History of Preble County, Ohio,* p. 310.

32. *History of Preble County, Ohio,* p. 310; Utter, *The Frontier State,* p. 238; Neff, "A History of Camden, Ohio," pp. 125–27.

33. "Census of 1850 for Preble County, Ohio."

34. Lowery, *A History of Preble County, Ohio,* pp. 295–300; Neff, "A History of Camden, Ohio," pp. 128–34; *Eaton Weekly Register,* September 6, 1855.

35. *Eaton Weekly Register,* September 6, 1855.

36. *A History of Preble County, Ohio,* pp. 307, 310; Neff, "A History of Camden, Ohio," pp. 133–34.

37. "Camden Sesquicentennial Souvenir," pp. 41–44; Neff, "A History of Camden, Ohio," pp. 134–41.

38. Weisenburger, *The Passing of the Frontier,* pp. 90–107; Knepper, *Ohio and Its People,* pp. 149–59; George Rogers Taylor, *The Transportation Revolution, 1815–1860;* Shaw, *Canals for a Nation,* pp. 126–54.

39. Weisenburger, *The Passing of the Frontier,* pp. 110–18; Knepper, *Ohio and Its People,* pp. 159–62.

40. *History of Preble County, Ohio,* p. 94; Neff, "A History of Camden, Ohio," pp. 53–54; "Camden Sesquicentennial Souvenir," p. 5; "Requiescat in Pace, Hon. David Barnet," newspaper clipping, November 8, 1883, Camden Archives; *History of Preble County, Ohio,* p. 310. The young sharpshooter, Ben Lamm, later served with distinction as a member of Company E, 156th O.V.I., during the Civil War and became a prominent local farmer and member of the Republican Party. Camden Archives.

41. Neff, "A History of Camden, Ohio," p. 129.

42. Glaab and Brown, *A History of Urban America,* pp. 112–13.

43. Neff, "A History of Camden, Ohio," pp. 196–201.

44. Ibid., pp. 203–7.

45. Ibid., pp. 206–7.

46. *Camden Gazette,* March 25, 1897; *Preble County News,* March 20, 1913, and March 19, 1931; Heistand, *Preble County, Ohio,* pp. 252–54; Charles, *Service Clubs in American Society,* pp. 25–29.

47. *Camden Gazette,* October 3, 1881, March 2, 1899, July 6, 1899, and May 15, 1902; *History of Preble County, Ohio,* p. 194; *Preble County News,* April 30, 1903; Neff, "A History of Camden, Ohio," pp. 62–65.

48. Neff, "A History of Camden, Ohio," p. 58.

49. *Camden Gazette,* May 11, 1899, July 6, 1899, and August 17, 1899; *Preble County News,* December 8, 1904, and December 23, 1915; Neff, "A History of Camden, Ohio," pp. 59–61.

50. See the final edition of the *Camden Gazette,* November 7, 1879, for Hartpence's angry denunciation of the local community for its failure to support his newspaper. Neff, "A History of Camden, Ohio," pp. 67–68.

51. Sinclair, *The Available Man,* p. 1.

52. *Camden Gazette,* October 11, 1900.

53. Ibid., October 15, 22, and 29, 1896; Neff, "A History of Camden, Ohio," pp. 95–96.

54. *Camden Gazette,* November 5, 1896.

55. Ibid., October 7 and 21, 1902. See Camden Archives for several pictures of this event.

Chapter 2. Winesburg: Life along Main Street

1. Klein, *The Flowering of the Third America,* p. 196.

2. Ibid.

3. Frymer, "Wal-Mart Hammered by Small Town Values"; Roberts, "Yes, A Small Town Is Different"; Kunstler, "They Came, They Conquered, They Closed"; Goodman, "Sturbridge Folk vs. Wal-Mart."

4. Weibe, *The Search for Order, 1877–1920*, pp. 2–3, 44–52.

5. Atherton, *Main Street on the Middle Border*, pp. 3–108; Lingeman, *Small Town America*, pp. 258–320.

6. Love, *The Situation in Flushing*, p. 102.

7. Welter, "The Cult of True Womanhood, 1820–1860."

8. Atherton, *Main Street on the Middle Border*, pp. 65–88.

9. Ibid., pp 1–88.

10. Ibid., p. 355.

11. Anderson, *Winesburg, Ohio*, pp. 136–37.

12. Garland, *Daughter of the Middle Border*, pp. 14–15; Atherton, *Main Street on the Middle Border*, p. 184; Anderson, *Winesburg, Ohio*, pp. 190–201.

13. Atherton, *Main Street on the Middle Border*, pp. 186–89, 255–59; P. Smith, *As a City upon a Hill*, pp. 157–58.

14. Atherton, *Main Street on the Middle Border*, pp. 173–74, 189–90; McClure, "The Masonic Order."

15. Glenway Wescott, quoted in Rifkind, *Main Street*, p. 187.

16. Rifkind, *Main Street*, pp. 194–95; Atherton, *Main Street on the Middle Border*, pp. 147–48.

17. Cather, *My Ántonia*, pp. 94, 111.

18. Lewis, *Main Street*, p. 37.

19. Ibid., p. 41.

20. Schorer, *Sinclair Lewis*, p. 5.

21. Lingeman, *Small Town America*, pp. 241–42, 280–86.

22. Eikenberry, "My Life and Times." Copy in the possession of the author.

23. Lingeman, *Small Town America*, pp. 291–92; Eikenberry, "My Life and Times."

24. Glaab and Brown, *A History of Urban America*, pp. 6–9; Wade, *The Urban Frontier*, pp. 27–29; Reps, *The Making of Urban America*, pp. 32–34.

25. Atherton, *Main Street on the Middle Border*, pp. 33–41; Lingeman, *Main Street America*, pp. 263–65.

26. Schorer, *Sinclair Lewis*, p. 7; Flink, *America Adopts the Automobile, 1895–1910*, pp. 104–12, 202–13, 216–25; Rae, *The American Automobile*, pp. 29–32, 92–95; Atherton, *Main Street on the Middle Border*, pp. 237–40.

27. Atherton, *Main Street on the Middle Border*, pp. 321–22.

28. Stowe, *Oldtown Folks*, pp. 1–2.

29. See P. Smith, *As a City upon a Hill*, pp. 258–83, for a thoughtful examination of novelists' treatments of the nineteenth-century town.

30. Veblen, "The Country Town."

31. Quoted in Webb, *The Great Plains*, p. 473.

32. Cather, *My Ántonia*, pp. 93 ff.; Anderson, *Poor White*, pp. 178–357; Masters quoted in Smith, *As a City upon a Hill*, p. 264.

33. Schorer, *Sinclair Lewis*, pp. 267–307.

34. Quoted in ibid., p. 272.

35. Lewis, *Babbitt;* Schorer, *Sinclair Lewis*, pp. 308–42.

Chapter 3. Camden: The Halcyon Days of the 1920s

1. The Camden Archives contain data, much of it newspaper clippings, about each enterprise in the community that lasted long enough to achieve local acceptance. For Bryson's drugstore, see *Preble County News,* May 14, 1925, April 12, 1928, and August 22, 1929.

2. See postcard picture of Town Hall, 1900, Camden Archives; *Preble County News,* May 22, 1902, September 10, 1903, September 15, 1905, March 20, 1913, March 24, 1927, and January 19, 1933; Mayor O. T. Taylor to State Department of Building Inspection, December 2, 1929, Camden Archives; Ruthayn Dearth, "Camden City Hall and Opera House," Camden Archives.

3. *Preble County News,* January 15, and May 14, 1931. In 1937 Van Skiver was convicted on a new charge of cashing fraudulent checks. This time he was sentenced to three years in the state penitentiary. *Preble County News,* January 28, 1937; Neff, "A History of Camden, Ohio," p. 67.

4. *Preble County News,* April 6, 1916, May 15, 1919, August 17, 1933, April 3, 1952, November 15, 1956; Heistand, *Preble County, Ohio,* p. 266.

5. *Preble County News,* November 30, 1911, May 14, 1914, May 5, 1927, and September 28, 1928.

6. Ibid., May 20, 1909, July 25, 1912, August 10, 1916; Neff, "A History of Camden, Ohio," pp. 149–52.

7. *Preble County News,* n.d., William Matt file, Camden Archives. It is interesting that this same advertisement was used by pioneer automobile dealer Robert Duvall in 1919 to urge purchase of the Overland automobile, which he was then selling. Duvall file, Camden Archives.

8. *Preble County News,* August 8, 1929.

9. Bailey file, Camden Archives.

10. See the large Eikenberry file, Camden Archives; and Eikenberry, "My Life and Times."

11. Eikenberry file, Camden Archives. See also *Preble County News,* July 18, 1918, June 16, 1921, August 2, 1928, November 15, 1934.

12. *Preble County News,* January 13, March 2, April 6, and June 8, 1916; January 4, 1917, January 9, 1947.

13. Ibid., January 13, 1916.

14. Ibid., May 9, and November 14, 1918.

15. Ibid., October 25, 1923, July 3, 1925, August 25, 1932, and August 18, 1933.

16. Dearth, "Camden Town Hall and Opera House."

17. Neff, "A History of Camden, Ohio," pp. 208–9.

18. See Genevieve White, "Preble County During the Civil War," master's thesis, Miami University, 1944. White taught English and social studies in the local high school from 1938 until 1963, and her classes were filled with local lore about antislavery and underground railroad activities, much of it drawn from her thesis research.

19. *Preble County News,* September 14 and 21, 1921.

20. Ibid., September 15, and November 8, 1921; Michael Simpson, to author, June 19, 1995.

21. *Preble County News,* November 8, 1923. See also Moore, *Citizen Klansmen;* Jackson, *The Ku Klux Klan in the Cities, 1915-1930.*

22. *Preble County News,* July 24, 1924, and July 30, 1925.

23. Belcher, "History of Camden's Nine Churches."

24. The Camden Archives contain extensive data on each of Camden's churches. See also Belcher, "History of Camden's Nine Churches."

25. P. Smith, *As a City upon a Hill,* p. 123.

26. Camden Village Council Minutes, May 17, 1926; *Preble County News,* July 12, 1926, and August 25, 1930.

27. *Preble County News,* July 12, 1926.

28. See Camden Archives for extensive data about the Camden Volunteer Fire Department.

29. *Preble County News,* May 28, 1903.

30. Ibid., April 10, 1913, and May 7, 1914; see August 24, 1942, for an article on Dr. Combs. Neff, "A History of Camden, Ohio," pp. 149-52, provides a brief overview of the automobile in the early twentieth century.

31. *Preble County News,* August 23, 1903.

32. Ibid., July 10, 1930.

33. Ibid., May 14, 1931. Pottenger refused to drive ever again and never purchased another automobile. He only reluctantly, and very nervously, entered an automobile to travel to out-of-town engagements with his band. For the next thirty years, he was a familiar figure as he walked throughout town to give piano lessons and do his errands.

34. *Preble County News,* March 26, 1931.

35. Village Council Minutes, March 13, 1933.

36. Rae, *The American Automobile,* pp. 87-88, 93-94; and Flink, *America Adopts the Automobile,* pp. 166-74, 203-13.

37. *Preble County News,* September 27, 1928.

38. Ibid., March 4, 1926.

39. Lynd and Lynd, *Middletown,* pp. 251-63.

40. Blumenthal, *Small Town Stuff,* p. 384.

41. *Preble County News,* July 10, 1930.

42. Ibid., March 26, 1931.

43. Ibid., August 7, 1930.

44. Ivan Greenfill, to author, October 1, 1994.

45. Quotation taken from a 1927 article in the *Richmond Palladium-Item,* reprinted in a *Palladium-Item* article of January 13, 1979, clipping in General Folder #2, Camden Archives.

46. Rifkind, *Main Street,* p. 213.

Chapter 4. Depression: "The Worst of Times"

1. *Preble County News,* July 2, 1931.

2. Ibid., December 7, 1933; Schlesinger, *The Crisis of the Old Order, 1919-1933,* pp. 174-75; *Preble County News,* November 26, 1931, and March 10, 1932.

3. Quoted in Schlesinger, *The Crisis of the Old Order,* p. 175. The *Preble County News,* July 8, 1937, reported that the average size of property taken by financial institutions averaged $2,509 in value.

4. *Preble County News,* January 28, and March 31, 1932; March 9, and July 6, 1933; and November 15, 1934.

5. Joseph Barnet, to author, October 1994; *Preble County News,* March 31, 1932, January 26, 1933.

6. *Preble County News,* November 30, 1933, and March 1, 1934.

7. Ibid., March 19, 1931.

8. See the Camden Archives for a large collection of materials related to everyday life in the 1930s. Also, I am especially indebted to the following individuals for sharing their memories with me: Edith DeCamp, Marion DeCamp, Julia Deem, and Ivan Greenfill.

9. Robert Davies, comment to author, June 1981.

10. *Preble County News,* March 31, 1932, and April 13, 1933.

11. Ibid., July 31, 1930, and August 14, 1930.

12. Ibid., January 21, 1932, July 23, 1931, and July 14, 1932.

13. Lynd and Lynd, *Middletown in Transition,* pp. 266–67.

14. Dale Major, to author, October 1994.

15. Helen Yochum Hamilton, to author, October 1994.

16. *Preble County News,* May 31, 1934; Ivan Greenfill, to author, October 1994.

17. Sue Silvers Knicker, to author, November 1994.

18. Nash, *The Crucial Era,* pp. 104–5.

19. *Preble County News,* November 29, 1934, and March 28, 1935.

20. Ibid., December 22, 1932; April 6, and December 7, 1933; Withers, *Plainville, U.S.A.,* p. 83. Some speculation later developed about the reasons why this group of men did not affiliate with a recognized international service club, such as Kiwanis. Veteran club members recalled that the group moved so rapidly that they did not want to bother with the necessary protocol for establishing an affiliation, and that they did not want to comply with rules established externally or to share any revenues with an outside organization. Herschel Brown, interview, June 3, 1994.

21. *Preble County News,* January 19, February 23, March 9, and June 15, 1933; Dearth, "Camden City Hall and Opera House," p. 6.

22. *Preble County News,* January 19, March 9, March 30, and April 6, 1933; Dearth, "Camden Town Hall and Opera House," p. 6.

23. See Progressive Club files, Camden Archives; *Preble County News,* January 17, 1935; January 6, and February 6, 1936; *Eaton Register-Herald,* March 8, 1950.

24. *Preble County News,* July 13, August 3, and August 18, 1933.

25. For example, James Neff, to author, November 1994.

26. James Barnet, to author, November 1994.

27. *Preble County News,* December 7, 1933; see also Progressive Club Files, Camden Archives.

28. Herschel Brown, interview, June 16, 1994. Brown served on the fund's board from 1935 until it disbanded in 1986. Minute Book of Camden Relief Fund, Camden Archives.

29. *Preble County News,* March 23, 1933.

30. Ibid., March 12, 1931.

31. France B. Berger, to author, October 1994.

32. Quotations from Schlesinger, *Crisis of the Old Order,* p. 3.

33. Ibid., pp. 7–8. The view of the New Deal from Camden was typical of small towns everywhere; see, e.g., Stock, *Main Street in Crisis,* pp. 86–127, for a discussion of similar ambivalence of small-town residents in North and South Dakota; and Adams, *The Transformation of Rural Life,* pp. 144–61, on the towns of southern Illinois.

34. *Preble County News,* March 9, and March 16, 1933; January 10, 1935.

35. See Schlesinger, *The Coming of the New Deal,* pp. 87–135, for a sprightly account of the short-lived National Recovery Administration.

36. *Preble County News,* August 31, 1933.

37. Ibid., August 10, 1933.

38. Ibid., August 31, 1934.

39. Schlesinger, *Coming of the New Deal,* p. 118.

40. *Preble County News,* June 6, and August 29, 1935.

41. Ibid., November 23, and December 7, 1933.

42. The literature on the New Deal farm program has attracted a large number of scholars. For example, see Kirkendall, *Social Scientists and Farm Politics in the Age of Roosevelt;* Schlesinger, *The Coming of the New Deal,* pp. 27–84; Fite, *George N. Peek and the Fight for Farm Parity;* and Rowley, *M. L. Wilson and the Campaign for the Domestic Allotment.*

43. Schlesinger, *The Coming of the New Deal,* pp. 62–63.

44. Stock, *Main Street in Crisis,* p. 87.

45. *Preble County News,* February 18, 1934.

46. Harry Neff, letter to village council, Village Council Minutes, September 26, 1933; see also Village Council Minutes, September 6, 1933.

47. *Preble County News,* September 14, 1933, and September 20, 1934.

48. Ibid., July 13, 1933, and October 31, 1936.

49. Ibid., October 31, 1936.

50. Ibid., November 7, 1936.

51. Ibid., November 14, 1936.

52. Ibid.

53. Board of Public Affairs, minutes, April 1936.

54. *Preble County News,* April 17, 1941.

55. Ibid., December 15, 1904.

56. Ibid., February 2, February 23, and March 16, 1905.

57. Ibid., December 22, 1910, March 2, 1916, October 25, 1917, February 17, 1921. See Camden Archives, basketball file, for picture of 1915–16 team.

58. Despite its limited personnel, the high school did field a football team—sporadically—from 1915 until 1925. The Camden Archives contains a picture of the 1916 team, which had a 2–3 record. The picture indicates that the team comprised a starting eleven, one substitute, and a manager. In its victory over College Corner in 1917, the team scored 26 points and, as the newspaper reported, would have scored more "if the coach had been there to help the team, he being in Cincinnati." *Preble County News,* November 1, 1917.

59. *Preble County News,* October 28, 1937; January 5, and March 9, 1939; and February 29, 1940. Robert Davies, comments to author, June 1981; Sue Silvers Knicker, to author, November 1994. No mention of the brawl appeared on the

decorous pages of the *Preble County News,* although the fight and the dousing of the lights remain a living part of the memory of many residents. Recollections have grown hazy with the passage of time: some recall the opposition as Germantown, but the consensus seems to be West Elkton. The date remains in question, but it was apparently in 1945, or perhaps a year or two earlier. By this time, I wouldn't place a large bet on the actual date or opponent, but I can recall my father telling and retelling the humorous story many times—and the emphasis was always on the dousing of the lights.

60. *Preble County News,* January 13, 1938.

61. *Camden Gazette,* September 13, 1894.

62. *Preble County News,* August 29, 1935.

63. *Preble County News,* March 31, 1932, September 14, 1933; January 10, May 9, June 6, and August 29, 1935.

64. Ibid., January 13, 1938.

Chapter 5. War: "Camden Behind the Men Behind the Guns"

1. *Preble County News,* March 5, 1931.

2. Ibid.

3. Ibid.

4. Ibid., May 23, 1940. Among those individuals contributing to the population increase reported in the 1940 census is the author of this book, born October 26, 1937, an event that was duly reported in the *Preble County News,* October 28, 1937.

5. See Patterson, *Mr. Republican,* pp. 160–79; and Davies, *Defender of the Old Guard,* pp. 29–47.

6. *Preble County News,* January 16, 1936, and October 28, 1937.

7. Ibid., January 16, and October 29, 1936; July 15, and September 7, 1937.

8. Ibid., November 20, 1941.

9. Elois Johnson, to author, November 1994.

10. Donald Shields, to author, November 1994.

11. Jacquelyn Overholser Sylvia, to author, November 1994.

12. Donald Shields, to author, November 1994; Elois Johnson, to author, November 1994. For a detailed examination of small-town values during this era, see Withers, *Plainville, U.S.A,* pp. 107–14; and Lynd and Lynd, *Middletown in Transition,* pp. 112–15.

13. In responses to the large questionnaire sent by the author to all Camden High School graduates from 1930 to 1960, more than 150 graduates answered with almost total unanimity to questions regarding sexual mores. More than 98 percent "disagreed strongly" with the statement, "When I was in high school pre-marital sex was accepted as 'the thing to do.'"

14. *Preble County News,* July 5, 1930.

15. Anti-interventionist sentiment is strongly indicated in the responses to the questionnaire from Camden High School graduates from the 1930s and 1940s. See cartoon in *Preble County News,* March 24, 1940.

16. *Preble County News,* December 7, 1940.

17. Ibid., May 29, 1941.

18. Ibid., May 1, July 19, and November 13, 1941.

19. Ambrose, *D-Day, June 6, 1944*, p. 26.

20. *Preble County News*, March 5, 1942.

21. Ibid., July 23, 1942, and June 1, 1944.

22. Ibid., November 25, December 2, December 9, and December 30, 1943; and January 20, 1944.

23. Even something as ordinary as a 100-pound cement practice bomb can have an interesting history. Some of the unused cement practice bombs became part of the permanent postwar Camden landscape: among other ingenious things, they were painted and placed as decorations in flower beds or alongside driveways, employed as short (if squat) decorative fence posts, and used to keep old gates shut. Some of these bombs contributed to the near demise of a small Nebraska town. One night in December of 1943, pilots in training mistook a few lights left on in Dickens, Nebraska, for a lighted bombing range some fifteen miles distant. Several cement bombs did some damage, but fortunately no one was injured. "We had three street lights in town then, in sort of a triangle," a survivor recalled. "I guess they looked like the lights at the bombing range. So we got bombed. They even made two passes at us, to make sure they got everything. Trouble was they missed everything but the lumber yard and the water tower." *A Century of Memories, Dickens, Nebraska, 1889–1989*, p. 520. For a summary of the history of the J. H. Gwynne Company, see minutes of Philomathean Club, February 6, 1968, Camden Archives.

24. *Preble County News*, April 9, 1942; April 29, and July 29, 1943.

25. Baritz, *The Good Life*, pp. 176–78.

26. For example, see *Preble County News*, July 27, 1944.

27. Ibid., September 17, 1942.

28. Ibid., December 18, 1941.

29. Ibid., August 27, and October 8, 1942.

30. Ibid., August 17, 1942.

31. Ibid., January 14, 1943.

32. Ibid., October 29, 1942; January 14, March 21, April 29, and May 27, 1943.

33. Ibid., October 29, 1942, and January 14, 1943.

34. *Preble County News*, January 14, and March 14, 1943.

35. Ibid., July 29, 1943.

36. Ibid., July 1, 1943.

37. Ibid, July 1, 1943, and March 9, 1944.

38. Ibid., June 8, 1944.

39. Ibid., June 8, and June 15, 1944.

40. Ibid., July 27, and August 17, 1944; February 1, 1945; "Service Record, World War I and II, Camden and Vicinity."

41. "Service Record, World War I and II"; *Dayton Daily News*, May 23, 1965; *Hamilton Journal News*, February 10, 1985; *Preble County News*, January 27, and March 22, 1945. See Ross, *Iwo Jima*; Newcomb, *Iwo Jima*; and Leckie, *The Battle for Iwo Jima*.

42. *Dayton Daily News*, May 23, 1965.

43. *Hamilton Journal News*, February 10, 1985.

44. *Preble County News*, August 16, 1945.

45. Ibid., May 24, 1945.

46. Ibid., August 9, August 23, and September 6, 1945.

47. Ibid., August 9, 1945.

48. Ibid., May 17, 1945.

Chapter 6. The Last Picture Show

1. The body of literature detailing the important expansion of metropolitan America, including suburbanization, is both large and rewarding. Among the many excellent studies are Jackson, *The Crabgrass Frontier;* Gottmann, *Megalopolis;* Halberstam, *The Fifties,* pp. 131–79; and Gans, *The Levittowners.*

2. This discussion is based upon observations by the author, but it is also supported by the responses to the questionnaire sent to high school graduates. More than a 20 percent response to the questionnaire—165 returned out of 595 mailed—demonstrates this phenomenon clearly.

3. *Preble County News,* December 20, 1945.

4. Humphrey's career pattern is quite typical of the returning veteran. He was drawn, as if by a magnet, to return to his hometown. After graduating from Ohio University in 1949 with a bachelor's degree in education, he taught and coached at Camden High School for two years. But once he compared pay scales and career potential, he moved to Conneaut, Ohio, where he taught social studies and physical education and coached championship baseball teams until his retirement in 1984. Stanley Humphrey, to author, November 1994.

5. Colladay, "The Passing of the American Village."

6. Ibid., p. 364.

7. Davies, *Housing Reform during the Truman Administration,* pp. 40–59.

8. The expected, and apparently willing, return of Camden women to their domestic roles was part of a national phenomenon. See Baritz, *The Good Life,* pp. 176–88; and Hartmann, *Home Front.*

9. *Preble County News,* September 20, 1945, and August 26, 1946.

10. Ibid., September 27, 1945.

11. *Preble County News,* July 18, 1946.

12. Gallaher, *Plainville Fifteen Years Later,* p. 56.

13. *Preble County News,* October 18, November 1, and November 8, 1945.

14. Ibid., September 5, 1946.

15. The other pitcher was Max DeCamp, whose career ended at the AA level with an injured arm. Elston was the only Camden native ever to make the "big leagues."

16. *Preble County News,* September 25, 1947.

17. Ibid., May 1, 1947.

18. Ibid., August 16, September 25, and October 23, 1947.

19. Ibid., December 25, 1947.

20. Ibid.

21. Ibid., April 29, 1948, and January 13, 1949.

22. I have re-created this episode from memory; the date is an educated guess, but the time of the year and the date are reasonably accurate based upon other oral histories and documents in the Camden Archives. In a retrospective essay that appeared on April 3, 1952, the *Preble County News* reported that "Smitty was

the first television expert in Preble County and opened the Camden Radio and Television Shop in March of 1948."

23. *Preble County News,* November 27, 1947, and September 1, 1949; see also December 8, 1949.

24. For a good overview of the impact of television on American society, see Halberstam, *The Fifties,* pp. 180–202; for the impact of television on sports, see Davies, *America's Obsession,* pp. 63–101.

25. Barnouw, *The Golden Web,* pp. 242–45, 283–303; Barnouw, *The Image Empire,* pp. 5–8, 65–84.

26. *Preble County News,* May 15, 1952.

27. *Preble County News,* November 3, 1950, April 19, 1951, and May 15, 1952; Halberstam, *The Fifties,* p. 185; McMurtry, *The Last Picture Show,* pp. 291–92.

28. *Preble County News,* September 2, 1937; O'Neill, *American High,* pp. 136–39.

29. *Preble County News,* June 29, 1950.

30. Ibid., August 25, 1949.

31. This perception is strongly identified by more than fifty graduates of the high school from the years 1950–60 in a questionnaire conducted by the author.

32. Suprisingly, there is little in the historical literature regarding the phenomenon of town baseball. Atherton, *Main Street on the Middle Border,* pp. 200–202, 318–19, talks of its importance to town morale; see also Amato, *The Decline of Rural Minnesota,* pp. 52–54.

33. *Preble County News,* November 1, 1951.

34. Ibid., November 8, 1951, November 4, 1952, and March 20, 1955.

35. These observations are based on the author's memory, the general tenor of reports and advertisements in the *Preble County News,* and questionnaires distributed to high school graduates. For comparable studies that report the same phenomenon, see Gallaher, *Plainville Fifteen Years Later,* pp. 17, 25; Vidich and Bensman, *Small Town in Mass Society,* pp. 299–30. Although published in 1954, Atherton's *Main Street on the Middle Border,* pp. 222–29, 348–52, perceptively identified this trend.

36. *Preble County News,* February 22, 1951. The perceptions in these two paragraphs are also based on my own memories, especially of conversations regarding teenage behavior with my father, who was superintendent of the local schools from 1946 until 1955. For a detailed analysis of a similar social phenomenon occurring at the same time in Missouri, see Gallaher, *Plainville Fifteen Years Later,* pp. 10–167.

37. *Preble County News,* December 7, 1950, and December 6, 1951.

38. Ibid., December 21, 1950.

39. Ibid., November 22, 1951. I myself was a member, however briefly, of this cold war defense system.

40. Ibid., April 27, and August 25, 1950; February 22, 1951.

41. Ibid., October 18, 1951.

42. Ibid., February 8, 1951.

43. "A Business of My Own," reprinted in ibid., February 2, 1946; January 5, 1950, April 3, 1952. "Camden's Foremost and Oldest Industry," *Forward Magazine,* December 1950.

44. *Preble County News,* January 9, 1947, and February 18, 1950.

45. Julia Deem, long-time secretary of the board of directors of Neff and Fry Company, to author, February 24, 1995.

46. Ibid.

47. *Preble County News,* February 12, 1953.

48. Ibid., November 18, 1948, and December 7, 1950.

49. Ibid., December 6, 1951.

Chapter 7. Main Street in Repose

1. *Preble County News,* November 3, 1955.

2. Ibid., April 17, 1952.

3. Ibid., August 23, 1956, and March 21, 1957.

4. Ibid., August 23, 1956, and March 21, 1957.

5. Ibid., December 31, 1957. For a concise discussion of the movement to build the Interstate and Defense Highway System, see Davies, *The Age of Asphalt,* pp. 13–18.

6. *Preble County News,* October 30, 1958.

7. *Dayton Daily News,* May 15, 1960; *Preble County News,* May 5, 1960.

8. *Dayton Daily News,* May 15, 1961; *Preble County News,* May 5, May 12, August 18, and December 15, 1960; July 19, and September 6, 1962. A last-ditch effort to reverse the decision in 1967 was unsuccessful. *Preble County News,* July 27, 1967.

9. *Preble County News,* November 17, 1955.

10. *Dayton Daily News,* October 10, 1982.

11. Ibid., March 23, 1958.

12. *Preble County News,* March 23, 1958. See also *Dayton Daily News,* July 16, 1959.

13. *Eaton Register-Herald,* March 8, 1950. See also *Dayton Daily News,* July 22, 1950, which reported on the positive economic environment its reporter found in Camden.

14. *Dayton Daily News,* September 8, 1961.

15. *Preble County News,* January 14, 1960; *Hamilton Journal,* October 7, 1973; *Preble County News,* May 8, 1980.

16. *Preble County News,* July 27, 1961.

17. Ibid., January 30, 1969, April 30, 1970.

18. Ibid., November 10, 1960.

19. Ibid., throughout 1971.

20. *Dayton Daily News,* October 18, 1985.

21. *Dayton Journal Herald,* September 11, 1972.

22. Ibid.; *Richmond Palladium-Item,* January 13, 1979. Camden's unsightly appearance was not unusual. In his study of small towns in Nebraska during the 1950s, the sociologist Otto G. Hoiberg criticized them for their run-down appearance. *Exploring the Small Town,* pp. 176–83.

23. *Eaton Register-Herald,* June 8, 1995.

24. *Richmond Palladium-Item,* December 20, 1955; *Dayton Daily News,* November 7, 1965, and April 3, 1975; *Preble County News,* August 18, 1966.

25. *Richmond Palladium-Item,* March 3, 1993.

26. *Preble County News,* December 7, 1972.

27. Ibid., August 1, 1980, and April 8, 1982.

28. Ibid., April 22, 1971.

29. Ibid., February 2, 1990.

30. Ibid., and February 9, 1990; *Middletown Journal,* June 21, 1991; *Dayton Daily News,* April 1, 1992; *Eaton Register-Herald,* July 28, 1993.

31. *Richmond Palladium-Item,* August 22, 1994.

32. *Dayton Journal Herald,* September 10, 11, and 12, 1972.

33. *Middletown Journal,* March 31, 1985.

34. *Preble County News,* June 10 and 17, 1988; Heistand, *Preble County, Ohio,* pp. 250–54.

35. Amato, *The Decline of Rural Minnesota,* p. 50.

36. *Preble County News,* November 21, 1985, January 9, 1986; May 4, and August 8, 1990; August 29, and October 31, 1991.

37. Herschel Brown, interview, June 6, 1994.

Epilogue. Camden: The Town We Left Behind

1. Comments to author by a random number of respondents to 1994 questionnaire and 1995 interviews.

2. Jerry Wood, comments to author, June 15, 1995.

3. Jack White, to author, November 1994.

4. Vance and Scott, "Sam Walton and Wal-Mart Stores, Inc.: A Study in Modern Southern Entrepreneurship." For a sampling of the anti-Wal-Mart sentiment, see Ellen Goodman, "Sturbridge Folk vs. Wal-Mart"; Kuntsler, "They Came, They Conquered, They Closed"; and Frymer, "Wal-Mart Hammered by Small Town Values."

5. Francaviglia, *Main Street Revisited,* p. 188.

6. Stock, *Main Street in Crisis.*

7. These comments are based on the my visits to these—and several other—communities during the spring of 1995. I am indebted to area residents for sharing with me both information and their personal views. I am especially appreciative of the assistance of librarians who made local materials, including newspapers and histories, available. Newspaper editors Randy Murphey of the *Elkton Banner* and Dewaine Gahan of the *Oakland Independent* were very helpful, and I am equally indebted to a lifelong friend and Camden native, Michael Simpson, who lives in Rising Sun and, like many Rising Sun residents, became an employee of the Hyatt Corporation.

8. Larry B. Russell, superintendent of Preble Shawnee Local Schools, to author, August 21, 1995; *New York Times,* August 27, 1995.

9. Stock, *Main Street in Crisis,* pp. 210–11.

Bibliography

Books

Aaron, Daniel. *Cincinnati: Queen City of the West, 1819–1838*. Columbus: Ohio State University Press, 1992.

Adams, Jane. *The Transformation of Rural Life: Southern Illinois, 1890–1990*. Chapel Hill: University of North Carolina Press, 1994.

Amato, Joseph, with John W. Meyer. *The Decline of Rural Minnesota*. Marshall, Minn.: Crossing Press, 1993.

Ambrose, Stephen E. *D-Day, June 6, 1944: The Climactic Battle of World War II*. New York: Simon & Schuster, 1994.

Anderson, David D. *Critical Essays on Sherwood Anderson*. Boston: G. K. Hall, 1981.

Anderson, Martin. *The Federal Bulldozer*. Cambridge, Mass.: MIT Press, 1964.

Anderson, Sherwood. *Hello Towns!* New York: Horace Liveright, 1929.

———. *Home Town*. New York: Alliance Book Corporation, 1940.

———. *Poor White*. New York: B. W. Huebsch, 1920.

———. *Sherwood Anderson's Memoirs*. New York: Harcourt, Brace, 1942. *A Critical Edition*. Edited by Ray Lewis White. Chapel Hill: University of North Carolina Press, 1969.

———. *Tar: A Midwest Childhood*. 1926. *A Critical Edition*. Edited by Ray Lewis White. Cleveland: The Press of Western Reserve University, 1969.

———. *Winesburg, Ohio*. 1919. With an introduction by Malcolm Cowley. New York: Penguin Books, 1987.

Atherton, Lewis E. *Main Street on the Middle Border*. Bloomington: Indiana University Press, 1954.

Baritz, Loren. *The Good Life: The Meaning of Success for the American Middle Class*. New York: Harper & Row, 1982.

Barnouw, Eric. *The Golden Web*. Vol. 2 of *A History of Broadcasting in the United States*. New York: Oxford University Press, 1968.

———. *The Image Empire*. Vol. 3 of *A History of Broadcasting in the United States*. New York: Oxford University Press, 1970.

Bender, Thomas. *Community and Social Change in America.* New Brunswick, N.J.: Rutgers University Press, 1978.

Berger, Michael L. *The Devil Wagon in God's Country: The Automobile and Social Change in Rural America, 1893–1929.* Hamden, Conn.: Archon Books, 1970.

Bertrens, Hans, and Theo D'Haen, eds. *The Small Town in America: A Multidisciplinary Revisit.* Amsterdam: VU University Press, 1995.

Blumenthal, Albert. *Small Town Stuff.* Chicago: University of Chicago Press, 1932.

Bond, Beverley W. *The Foundations of Ohio.* Columbus: Ohio State Archaeological and Historical Society, 1941.

Burbank, Rex. *Sherwood Anderson.* New York: Twayne Publishers, 1964.

Cather, Willa. *My Ántonia.* Boston: Houghton Mifflin, 1918, 1988.

Cayton, Andrew R. L., and Peter S. Onuf. *The Midwest and the Nation: Rethinking the History of an American Region.* Bloomington: Indiana University Press, 1990.

Census of 1850 for Preble County, Ohio. Mansfield, Ohio: Ohio Genealogical Society, 1974. Copy available at Ohio Historical Society.

A Century of Memories, Dickens, Nebraska, 1889–1989. Dickens, Nebraska, 1989.

Charles, Jeffrey. *Service Clubs in American Society: Rotary, Kiwanis, and Lions.* Urbana: University of Illinois Press, 1993.

Cronon, William. *Nature's Metropolis: Chicago and the Great West.* New York: W. W. Norton, 1991.

Davidson, Osha. *Broken Heartland: Rise of America's Rural Ghetto.* New York: Free Press, 1990.

Davies, Richard O. *The Age of Asphalt: The Automobile, the Freeway, and the Condition of Urban America.* Philadelphia: Lippincott, 1975.

———. *America's Obsession: Sports and Society since 1945.* New York: Harcourt Brace, 1994.

———. *Defender of the Old Guard: John Bricker and American Politics.* Columbus: Ohio State University Press, 1993.

———. *Housing Reform during the Truman Administration.* Columbia: University of Missouri Press, 1966.

Dumenil, Lynn. *Freemasonry and American Culture, 1880–1930.* Princeton: Princeton University Press, 1984.

Editors of *Fortune. The Exploding Metropolis.* Garden City, N.Y.: Doubleday, 1959.

Eliot, Marc. *Walt Disney: Hollywood's Dark Prince.* New York: Birch Lane Press, 1993.

Faragher, John Mack. *Sugar Creek: Life on the Illinois Prairie.* New Haven: Yale University Press, 1986.

Findlay, John M. *Magic Lands: Western Cityscapes and American Culture after 1940.* Berkeley and Los Angeles: University of California Press, 1992.

Fite, Gilbert. *American Farmers: The New Minority.* Bloomington: Indiana University Press, 1981.

———. *George N. Peek and the Fight for Farm Parity.* Norman: University of Oklahoma Press, 1954.

Flink, James, *America Adopts the Automobile, 1895–1910.* Cambridge, Mass.: MIT Press, 1970.

———. *The Car Culture.* Cambridge, Mass.: MIT Press, 1975.

Francaviglia, Richard V. *Main Street Revisited: Time, Space, and Image Building in Small-Town America.* Iowa City: University of Iowa Press, 1996.

Gale, Zona. *Friendship Village Love Stories.* New York: Macmillan, 1908.

———. *Miss Lulu Betts.* New York: Macmillan, 1920.

Gallaher, Art. *Plainville Fifteen Years Later.* New York: Columbia University Press, 1961.

Gans, Herbert J. *The Levittowners: Ways of Life and Politics in a New Suburban Community.* New York: Pantheon Books, 1967.

Garland, Hamlin. *Daughter of the Middle Border.* New York: Harper, 1921.

———. *Main-Travelled Roads.* New York: Harper, 1891.

———. *Son of the Middle Border.* New York: Harper, 1917.

Glaab, Charles, and A. Theodore Brown. *A History of Urban America.* New York: Macmillan, 1967.

Gottmann, Jean. *Megalopolis: The Urbanized Northeastern Seaboard of the United States.* New York: Twentieth Century Fund, 1961.

Hahn, Steven, and Jonathan Prude, eds. *The Countryside in the Age of Capitalist Transformation: Essays in the Social History of Rural America.* Chapel Hill: University of North Carolina Press, 1985.

Halberstam, David. *The Fifties.* New York: Villard Books, 1993.

Harper, Arthur R. *The Making of Ohio.* Columbus: Ohio State University Press, 1948.

Hartmann, Susan. *The Home Front: American Women in the 1940s.* Boston: Twayne Publishers, 1982.

Hearn, Charles. *The American Dream in the Great Depression.* Westport, Conn.: Greenwood Press, 1977.

Heat-Moon, William Least. *Blue Highways: A Journey into America.* Boston: Little, Brown, 1982.

Heistand, Ione Sell, ed. *Preble County, Ohio.* Eaton, Ohio: Preble County Historical Society, 1992.

Herron, Ima. *The Small Town in American Literature.* Durham, N.C.: Duke University Press, 1939.

History of Preble County, Ohio, with Illustrations and Biographical Sketches. Cleveland: H. Z. Williams, 1881.

Hoiberg, Otto. *Exploring the Small Town.* Lincoln: University of Nebraska Press, 1955.

Howe, Irving. *Sherwood Anderson.* New York: William Sloane Associates, 1951.

Hudson, John. *Plains Country Towns.* Minneapolis: University of Minnesota Press, 1985.

Hurt, R. Douglas. *The Ohio Frontier: Crucible of the Old Northwest, 1720–1830.* Bloomington: Indiana University Press, 1996.

Jackson, Kenneth. *The Crabgrass Frontier: The Suburbanization of the United States.* New York: Oxford University Press, 1985.

———. *The Ku Klux Klan in the City, 1915–1930.* New York: Oxford University Press, 1967.

Jacobs, Jane. *The Death and Life of Great Cities.* New York: Random House, 1963.

Jordan, Philip D. *Ohio Comes of Age, 1873–1900.* Columbus: Ohio State Archaeological and Historical Society, 1943.

Keats, John. *The Crack in the Picture Window.* Boston: Houghton Mifflin, 1956.

Keillor, Garrison. *Lake Wobegon Days.* New York: Penguin Books, 1985.

Kirkendall, Richard S. *Social Scientists and Farm Politics in the Age of Roosevelt.* Columbia: University of Missouri Press, 1966.

———, ed. *The Harry S. Truman Encyclopedia.* Boston: G. K. Hall, 1989.

Klein, Maury. *The Flowering of the Third America: The Making of an Organizational Society, 1850–1920.* Chicago: Ivan R. Dee, 1993.

Knepper, George. *Ohio and Its People.* Kent, Ohio: Kent State University Press, 1989.

Kuralt, Charles. *On the Road with Charles Kuralt.* New York: Fawcett, 1985.

Lebhar, Godfrey. *The Chain Store in America, 1859–1959.* New York: Chain Store Publishing Company, 1959.

Leckie, William. *The Battle for Iwo Jima.* New York: Random House, 1967.

Lewis, Sinclair. *Babbitt.* 1922. New York: Signet Classics, 1980.

———. *Main Street.* 1920. New York: Signet Classics, 1980.

Lindley, Harlow. *Ohio in the Twentieth Century, 1900–1938.* Columbus: Ohio State Archaeological and Historical Society, 1942.

Lingeman, Richard. *Don't You Know There's a War Going On?* New York: G. P. Putnam's Sons, 1970.

———. *Small Town America.* New York: G. P. Putnam's Sons, 1980.

Love, E. G. *The Situation in Flushing.* New York: Harper & Row, 1963.

Lowery, R. E. *A History of Preble County, Ohio.* Indianapolis: B. F. Bowen, 1915.

Lyford, Joseph P. *The Talk in Vandalia.* Charlotte, N.C.: McNally and Loftin, 1962.

Lynd, Robert, and Helen Merrell Lynd. *Middletown: A Study in Modern American Culture.* New York: Harcourt, Brace, 1929.

———. *Middletown in Transition: A Study in Cultural Conflicts.* New York: Harcourt, Brace, 1937.

Martindale, Don, and R. Galen Hanson. *Small Town and the Nation: The Conflict of Local and Translocal Forces.* Westport, Conn.: Greenwood Press, 1969.

Masters, Edgar Lee. *Domesday Book.* New York: Macmillan, 1920.

———. *Spoon River Anthology.* New York: Macmillan, 1914.

McMurtry, Larry. *The Last Picture Show.* New York: Pocket Books, 1966.

Metalious, Grace. *Peyton Place.* New York: Dell Books, 1956.

Miller, Henry. *The Colossus of Maroussi.* New York: New Directions, 1941.

Moore, Leonard. *Citizen Klansmen: The Ku Klux Klan in Indiana, 1921–1928.* Chapel Hill: University of North Carolina Press, 1991.

Morgan, Arthur E. *The Small Community, Foundation of Democratic Life: What It Is and How to Achieve It.* New York: Harper, 1942.

Morgan, B. F. *Directory of Preble County, O.* Eaton: *Eaton Weekly Register* Power Press Printer, 1875.

Mosier, Richard D. *Making the American Mind: Social and Moral Ideas in the McGuffey Readers.* New York: King's Crown Press, Columbia University, 1947.

Nash, Gerald D. *The Crucial Era: The Great Depression and World War II, 1929–1945.* New York: St. Martin's Press, 1992.

Newcomb, Richard F. *Iwo Jima.* New York: Holt, Rinehart and Winston, 1965.

O'Neill, William L. *American High: The Years of Confidence, 1945–1960.* New York: Macmillan, 1986.

Patterson, James T. *Mr. Republican: A Biography of Robert A. Taft.* Boston: Houghton Mifflin, 1972.

Plowden, David. *Small Town America.* New York: Henry N. Adams, 1994.

Rae, John B. *The American Automobile: A Brief History.* Chicago: University of Chicago Press, 1965.

———. *The Road and the Car in American Life.* Cambridge, Mass.: MIT Press, 1971.

Reps, John W. *The Making of Urban America: A History of City Planning in the United States.* Princeton: Princeton University Press, 1965.

Rifkind, Carole. *Main Street: The Face of Urban America.* New York: Harper & Row, 1977.

Roseboom, Eugene H., and Francis P. Weisenburger. *A History of Ohio.* Columbus: Ohio Historical Society, 1976.

Ross, William. *Iwo Jima.* New York: Vanguard Press, 1985.

Rowley, William. *M. L. Wilson and the Campaign for the Domestic Allotment.* Lincoln: University of Nebraska Press, 1970.

Salamon, Sonya. *Prairie Patrimony: Family, Farming, and Community in the Midwest.* Chapel Hill: University of North Carolina Press, 1992.

Salisbury, Harrison. *The Shook-Up Generation.* Greenwich, Conn.: Fawcett Publications, 1958.

Santmyer, Helen. " . . . *And Ladies of the Club.*" Columbus: Ohio State University Press, 1982.

———. *Ohio Town.* Columbus: Ohio State University Press, 1962, 1998.

Schlesinger, Arthur M., Jr. *The Coming of the New Deal.* Vol. 2 of *The Age of Roosevelt.* Boston: Houghton Mifflin, 1958.

———. *The Crisis of the Old Order, 1919–1933.* Vol. 1 of *The Age of Roosevelt.* Boston: Houghton Mifflin, 1957.

Schorer, Mark. *Sinclair Lewis: An American Life.* New York: McGraw Hill, 1961.

Shaw, Ronald E. *Canals for a Nation: The Canal Era in the United States, 1790–1860.* Lexington: University of Kentucky Press, 1990.

Shortridge, James. *The Middle West: Its Meaning in American Culture.* Lawrence: University of Kansas Press, 1989.

Sinclair, Andrew. *The Available Man: The Life behind the Mask of Warren Gamaliel Harding.* New York: Macmillan, 1965.

Slotkin, Richard. *Fatal Environment: The Myth of the Frontier in the Age of Industrialization, 1800–1890.* New York: Atheneum, 1985.

Smith, Page. *As a City upon a Hill: The Town in American History.* New York: Alfred A. Knopf, 1966.

Smith, William E. *History of Southwestern Ohio: The Miami Valleys.* 2 vols. New York: Lewis Historical Publishing Company, 1964.

Snyder, Margaret. *The Chosen Valley: The Story of a Pioneer Town.* New York: W. W. Norton, 1948.

Steinbeck, John. *Travels with Charlie: In Search of America.* New York: Viking Press, 1962.

Sternsher, Bernard. *Hitting Home: The Great Depression in Town and Country.* Chicago: Quadrangle Books, 1970.

Stock, Catherine McNicol. *Main Street in Crisis: The Great Depression and the Old*

Middle Class on the Northern Plains. Chapel Hill: University of North Carolina Press, 1992.

Stowe, Harriet. *Oldtown Folks.* Boston: Fields and Osgood, 1869.

Taylor, George Rogers. *The Transportation Revolution, 1815–1860.* Armonk, N.Y.: M. E. Sharpe, 1951.

Taylor, Welford Dunaway. *Sherwood Anderson.* New York: Frederick Unger, 1977.

Thoreau, Henry David. *Walden; and, Resistance to Civil Government.* Edited by William Rossi. New York: W. W. Norton, 1992.

Townsend, Kim. *Sherwood Anderson.* Boston: Houghton Mifflin, 1987.

Trollope, Frances. *Domestic Manners of the Americans.* 1832. New York: Vintage, 1960.

Utter, William T. *The Frontier State, 1803–1825.* Columbus: Ohio State Archaeological and Historical Society, 1942.

Veblen, Thorstein. *The Portable Veblen.* Edited by Max Lerner. New York: Pocket Books, 1966.

Vidich, Arthur, and Joseph Bensman. *Reflections on Community Studies.* New York: John Wiley & Sons, 1964.

———. *Small Town in Mass Society: Class, Power, and Religion in a Rural Community.* Princeton: Princeton University Press, 1968.

Wade, Richard. *The Urban Frontier: The Rise of Western Cities, 1790–1830.* Cambridge, Mass.: Harvard University Press, 1959.

Webb, Walter Prescott. *The Great Plains.* Boston and New York: Ginn and Company, 1931.

Weibe, Robert. *The Search for Order, 1877–1920.* New York: Hill and Wang, 1967.

Weisenburger, Francis P. *The Passing of the Frontier.* Columbus: Ohio State Archaeological and Historical Society, 1941.

Wescott, Glenway. *Good-bye Wisconsin.* New York: Harper, 1928.

White, Ray Lewis. *The Achievement of Sherwood Anderson.* Chapel Hill: University of North Carolina Press, 1966.

———. *Winesburg, Ohio: An Exploration.* Boston: Twayne Company, 1990.

White, William Allen. *The Autobiography of William Allen White.* New York: Macmillan, 1946.

Whittlesey, Charles. *Geology of Ohio.* Cleveland: Fairbanks, Benedict, 1869.

Withers, Carl [James West, pseud.]. *Plainville, U.S.A.* New York: Columbia University Press, 1945.

Articles

"Are Small Towns Doomed?" *American Mercury,* May 1934, pp. 74–79.

Colladay, Morrison. "The Passing of the American Village." *Commonweal,* July 18, 1952, pp. 363–64.

Frymer, Murray. "Wal-Mart Hammered by Small Town Values." *Sacramento Bee,* October 15, 1994.

Goodman, Ellen, "Sturbridge Folk vs. Wal-Mart." *San Francisco Chronicle,* September 27, 1994.

Griswold, Robert. "Western Women and the Use of Domestic Ideology." In

Women: Their Land, Their Lives, edited by Lillian Schlissel, Vicki L. Ruiz, and Janice Monk, pp. 15–29. Albuquerque: University of New Mexico Press.

Heath, Thomas. "Parts of Nebraska Are Just Plain Deserted." *Washington Post National Weekly,* November 13, 1995, pp. 33–34.

Johnson, Dirk. "It's Not Hep to Stay." *New York Times,* September 5, 1994.

Jones, Robert Leslie. "The Introduction of Farm Machinery into Ohio Prior to 1865." *Ohio State Archeological and Historical Society Quarterly,* January 1949, pp. 1–20.

Kuntsler, Howard. "They Came, They Conquered, They Closed." *New York Times,* June 10, 1995.

McClure, Arthur F., III. "The Masonic Order." In *The Harry S. Truman Encyclopedia,* edited by Richard S. Kirkendall, pp. 234–35. Boston: G. K. Hall, 1989.

Roberts, Sam. "Yes, a Small Town Is Different." *New York Times,* August 27, 1995.

Sinks, Alfred. "The Home Town Fights to Live." *Colliers,* July 2, 1947, pp. 28 ff.

Sutton, William Alfred. "Sherwood Anderson, The Clyde Years, 1884–1896." *Northwest Ohio Quarterly* 19 (July 1947): 99–114.

Tavernini, Rebecca. "Our Town." *American Times,* August 1993, pp. 5–10.

Vance, Sandra S., and Roy V. Scott. "Sam Walton and Wal-Mart Stores, Inc.: A Study in Modern Southern Entrepreneurship." *Journal of Southern History* 58 (May 1992): 231–52.

Veblen, Thorstein. "The Country Town." *Freeman,* July 11 and 18, 1923, pp. 417–20, 440–43.

Watts, Steven. "Walt Disney: Art and Politics in the American Century." *Journal of American History* 82 (June 1995), pp. 84–110.

Welter, Barbara, "The Cult of True Womanhood, 1820–1860." *American Quarterly* 18 (1966): 151–74.

Newspapers

Camden Gazette, 1880–1902
Camden Herald, 1877–80
Dayton Daily News
Dayton Journal Herald, 1972
Eaton Register-Herald
Eaton Weekly Register, 1855
Hamilton Journal News, 1985
Preble County News, 1902–89
Richmond Palladium-Item

Unpublished materials

Belcher, Shirley. "History of Camden's Nine Churches." Typescript, 1994. Camden Archives.

"Camden Sesquicentennial Souvenir." 1968. Camden Archives.

Dearth, Ruthayn. "Camden Town Hall and Opera House." 1994. Camden Archives.

Eikenberry, William. "My Life and Times." N.d. Copy in possession of the author.

Minute Books of Camden Village Council, Town Hall, Camden, Ohio.

Minute Books of the Camden Board of Public Affairs, Town Hall, Camden, Ohio.

Neff, Ruth N. "A History of Camden, Ohio." Master's thesis, Miami University, 1955.

"Service Record, World War I and II, Camden and Vicinity." Camden, Justice-Liebolt American Legion Post 377, 1948. Camden Archives.

White, Genevieve. "Preble County During the Civil War." Master's thesis, Miami University, 1944.

Index

Aaron, Daniel, 25
"Acres of Diamonds" (Conwell), 56
adults, young: changing postwar behavior, 156–57; jobs during high
school, 121; opportunities, 1–2; out-
migration, 4, 5; postwar local incentives for college graduates, 139–40;
social behavior of, 46, 121–22
Agricultural Adjustment Administration (AAA), 104–5
agricultural areas: changing technology,
15, 27, 66, 82, 83, 143–44; decline of
towns, 5; destruction of virgin forests, 21–22; early trading in farm
commodities, 29; price drops during
Great Depression, 90–91; as served
by small-town businesses, 1, 3, 44. *See
also* farms
Agriculture, U.S. Department of, aid
during Great Depression, 105, 119
Aid for Dependent Children, programs
during Great Depression, 89
Alcorn, Marvin (World War II serviceman), 131
Amato, Joseph, 5, 182
Ambrose, Stephen, 125
American Automobile Association, 168
American Legion: membership in, 76;
women's auxiliary, 76; World War II
activities, 128
American Red Cross, 129
Anderson, Irwin, 9, 66

Anderson, Sherwood, 10–12, 11 *il.*, 50,
56, 58; Camden as birthplace, 2, 7–8,
9, 61, 162; *Poor White,* 12, 14, 59;
Tar: A Midwest Childhood, 13–14;
Winesburg, Ohio, 8, 10–12, 14, 46–47
Andrews, Clayton (World War II serviceman), 132
Anselmo, NE, 1995 study of, 6
antique shops, as small-town businesses, 176, 194
apartments, conversions of vacant
stores, 176, 192
appearance, physical: of present-day
small towns, 176, 181, 185, 193,
210 n. 22; of turn-of-the-century
small towns, 50–51
appliances, household, postwar demands, 141
Ashland, OR, Shakespeare Festival as
prosperity catalyst, 190–91
Atherton, Lewis E., 4, 46, 56
Atlas Plywood Company, Camden, 159,
172, 175
atomic bombs, use to end war, 134–35
automobiles: accidents in prewar Camden, 81–82; agencies in Camden, 67,
68–69, 85, 119, 147, 154, 175; for
commuting to jobs, 139, 140, 156,
192, 194; early ownership in Preble
County, 80–81; effect on Camden's
economic life, 66–69, 80–85; influence on street paving and new ser-

wildlife, in early Ohio, 17, 21–22
"Willard, George" (character, *Winesburg, Ohio*), 8
Willeford, Adolph (World War II serviceman), 132
Willson, Meredith, 50
Wilson, John, 105
Wilson, M. L., 105
Winesburg, Ohio (Anderson), 8, 10–12, 14, 46–47
Wisconsin Glacier, imprint on Ohio, 18–19
Witherby, Orma (telephone operator), 63
Withers, Carl, 4, 96
women: class status and activities, 75–77; girlhood education, 121; postwar status as homemakers, 142, 208 n. 8; role in the home, 45; as tavern patrons, 120; as war workers, 127
Women's Christian Temperance Union, Camden, 120
Wood, Jerry (mayor), 185

Wood, Orville (businessman), 93, 95, 96, 151; attempted draft evasion during World War II, 126–27; backyard radio tower, 163–64, 164 *il.*; as mayor, 170–71; opposition to proposed water and sewer system, 107, 108–9
"Woody's Tower," 163–64, 164 *il.*
World War II, effect on Camden, 124–36
WPA (Works Progress Administration), building programs and job opportunities, 89, 104
wrestling, as early TV fare, 149–50
Wright-Patterson Air Force Base, postwar job opportunities, 138, 142

Young, Roz, 180–81
youth. *See* adults, young

Zech, Edward (World War II serviceman), 124
"Zenith" (fictional city, *Babbitt*), 59–60

Urban Life and Urban Landscape Series
Zane L. Miller, General Editor

The series examines the history of urban life and the development of the urban landscape through works that place social, economic, and political issues in the intellectual and cultural context of their times.

Designing Modern America: The Regional Planning Association and Its Members
Edward K. Spann

Hopedale: From Commune to Company Town, 1840–1920
Edward K. Spann

Visions of Eden: Environmentalism, Urban Planning, and City Building in St. Petersburg, Florida, 1900–1995
R. Bruce Stephenson

Welcome to Heights High: The Crippling Politics of Restructuring America's Public Schools
Diana Tittle

Washing "The Great Unwashed": Public Baths in Urban America, 1840–1920
Marilyn Thornton Williams